EASTBOUND THROUGH SIBERIA

EASTBOUND THROUGH SIBERIA

Observations from the Great Northern Expedition

Georg Wilhelm Steller

Translated and Annotated by
Margritt A. Engel and Karen E. Willmore

INDIANA UNIVERSITY PRESS

This book is a publication of

Indiana University Press
Office of Scholarly Publishing
Herman B Wells Library 350
1320 East 10th Street
Bloomington, Indiana 47405 USA

iupress.org

© 2020 by Margritt Engel and Karen Willmore

All rights reserved

No part of this book may be reproduced or utilized in any form or by any means, electronic or mechanical, including photocopying and recording, or by any information storage and retrieval system, without permission in writing from the publisher. The paper used in this publication meets the minimum requirements of the American National Standard for Information Sciences—Permanence of Paper for Printed Library Materials, ANSI Z39.48-1992.

Manufactured in the United States of America

Cataloging information is available from the Library of Congress.

ISBN 978-0-253-04777-9 (hardback)
ISBN 978-0-253-04778-6 (paperback)
ISBN 978-0-253-04784-7 (ebook)

1 2 3 4 5   24 23 22 21 20

CONTENTS

Foreword: The Steller Legacy /
Jonathan C. Slaght   vii

Translators' Preface   xv

Acknowledgments   xxiii

Introduction   1

Instructions for Georg Wilhelm Steller from February 18, 1739, from Yeniseysk / Johann Georg Gmelin and Gerhard Friedrich Müller   9

Part I Description of Irkutsk and Its Surroundings

1. About Irkutsk and Its Surroundings   27
2. About Irkutsk Itself   39
3. About the Public Offices   46
4. About the Clergy   52
5. About the Chinese Trade and Chinese Trade Goods   53
6. About Customs and Lifestyle in Irkutsk   59
7. About Transbaikalia   67
8. Report from the Uda River   75

vi | Contents

Part II Travel Journal from Irkutsk to Kamchatka

9   From Irkutsk to Ust'Ilginskaya (3/4–3/13)   *81*

10 From Ust'Ilginskaya to Kirensk (3/14–5/1)   *93*

11 From Kirensk to Yakutsk (5/2–5/24)   *99*

12 In Yakutsk and Yarmanka (5/25–6/19)   *107*

13 From Yarmanka to the Amga River (6/20–7/2)   *119*

14 From the Amga to the Yuna River (7/3–7/21)   *126*

15 From the Yuna River to Yudoma Cross (7/22–8/8)   *139*

16 From Yudoma Cross to Okhotsk (8/9–8/13)   *152*

17 In Okhotsk (8/14–8/26)   *160*

18 Salmon Fishing and Preserving (8/27)   *165*

19 From Okhotsk to Bol'sheretsk (8/28–9/16)   *172*

Afterword   174

Appendix A: Georg Wilhelm Steller's Life   179

Appendix B: Schnurbuch Account Ledger   183

Appendix C: Letter to Johann Daniel Schumacher   185

Appendix D: Plants Named after Steller   189

Glossary of Foreign Words   191

Glossary of People   195

Bibliography   197

Plant Index   207

Index   211

FOREWORD: THE STELLER LEGACY

Jonathan C. Slaght

THE EARLIEST EXPLORERS OF SIBERIA AND THE RUSSIAN Far East were the fur traders and Cossacks, hard men of rust and mud. Leaning heavily on firearms and steel, they established a chain of Russian outposts winding from Irkutsk in Siberia to Yakutsk and Kamchatka in the Russian Far East. Among them were Ivan Moskvitin, the first Russian to reach the Sea of Okhotsk (in 1639); Kurbat Ivanov, the first Russian to stumble upon the shores of Lake Baikal (in 1643); Vassili Poyarkov, the first Russian to reach the Amur River (in 1644); and Vladimir Atlasov, among the bloodiest of the Cossacks, the first to organize explorations of Kamchatka. Some of these explorers died peacefully, whereas others, like the morally ambiguous Atlasov, died violently while cementing the Russian Empire's hold on this frontier.

Once a network of Russian fortresses and peasant villages had been established across the lands of the eastern half of the Russian Empire, another group of explorers came. Armed with journals, notepads, and specimen cases instead of weapons, these were the naturalists. Georg Steller was part of this wave, joining adventurous Russians, Danes, Germans, Poles, Scots, and Swedes hired by the Russian Empire to catalog its natural riches. The legacies of these explorers are intertwined with the history of science and exploration in Russia; their names peer back at us from the plants, birds, and mammals seen there today: Dybowski's frog, Gmelin's buttercup, and Pallas's reed bunting among them. Later explorers who fine-tuned our knowledge of these vast landscapes included Nikolai Przhevalskii, Alexander von Middendorff, Carl Maksimovich, George Kennan, and Vladimir Arsenyev.

Georg Steller's contributions to natural and social history in Russia have been, I believe, undervalued. This is due partly to the thunderclap of discovery that defined his time with Vitus Bering—the first European exploration of Alaska would overshadow anyone's other work—but also to how his records were handled by the Russian authorities Steller answered to. At the time of his expeditions, the Russian Empire was jealous of the information Steller (and all the other scientists) put to paper, keeping it hidden from foreign powers also eager to exploit the riches of the North Pacific.

Other specifics in Steller's journals on Siberia and the Russian Far East, particularly of life in these wild regions far from the gilded palaces of St. Petersburg, contained details the government likely preferred remain quiet. Corruption was rampant, laws were haphazardly designed, and services such as rudimentary health care were often absent. In the passages here, Steller documented a months-long epidemic that killed Russians (but did not affect the indigenous Buryats) and saw injustice in the burden of taxes levied on the neediest peasants. Comparing the poor with the rich in March 1740, he wrote that

> as a general rule about Siberia, it can be noted that the people in poor and bad places are much more industrious and of a better mind-set than in rich places and those of abundance. There is no house in these parts where hemp and burlap are not spun and woven for shirts and pants; young and old are intent on saving themselves from poverty as much as possible. Whereas in Irkutsk the womenfolk—as soon as the tea and cabbage soup have been prepared—can be found lying together on the stove like sausages in a frying pan, smoking their asses so they don't rot and fall apart from all the moving and whoring.

Although some of Steller's documents were released soon after his death and acted as vital references for future explorers of the North Pacific, the sensitive nature of Steller's texts meant that the breadth of his discoveries and observations remained—and to some degree still remains—unexplored. His notes were locked away; some were lost to subsequent decay or misplaced, while others sat near-indecipherable in the Latin and eighteenth-century German they were written in. Remarkably, the dissolution of the Soviet Union cracked these long-sealed vaults as well, and a number of Steller's records have come to light in recent decades. This volume was among that valuable cache.

* * *

Steller's legacy in the North Pacific is subtle but deeply pervasive. Like Vladimir Arsenyev, who detailed explorations of the areas south of the Amur River in *Across the Ussuri Kray* (Indiana University Press, 2016), Steller seemed most comfortable describing vegetation when he wrote about nature. It is therefore unsurprising that the greatest number of taxa named after him today are plants. In Appendix D of this volume, translators Margritt Engel and Karen Willmore list two genera (*Dendrostellera* and *Stellera*) and ten species that still carry his name, from Steller's leek to a perennial herb called *Veronica stelleri*, and note an additional fifteen species that, given the ever-evolving nature of scientific and common species names, were once called "Steller" but no longer are.

Steller's detailed lists of plants—important for understanding how vegetation communities may have changed in the last three hundred years—are ample, and his descriptions of the natural world are thoughtful. For example, somewhere in eastern Yakutia (near the Ancha River, a tributary of the Allakh-Yun River), Steller encountered permafrost for the first time and, not knowing what it was but recognizing it as special, wrote the following: "I saw a curious phenomenon in the woods. A stream flowed between two mountains separated from each other by half a kilometer. On both sides the cut banks were made of ice up to two feet thick. On top of the ice were soil and muskeg and very tall larch trees. I gathered that this ice has never thawed and has been lying here since times immemorial and represents solid ground."

Steller recorded few birds in his journals here. As an ornithologist with twenty years of experience in the Russian Far East, one of my joys in translating *Across the Ussuri Kray* was deciphering the birds Vladimir Arsenyev saw but could not identify. For example, Arsenyev wrote about "grebes here and there in the pools of standing water, these birds had protruding ear tufts and a collar of colorful feathers."[1] These key characteristics allowed me to confidently identify these birds as great crested grebes (*Podiceps cristatus*). Steller, unfortunately, gives readers less information to work with. At one point he noticed "two kinds of gulls that live on the sea: one was black-and-white spotted on the back; the other was all black, longish, and gaunt with long, narrow wings." Heinrich Springer, an Alaskan ornithologist who helped the translators with bird identifications in this text, was justifiably perplexed. In his notes he suggested that the first bird, the "black-and-white spotted" one, might be a juvenile gull, as many young gulls are mottled in their plumage. The second bird, he proposed, was perhaps a storm petrel or maybe a black tern. But if Steller is confusing a petrel or a tern with a gull, this second mystery bird might be a wide range of things. Certain color morphs of the parasitic (*Stercorarius parasiticus*) or long-tailed (*S. longicaudus*) jaegers, for example, meet his descriptions, as does a sooty shearwater (*Puffinus griseus*), a short-tailed shearwater (*P. tenuirostris*), or a dark phase of the northern fulmar (*Fulmarus glacialis*). It could even be something far more exotic, like a lesser frigatebird (*Fregata ariel*)—a highly nomadic, lithe species documented as far north as the Tartary Strait and the Amur River mouth, but never as far north in the Sea of Okhotsk as Steller was at the time.[2]

Steller's clumsiness with bird identification is somewhat ironic, given that he is perhaps best recognized today by ornithologists and birdwatchers for the three striking avian species that carry his name. There is Steller's sea eagle (*Haliaeetus pelagicus*), a gorgeous raptor and close relative of North America's bald eagle (*H. leucocephalus*), unmistakable with its enormous orange bill and patterned plumage of rich blacks and bright whites. The largest eagle in the world (by mass) and a salmon eater, it breeds along the Sea of Okhotsk and eastern Kamchatka coasts and was likely a common sight for Steller throughout much of his time in the region. He mentioned these eagles in his journals, but the species was not formally described to science until Peter Pallas, an accomplished naturalist in his own right who had idolized Steller as a child, published *Zoographia Rosso-Asiatica* and named this bird in Steller's honor.[3]

Next is Steller's eider (*Polysticta stelleri*)—also named by Pallas—a beautiful, enigmatic creature of the northern seas. It breeds in the high Arctic on both sides of the Bering Strait and winters off the coasts of southern Alaska, Kamchatka, the Kuril Islands, and the Commander Islands. The latter of these contain what is now called Bering Island, where Steller, Bering, and others were stranded when their ship, the *St. Peter*, crashed into it; this island is the site of Bering's grave.

Last is Steller's jay (*Cyanocitta stelleri*)—the first bird in Alaska to be felled by a bullet, when Steller's assistant brought one down along the shores of Kayak Island a year after the adventures described here.[4] Steller recognized this jay's similarity in plumage to the ubiquitous North American blue jay (*C. cristata*) he'd seen renderings of, and he felt certain this bird was a representative of American fauna. The *St. Peter* was indeed moored along the continent they had sought. Steller was also the first person to describe to science the spectacled cormorant (*Phalacrocorax perspicillatus*)—the largest known cormorant species—and the northern fur seal (*Callorhinus ursinus*).

If we assemble the birds and mammals Steller described or that carry his name, we see that most are in conservation trouble today, with Steller's jay being the only exception. Steller's sea cow (*Hydrodamalis gigas*), now extinct, was a relative of the manatee and dugong so large that a recently recovered skeleton on Bering Island revealed a ribcage nearly the size of a minivan.[5] Steller's sea lion (*Eumetopias jubatus*), among the largest of the eared seal species, breeds on island beaches throughout the North Pacific, but their numbers have drastically declined since Steller's day. Sea otters (*Enhydra lutris*) were unknown to science before Steller described them, and the pelts brought back to the Russian mainland from Bering Island became the basis of a sustained, hundred-year hunt that nearly drove this species to extinction.[6]

In the search for commercially valuable sea otter pelts, Steller's sea cow and the spectacled cormorant were casualties of association: the hordes of fur hunters drawn to the North Pacific in search of Steller's discoveries needed something to eat, and the slow-moving sea cows and reluctant-to-fly cormorants were favored targets. The sea cow—the meat from a single individual rumored to feed thirty-three men for a month—disappeared less than three decades after Steller first described it.[7] The cormorant made it just more than a century, with the last individuals seen around 1850.[8] While new fossil evidence suggests that these birds were a vestige of an already-dying population—relicts of an ice age that only slightly, in geological time, outlasted the wooly mammoths of Wrangel Island—it's indisputable that Steller was an unwitting harbinger of a conservation cataclysm in this Arctic ecosystem.[9] In some respects, Steller's legacy in the North Pacific is one of death.

* * *

In Siberia and the Russian Far East, Steller was a foreigner twice removed: the ways of the rural Russians were almost as intriguing as the customs of the indigenous Buryat, Yakut, Koryak, or Tungus. He seemingly detailed every encounter from Irkutsk to Okhotsk, a direct distance of more than 2,500 kilometers, occasionally with a touch of humor as evidenced by this exchange at a Yakut yurt he stumbled upon after becoming disoriented in the forest: "I exchanged a few Yakut words with them; the rest I communicated with hands, feet, and gestures, and they caught on that I was lost. Pointing with their fingers, they asked if I had fallen off my horse, because I had covered almost fifty kilometers on foot. However, I understood them to ask if I was looking for love and wanted to sleep with a Yakut woman. I therefore answered, 'No.'"

The journal notes published here in English for the first time add to Steller's legacy by building on his other recently translated works, notably

Journal of a Voyage with Bering, 1741–1742 (Stanford University Press, 1988, translated by Margritt Engel and O. W. Frost) and *Steller's History of Kamchatka* (University of Alaska Press, 2003, translated by Margritt Engel and Karen Willmore). They are a further exploration of the man's character, temperament, and skill as a natural and social scientist. Steller described the crippling debt of peasants in the Lena River basin, the logistics of bringing provisions to Okhotsk, the ancient petroglyphs he passed on cliff faces, and how the Yakut hunt waterfowl and pay tribute to vengeful gods. An entire chapter is devoted to the capture and preparation of salmon at Okhotsk's fishery. He documented geophagy among the Tungus—the process of eating clay soils—in this case to ease diarrhea resulting from excessive phosphorus in their salmon-rich diets.[10] Such observations act as a complement to his encounters with (and descriptions of) the indigenous Kamchadals of Kamchatka in 1743 and 1744, after returning to northeast Asia from Alaska.[11] From a historical perspective, these vignettes are invaluable.

Steller's journal entries are worthy texts in their own right: these notes of hospitable peasants, entranced shamans, and descriptions of new plants and landscapes expand our knowledge of a unique time and place. But they are more than just that. His journals from 1739 and 1740 represent the calm before the storm—the steady path toward the frontier town of Okhotsk that culminated in Steller's first meeting with Vitus Bering. His journals make casual mention of future shipmates such as Sven Waxell, who assumed command of the *St. Peter*'s wreck upon Bering's death, and Safron Khitrov—an apt last name meaning "sly" or "devious" in Russian—tantalizing cameos for anyone familiar with the epic to come. These words are the first tendrils of complicated relationships now tightly intertwined in history. Few tales of exploration and survival can match the experiences these men shared on the *St. Peter* during the Great Northern Expedition. The texts here set the stage for this monumental event, a story of near unimaginable peril and discovery; one that crafted the course of modern history by heralding the extinction of some species, the near extinction of others, and an irreversible bridging of the Old and New Worlds.

Notes

1. V. K. Arsenyev, *Across the Ussuri Kray*, trans. J. Slaght (Bloomington: Indiana University Press, 2016).

2. V. A. Nechaev and T. V. Gamova, *Ptitsy Dalnego Vostoka Rossii* [Birds of the Russian Far East] (Vladivostok: Dalnauka, 2009).

3. C. Ford, *Where the Sea Breaks Its Back* (Boston: Little, Brown, 1966); V. B. Masterov and M. S. Romanov, *Tikhookeanskii orlan Haliaeetus pelagicus—ekologiya, evolyutsia, okhrana* [Steller's sea eagle *Haliaeetus pelagicus*: ecology, evolution, and conservation] (Moscow: KMK Scientific, 2014).

4. W. B. Lincoln, *The Conquest of a Continent* (New York: Random House, 1994).

5. J. Daley, "Skeleton of a Massive Extinct Sea Cow Found on Siberian Island," Smithsonian.com, November 21, 2017, https://www.smithsonianmag.com/smart-news/massive-extince-sea-cow-skeleton-found-siberian-island-180967291/.

6. K. W. Kenyon, "The Sea Otter in the Eastern Pacific Ocean" (North American Fauna 68, US Government Printing Office, Washington, DC, 1969).

7. H. Marsh, T. J. O'Shea, and J. E. Reynolds, *Ecology and Conservation of the Sirenia: Dugongs and Manatees* (Cambridge: Cambridge University Press, 2011).

8. L. Stejneger, *Georg Wilhelm Steller, the Pioneer of Alaskan Natural History* (Cambridge, MA: Harvard University Press, 1936).

9. J. Watanabe, H. Matsuoka, and Y. Hasegawa, "Pleistocene Fossils from Japan Show That the Recently Extinct Spectacled Cormorant (*Phalacrocorax perspicillatus*) Was a Relict," *The Auk* 135 (2018): 895, doi:10.1642/AUK-18-54.1; N. Wade, "The Woolly Mammoth's Last Stand," *New York Times*, March 2, 2017, https://www.nytimes.com/2017/03/02/science/woolly-mammoth-extinct-genetics.html.

10. I. V. Seryodkin, A. M. Panichev, and J. C. Slaght, "Geophagy by Brown Bears in the Russian Far East," *Ursus* 27 (2016): 11–17.

11. G. Steller, *Steller's History of Kamchatka: Collected Information Concerning the History of Kamchatka, Its Peoples, Their Manners, Names, Lifestyles, and Various Customary Practices*, trans. M. Engel and K. Willmore, Historical Translation Series 12 (Fairbanks: University of Alaska Press, 2003).

TRANSLATORS' PREFACE

With the opening of the Iron Curtain in the 1990s, Russian archives once again became accessible to foreign scholars, and the veil of secrecy imposed on the members of the Second Kamchatka Expedition centuries ago was finally lifted. In 1992, Wieland Hintzsche, a natural scientist and historian from Halle, Germany, where Steller had been a student and docent in botany some 260 years earlier, went looking for Steller manuscripts in Russian archives. He found a treasure trove of letters and documents not only by Steller but also by other individuals and institutions involved in the Second Kamchatka Expedition, most of them previously unexamined and unpublished. They are now being published in a series called *Quellen zur Geschichte Sibiriens und Alaskas aus russischen Archiven* (Source materials concerning the history of Siberia and Alaska from Russian archives) by the Franckesche Stiftungen in Halle, Germany, in cooperation with the Archive of the Russian Academy of Sciences in St. Petersburg, with Wieland Hintzsche serving as main editor.

The two Steller texts of our current translation—"The Description of Irkutsk and Its Surroundings" and the "Travel Journal from Irkutsk to Kamchatka, 1740"—are found in the series's second volume, *Reisetagebücher, 1735–1743* (2000). The "Instructions" given to Steller by professors Gmelin and Müller, which we included because they explain the scope and details of the assignments given to the scientists and provide a better understanding of why Steller did what he did, are printed in volume 3, *Briefe und Dokumente, 1739* (2001). These translated texts contain historical and scientific information that deserves to become more widely known. While they will appeal most to historians and botanists, general readers who like a good wilderness adventure will also enjoy reading them.

Steller's observations in the role of social scientist are a particularly memorable aspect of the "Description of Irkutsk." He deplores the unfair treatment of poor people; appreciates the Cossacks' superb choice of the absolutely best place to found this town; and admires, rather idealistically, the hardworking promyshlenniks[1] and their fishing cooperative in which everything is harmoniously shared. Much of the journal, especially

Frontis. Though no portrait of Georg Wilhelm Steller is known to exist, several artists have depicted him as they imagined him to look. In our estimation this statue by Russian sculptor Ilya Vyuev, entitled *Infinitely Large in the Infinitely Small* (2011), most successfully captures Steller's unassuming appearance and his intense interest in scientific research. This work in plaster (70 centimeters) was initially presented in Moscow in 2011. In 2016, at the request of the Komandorskiy Nature Reserve, a full-scale Steller bronze monument (2.2 meters) was made based on the initial sculpture. The plan is to place this monument on Bering Island. Photo reprinted with permission of the artist.

beginning with the trip down the Lena River during breakup, relates an arduous trek with descriptions of rugged landscapes and their flora. Stejneger, who in his 1936 biography of Steller lamented the loss of this journal, would indeed have found in it "the wonderful commentary . . . on men and conditions as they prevailed during the time of the Second Kamchatka Expedition" that he assumed would be there.[2] From the wealth of letters and other documents we consulted in both *Quellen* volumes, we have added a sample of a *Schnurbuch* (account ledger; 3:317–21) and a letter to Schumacher (3:212–14) as appendices (B and C) to further illustrate how the expedition's byzantine administrative system affected Steller's work.

Translating Steller's texts has been its own arduous trek through the eighteenth-century linguistic landscape. First of all, these texts are essentially Steller's unrevised field notes, published in what the Germans call a *textkritische Ausgabe*, recording Steller's notes just as he wrote them but also carefully identifying lacunae and substitutions due to the condition of the manuscript. Eighteenth-century written German was not standardized with respect to spelling, grammar, or punctuation; helping verbs were frequently omitted, and the same word might be spelled three different ways on the same page. Steller's use of punctuation is totally erratic, so deciphering which words constituted a complete sentence became something of a guessing game. It is safe to assume that, had he lived and been given permission to publish his work, Steller himself would have eliminated many of the confusing aspects of the manuscripts. He suggests as much in his *Beasts of the Sea*, where he invites readers who object to the earthen vessel containing his written porridge to pour it into a gold or silver urn.[3] He was definitely sensitive to the shortcomings in his writing caused by lack of time, as evidenced in his letters—for example, the one to Schumacher (see appendix C). Switching number or tense; omitting nouns, pronouns, and articles; not putting events in a logical sequence—for example, observing that he drowned his beard in a lake before writing that he was getting a shave—are all examples of the haste with which he had to work much of the time and his superactive mind outracing his pen.

Despite his unpolished writing, his personal style comes through. He was fond of repetition, often piling one adjective on another— lovely, beautiful, pleasant—or using two nouns meaning the same thing—the rich and well-to-do. He had a wicked sense of understated humor—for example, ironically labeling it a misfortune that he and Aleksei "just barely escaped a watery grave" (114–15). He delighted in playing with language, as when he described himself as the meat in a muck soup after falling into a boggy hole with his horse or cited the need to let the horses "*ausruhen, ausfressen und ausheilen*" or "rest up, fill up, and pick up their health" (139). However, using *Berg*, mountain, interchangeably with *Gebirge*, mountain range, seemed out of character for a scientist. Here we tried to be more precise.

Steller had been schooled in Latin. It was the lingua franca among scholars; he read, wrote, and spoke it fluently. Not surprisingly, he used it almost exclusively in describing plants and minerals. Since he was traveling through Russia, he used Russian terms, writing them down as he heard them, not necessarily how they were actually spelled, his Russian apparently having been learned by ear. Using many French words was common in the eighteenth century, and Steller did that too. Quite a few words in all of these languages, including Steller's native German, are obsolete now, sending us to Hintzsche's *Anmerkungen* or the Grimm Brothers' *Deutsches Wörterbuch*.

Hintzsche transcribed the text painstakingly while supplying ample notes with explanations of outdated German words and expressions, corrections and translations of Russian words and phrases, translations of Latin and French words and phrases, geographic and historical explanations, and identification of people as well as a glossary of Russian terms. Wherever Hintzsche's notes helped, we used them, citing them as WH, Anm. However, he did not edit the text to clarify the meaning. That has been left to us.

We have had two competing goals. We wanted to faithfully convey the meaning that Steller intended. At the same time, we wanted to produce a translation that would be read with pleasure, without the stumbling blocks of antiquated and bureaucratic language and a host of foreign words and expressions or explanatory notes. Our process of translating was often like walking a knife-edged ridge, trying, on the one side, not to fall into misrepresenting Steller with our coherent, flowing prose and, on the other, not to leave readers confused or bored. We have of course standardized the spelling and the punctuation and supplied helping verbs that Steller omitted as well as pronouns, articles, nouns, and occasionally phrases to avoid ambiguity. Some of his repetitions we have retained; some we have shortened. We have usually reversed illogical sequences, and we have tried to match his creative use of language or at least note it. We have opted, wherever possible, for words most likely used in Steller's time, translating, for example, *Branntwein* consistently as *brandy*, while other translators or commentators use *vodka* or *whiskey*. To accurately reflect the range of Steller's language use from high society to barnyard, we have translated terms not used in polite society accordingly. We have used contractions to reflect Steller's informal language. We have retained the Russian terms for which there are no ready equivalents in English—for example, designations of officials and places—and kept the Russian for which Steller himself supplies the translation, correcting the spelling and transliterating it using the Modified Library of Congress system. We have taken the liberty of retaining the anglicized *sluzhiv/sluzhivs*, used also by Stejneger, in place of the Russian *sluzhivii* and *sluzhivye liudi* because Steller himself almost always Germanized the word; we consider *servitor/s*, the translation used by other translators and scholars, stilted and alien to contemporary American English.[4] We retain the spellings of Russian words as found in American dictionaries (e.g., *ukase* and *yurt*) and of cities as found in standard American atlases (e.g., Yeniseysk and Yakutsk). We have also retained the old adjective ending *-oi* (e.g., *boyarskoi* and *Olekminskoi*) typically used in Steller's time where today *-ii* is used. We italicize foreign words only the first time we use them. We have relied on Hintzsche's notes and Jäger's generous help in translating the Latin.

Language reflects society, and eighteenth-century Europe stood on ceremony; class distinctions and rank mattered greatly, but how much so was not immediately apparent to us. We were rather puzzled that Steller used two different words for *Diener*, servant, calling Herr Berckhan's a *Knecht*, today strictly meaning a farm laborer. These two servants were obviously in identical positions, albeit serving different masters. Then, perusing volumes 1 and 3 of the *Quellen*, we discovered that in letters to personages of higher rank Steller himself signs off as "*Ihr ergebener* (your devoted) *Knecht*," while the standard formula to a person of equal status used by him and by others is "*Ihr ergebener Diener*." So it turned out to be a question of rank in the eye of the beholder—Steller outranked Berckhan; thus, his servant presumably outranked Berckhan's. Another, rather amusing, example of the importance of rank is found in the sample ledger in appendix B. To our regret we did not find a better equivalent to *Euer Wohlgeboren* (literally, you, well-born person) *geruhten zu nehme*n (the servility of which made us both grin and cringe) than "you, sir, deigned to take." The importance of class distinctions in czarist Russia is borne out by the bizarre practice of classifying documents according to who was addressing whom, a *donoshenie* being one from a lower- to a higher-ranked individual, a *trebovanie* the opposite (Glossar, Quellen 1:332), and a *vedenie* a rank-neutral official communication from an institution to another or to a person (Glossar, Quellen 5:420).

The most frustrating puzzles were posed by two presumably German words, one of which, *Caper,* meaning pirate, seemed to cast aspersions on one of Steller's drivers, while the other, *jutschen,* seemed to be a nonexistent verb. Both words turned out to be disguised Russian, which we began to suspect on discovering that Steller occasionally confused letters in the Cyrillic and Roman alphabets. For example, he consistently misspelled Russian *zimov'e* (hut, way station) as *Simobhio* (our *b* being the Russian *v*). So, conjecturing that *Caper*'s C might be a Russian S, we found the Russian word *sapër*, meaning a sapper, a soldier in an engineering battalion, comparable to a Seabee in the US Navy. The verb *jutschen,* on the other hand, appears to be Steller's germanization of Russian *v'iuchit'*, to load a horse.

The greatest translation challenge by far was the pre-Linnaean nomenclature for the 155 plants Steller mentions in his travel journal. Retired botanist Eckehart J. Jäger graciously took on the huge task of identifying these plants by their current scientific names. According to Jäger (email, March 10, 2015), Steller knew that many of the plants he found had not yet been described and were thus new to science. In fact, from his excursions around Halle and St. Petersburg, Steller could not have known about 85 percent of the plants growing between Lake Baikal and Kayak Island on the west coast of the Pacific. Since in 1740 scientific names for plants had not yet been standardized by Linnaeus's *Species Plantarum* of 1753, Steller used working names that were useful for comparing with known Central European plants, often with short annotations of important characteristics. Steller did describe some of the plants he collected more extensively in his *Catalogus plantarum*, 1740 (*Flora Ochotensis*), but he often used different names from those in this travel journal. To give an idea of the huge amount of work that went into tracking down the present-day identity of these plants, our bibliography includes a separate list of references that Jäger used. Even though Steller was to investigate and describe everything concerning natural history (Instruction 1), botany was his first love, and he happily took every chance to go botanizing, whether up on a mountain or across a river filled with chunks of ice. He was particularly fond of gentians, saxifrages, louseworts, buttercups, and primroses, which he often described as *pulchra*

(Latin [L], beautiful) or even as *perpulchra* (L, exceedingly beautiful), sometimes even recommending them as ornamentals (Jäger).

As Steller described the various rivers, he listed the fish found in them as well as in Lake Baikal. He seemed most interested in the subsistence and commercial value of these fish. We lacked the help from a fisheries expert in identifying each of the twenty-eight fish Steller mentioned, though he often used Russian names, some of which were close enough to the modern Russian that we could eventually find the scientific name. The species of salmon were the easiest, the whitefish the toughest to figure out. Steller offered one amusing though erroneous theory that the rigidity of the Eurasian ruffe's dorsal fin kept it from swimming upriver against the current. Like the plants, Steller described the fish in Latin.

In the journal, Steller mentions fewer than twenty birds, sometimes with the German names, more often with a sketchy description. Luckily, a well-known Anchorage ornithologist, the late Heinrich Springer, could identify them for us or come up with a best guess. In the letter to Schumacher (December 24, 1739, *Quellen* 3:41; see appendix C) requesting birdshot, Steller gives a plausible explanation for the misleading low count. Having only small bullets, which tear small birds apart, he could stuff just one in twenty of the some three hundred birds he had examined and described to that point. Since he wrote this before he even left Irkutsk, it is safe to assume that he encountered and identified more birds than he recorded. Touchingly, however, when Steller reported that Berckhan had shot a young loon, he also commented that they "were surprised to hear the mother lament her young with the most pitiful cries" (chap. 14, July 13).

Quotes from the letters and documents Steller wrote and received during 1739 and 1740 are our translations, too. Dates throughout all the volumes of *Quellen* refer to the Julian calendar then in use in Russia (Hintzsche, pers. comm., January 2018). To convert to the Gregorian, eleven days should be added (Hintzsche, *Quellen* 4.2:823). Because the headings Steller applied to sections in the journal often seemed arbitrary, likely identifying notebooks used rather than sections traveled, we have replaced those with headings identifying segments of the journey. Where appropriate, we have supplied what information was available in Hintzsche's *Personenregister* (*Quellen* 2:490–507) to persons mentioned in the text. On pages—for example, in chapter 14—where the manuscript contained so many lacunae that the integrity of the text was questionable, we have retained Hintzsche's markings of [. . . .], noting other smaller omissions individually.

Notes

1. Contract workers drawn largely from the serf and townsman class who fished and hunted for furs in Siberia and later in Russian America.

2. L. Stejneger, *Georg Wilhelm Steller: The Pioneer of Alaskan Natural History* (Cambridge, MA: Harvard University Press, 1936), 135.

3. "Pressure of duties does not permit me to spend too much time in perfecting [my papers]. . . . I therefore set out my porridge in carefully made earthen vessels. If the vessel is an offense to anyone, he will perform for me and others a most friendly service if he will pour it all into a gold or silver urn." Quoted in D. Littlepage, *Steller's Island: Adventures of a Pioneer Naturalist in Alaska* (The Mountaineer's Books, 2006), 203.

4. *Sluzhiv*, from the verb *sluzhit'*, to serve. A general term applied to state employees in both civil and military service, mostly peasants and *posadskie* but also including Cossacks and streltsy, who were sent to Siberia to protect Russia's vital interests. Hintzsche, Glossar, Quellen 1:331–32; Dmytryshyn in A. Wood, ed., *The History of Siberia* (New York: Routledge, Chapman & Hall, 1991), 22; L. Kokaurov, pers. comm., November 2017.

ACKNOWLEDGMENTS

WE GRATEFULLY ACKNOWLEDGE THE HELP AND SUPPORT OF many people in our third Steller translation project. Foremost among them are Dr. Wieland Hintzsche, discoverer of lost documents and editor-in-chief of *Quellen zur Geschichte Sibiriens und Alaskas aus russischen Archiven*, and his wife and staunchest supporter, Dr. Elisabeth Hintzsche, a physician and the president of the International Georg-Wilhelm-Steller Society, which they founded twenty-two years ago together with scholars from the St. Petersburg Academy of Sciences. Under the auspices of the society, the Hintzsches have organized annual "German-Russian Encounters" in Halle, at which international scholars explore and share a multitude of topics related to the eighteenth-century history of Siberia and Alaska. While Elisabeth has been the driving force behind these and other regular Society-sponsored events, Wieland has shepherded the documents he located in Russian archives into print (fifteen volumes so far). His single-handed transcription of Steller's manuscripts in itself has been a monumental task we stand in awe of. For their devotion to Steller and all the encouragement given us, we salute and thank them both.

We owe Dr. Dr. h. c. Eckehart J. Jäger, Professor Emeritus of the Department of Biology (Geobotany und Botanical Garden), Martin-Luther-Universität, Halle, Germany, special thanks for his stellar help with Steller on several fronts. He graciously shared his botanical expertise and donated an enormous amount of time to hunting down the current scientific names of the some 155 plants Steller mentioned, who sometimes described the plant in detail, more often with just a few characteristics, occasionally with just one word. This identification process alone was a huge undertaking, especially considering how DNA analysis is changing how some plants are classified. It is one we could never have done ourselves. Unasked, Professor Jäger also edited our translation for accuracy, comparing our English with Steller's German, aided us in the transliteration of the Russian, drew and labeled the maps of Steller's journey, and reviewed the galley proofs for late-minute changes in classification. Finally, he described Steller's place in the history of botany. We are immeasurably thankful for his contribution, including for his and his wife's hospitality during our stays in Germany.

It is to Dr. O. W. (Jack) Frost, Professor Emeritus of Alaska Pacific University, Anchorage, AK, that we owe our involvement with Steller in the first place. Thirty-five years ago he asked for help in a new translation of Steller's Sea voyage, beginning with unpublished Steller manuscripts found in the Smithsonian. Frost's passion for all things Steller, culminating in his book, *Bering: The Russian Discovery of America*, started us on our own Steller journey.

We gratefully acknowledge the pictorial contributions of Ann Arnold, artist and writer, who graciously allowed us to use illustrations from her book *Sea Cows, Shamans, and Scurvy*; of Ilya Vyuev, Russian sculptor, and his wife, Inna Lipilina, who provided a photo of his Steller statue to use as frontispiece; of Drs. Irina Tunkina and Larissa Bondar, of the Russian Academy of Sciences, St, Petersburg branch, who located and gave us permission to use the sample of Steller's handwriting; and of Wikimedia Commons, which provided the other two illustrations.

While we relied primarily on Hintzsche's notes and Jäger's expertise in dealing with Steller's unorthodox use of the Russian language, local Russian teachers Delynne Chambers and Leonid Kokaurov; the late Dr. Roman R. Tchaikovsky (Professor Emeritus of German and English, Northern International University, Magadan, Russia), and Professor Dr. Swetlana Mengel (Martin-Luther-Universität Halle-Wittenberg, Seminar für Slavistik) helped us solve particular vocabulary puzzles.

For answers to other, primarily scientific, questions we turned for help to Dr. Robin A. Beebee, hydrologist for the US Geological Survey in Anchorage, who answered our questions about the accuracy of some of Steller's topographical descriptions; to Archpriest Michael J. Oleksa, Dean of St. Michael's Cathedral, Sitka, AK, who untangled the names of the Russian Orthodox churches Steller describes in Irkutsk and explained the religious terminology; to the late Heinrich Springer, a well-known Alaskan ornithologist, who happily identified the birds Steller mentions; and to Dr. Richard VanderHoek, archeologist for the Department of Natural Resources, State of Alaska, who helped with identifying the sheets of ice Steller describes, particularly those now known as ice patches. We thank them all for their help. We also gratefully acknowledge the posthumous assistance of the late Dr. Carl E. Bond, Professor Emeritus, Department of Fisheries and Wildlife, Oregon State University, who had identified the fish Steller mentions and describes in his Kamchatka manuscript, some of which we have used in this translation.

Last but not least we express our sincere appreciation for the assistance rendered by the Indiana University Press team who shepherded our work through the publication process, especially Jennika Baines, Acquisitions Editor, who enthusiastically recommended it for publication; Darja Malcolm-Clarke, Editorial Project Manager, who coordinated the publication process; Pete Feely, Amnet's Project Manager, who made sure we did not get hopelessly tangled up in the copyediting process; and Lizzie Troyer, the copyeditor, who managed to remove all our inconsistencies.

Not to be forgotten, we offer a huge thank-you to our families for good-humoredly tolerating our years-long preoccupation with Georg Wilhelm Steller and for patiently and wholeheartedly supporting us.

EASTBOUND THROUGH SIBERIA

INTRODUCTION

What comes to mind when Americans hear the name Steller depends on whether they live in Alaska, have an interest in the natural world, or are challenged spellers who think it is an adjective. Correctly spelled, his name has been affixed to a noisy jay, a huge sea eagle, a northern eider duck, a bellowing sea lion, an icy mountain rising from the Bering Glacier, a cove on Alaska's westernmost island, the largest chiton, the extinct northern sea cow, and many plants, such as the slender rockbrake. Apart from the natural world, a street and a high school in Anchorage are also named after him. Yet he is still not well known, his reputation still primarily defined by the journal of the voyage with Bering that landed him on Kayak Island in July of 1741.

What compelled us, after spending fifteen years on the translation of Steller's book about Kamchatka, to embark on the current translation project was both the fascinating subject matter and the desire to acquaint a larger audience with this extraordinary scientist, explorer, and human being. For almost a century, readers have been gaining the impression from the *Journal of the Sea Voyage* that he was ill-tempered and rather intolerant, sympathetic portrayals in the popular literature notwithstanding (see the bibliography). In the texts here translated, a much more nuanced image of a more likable man emerges. The journal in particular reveals his humanity, his strength of character, his intense dedication to scientific discovery, and his wry sense of humor. The stamina with which he endured both awkward and perilous situations and met the burdensome challenges he faced as a member of this expedition is extraordinary. The history of the colonization of Siberia can be found in many sources, so we have included here only enough historical context to help understand Steller's writing. By the time he arrived in St. Petersburg in 1734, Russia had, starting in the late sixteenth century, expanded its influence eastward across the Ural Mountains to the Pacific Ocean, bringing some ten million square kilometers of inhospitable territory, rich in natural resources and inhabited by various indigenous peoples, under Moscow's control.

Fig. Intro.1. Sweetvetch (Wikipedia, *Hedysarum hedysaroides*).

Though the Russian government tried to control settlement, administration, trade, and economic growth, it was the people who came and who were already there that shaped Siberian development. The first men (and they were almost exclusively men) to open up the region to settlement were the freebooting Cossacks and the independent Russian promyshlenniks who hunted and trapped fur-bearing animals.[1] They were followed by peasant settlers, dissident religious communities, and involuntary settlers—that is, convicts, political exiles, and prisoners of war dispatched to the region for "safekeeping" by the central authorities. There were the *sluzhivs*—state employees who encompassed both civil administrative officials and military personnel sent to protect Russia's vital interests. And since the czar was the nominal head of the Russian Orthodox Church, every *ostrog*[2] had either a chapel or a church that was supported by the government, as were the ecclesiastical personnel. The relationship between the natives and the invaders was one of conflict and coexistence. Some natives served voluntarily as guides and interpreters, and socializing and marriage took place between Russians and non-Russians, but much of this contact was unwelcome and painful for the indigenous people. As Hartley summarizes, "The opening up of Siberia in the seventeenth century and the expeditions of the eighteenth and nineteenth centuries were extraordinary feats of courage and endurance, but at the same time they were violent and traumatic, both for the participants and for the indigenous people with whom they came in contact" (xviii).

In theory, the czar wielded absolute authority over Siberia; in practice, the conquest, exploitation, administration, and defense of Siberia were supervised by two intertwined bureaucracies. One was centered in Moscow—the Siberian Office,[3] emerging slowly and haphazardly with no grand master plan. These officials were collectively in charge of the daily operations—they supervised appointments and the activities of the top Siberian officials, formulated rules for their personal behavior and treatment of the indigenous population, devised plans for permanent settlements, established *yasak*[4] quotas, and developed ways to protect their investment in Siberia.

The other level of administrative bureaucracy was dispersed throughout Siberia, far removed from central authority and so remote it might take two years for an official to reach his destination. It was headed by scores of *voevods*[5] with their own assistants, stationed in strategically located, fortified outposts. In addition to controlling all the supplies, they essentially had the power of life and death over those within their jurisdiction. Particularly in the remote regions of northeastern Siberia, trustworthy men were less willing to serve, and the corrupt ones were removed only when their abuses became unbearable. A voevod received generous remuneration, but he also expected to receive the essentials from the local inhabitants. All the native subjects were required to give him gifts on the holidays, and his subordinates also expected to receive their share. So indigenous people were under an enormous burden. It is understandable that they frequently expressed their anger (Dmytryshyn, Crownhart-Vaughan, and Vaughan, 18–20, 22; Hartley, xvi–xvii).

While the challenges and tensions of this conquest of Siberia were likely unknown to or ignored by the Europeans eager to receive any knowledge about foreign lands, what news trickled into Europe about the area was enthusiastically read and disseminated. An announcement about the Second Kamchatka Expedition, later named the Great Northern Expedition and, like the First Kamchatka Expedition, headed by the Danish captain Vitus Bering, appeared in the *Neue Leipziger gelehrte Anzeigen* of November 1733, while Steller was still in Halle. Since Halle is not very far from

Leipzig and one of his professors was closely connected to the St. Petersburg Academy of Sciences (Hintzsche, *Quellen* 1:xix), it is very likely that Steller heard of this enormous undertaking before leaving Halle in August of 1734 and possible that he resolved then to join it. Spanning ten years between 1733 and 1743 and involving directly or indirectly more than three thousand people with an estimated cost of 1.5 million rubles or one-sixth the income of the Russian government, its greatness lay in its size, the distance it had to go across the Northern Hemisphere, and the complexity of its goals.

Any systematic exploration and scientific discovery of Siberia was due in large part to Peter the Great, who, in order to implement his vision of expanding the Russian Empire, drew foreign scholars to Russia to create a scientific academy in St. Petersburg, inaugurated in 1725, that resembled those he had visited in Europe. Young and mostly German-speaking scholars initially formed the core of the academicians. One of their tasks was to organize and eventually accompany scientific expeditions to the unexplored lands east of the Urals. The German physician and naturalist Daniel Gottlieb Messerschmidt's journey from 1720 to 1727 to western and central Siberia marked the beginning of research into geography, mineralogy, botany, zoology, ethnography, and philology in this region as well as opening up the area to trade and economic development.

The possible existence of a land bridge between northeastern Asia and North America, posed by Gottfried Wilhelm Leibniz as a way of answering questions about the common origin of humans, among other interests, prompted Peter the Great to mount the First Kamchatka Expedition (1728–1730) after an initial expedition of two geodesists in 1719 had failed. After also failing to reach the North American coastline, Bering proposed a Second Kamchatka Expedition whose primary goals were to search for a sea route to North America and Japan and to survey the northern and eastern coast of Siberia. Under Czarina Anna these goals were greatly expanded into investigating the flora, fauna, minerals, and peoples of Siberia and opening up access to developing Siberia's resources. What had initially been a huge undertaking became for Bering an even bigger logistical nightmare. Because Russia viewed this expedition as providing information that would give it the strategic upper hand, especially in comparison to its neighboring countries, no one on the expedition was to reveal anything about its purpose or findings. It was this imposed secrecy that is largely responsible for the fact that much of the information gathered was published only much later, some of it not until today. Some of the information may still be lying unread or even undiscovered in the archives; some, unfortunately, may be lost forever.

Not surprisingly, these overly ambitious goals fell somewhat short, but amazingly much was actually achieved: the European discovery of Alaska (i.e., the Aleutian Islands and part of what is today known as Southeast Alaska) and the Commander Islands, notably Bering Island; a detailed cartographic assessment of the northern and northeastern coast of Russia and the Kurile Islands; considerable groundbreaking ethnographic, historic, and scientific research into Siberia and Kamchatka; and the refuted existence of a northeast passage and of the legendary land mass in the North Pacific.

In order to fulfill all these objectives, the expedition was divided into three independent detachments: (1) the Northern, charged with exploring the eastern sea route from the mouth of the Ob River to the Pacific; (2) the Pacific; and (3) the Academic. The Pacific or Maritime group was further divided into two. The first, led by Bering himself, was to sail to Kamchatka from Okhotsk and from there search for the legendary "Joao-da-Gama-Land," named after the Portuguese explorer who claimed to have discovered a land mass north of Japan. Then they were to sail farther east to the coast of North America. The other division, under the command of the Danish captain Martin Spangberg, was to investigate and chart the sea route from Okhotsk to Japan and China.

Steller eventually joined the third contingent—the Academic group, composed of a small number of scientists. The leaders—Professor Gerhard Friedrich Müller (history and ethnography), Johann Georg Gmelin (natural history), and Louis de l'Isle de la Croyère (astronomy and geodetics)—left St. Petersburg in August 1733, traveling together to Tobolsk, the seat of the Siberian Office. De la Croyère traveled separately from there, in March 1735 meeting up with Müller and Gmelin in Irkutsk, the center of Russian trade with China and an important stopping place for the expedition. Even though the local authorities, in this case the Irkutsk Provincial Government, were legally mandated to provide the researchers all the aid they required, neither boats nor food supplies were ready for the trip down the Lena to Yakutsk; thus, these three members took the opportunity to sail across Lake Baikal and to investigate the region from the eastern shore to the Chinese border, returning to Irkutsk for the winter.

They were finally able to continue their journey in 1736, getting as far as Yakutsk, where they were to meet Bering and travel together to Kamchatka, but they were again stuck without transportation and food supplies to get them to Okhotsk and then Kamchatka. Because of poor health, Müller and Gmelin eventually received permission to return to St. Petersburg, finally arriving in 1743. Before leaving Yakutsk, Müller and Gmelin had given the student Stepan Krasheninnikov detailed instructions for fulfilling his role as the preliminary researcher on Kamchatka. Beginning in 1737 Krasheninnikov studied mostly the southern part of the peninsula. He spent ten years as a member of the expedition, eventually became a professor at the Academy of Sciences, and was commissioned to write up the results of both his and Steller's research about Kamchatka, which appeared in 1755, the year of Krasheninnikov's death, with the title *Opisanie Zemli Kamchatki* or *Description of Kamchatka*.

By the end of 1737, Steller had been sent to assist Müller and Gmelin, receiving his instructions (found after this introduction) from them in Yeniseysk. Per these instructions, every three months Steller was to send to the Academy of Sciences written descriptions and drawings of everything he had investigated and of any preserved specimens, all cataloged, as well as an accounting of all his activities. These were then to be forwarded to the Academy of Sciences. In addition to his research, Steller carried heavy administrative obligations for the formidable logistics of the whole enterprise, the scope of which is also spelled out in the instructions. Number 2, for example, identifies the five people in his party for whom Steller had the responsibility, to be augmented in Irkutsk by three sluzhivs to serve as escorts and additional helpers. It was up to Steller to look out for them all, to stand up for them if they encountered problems, and, above all, to see to it that they received their meager pay and rations, preferably on time. Since both pay and provisions had to first be requested from various government agencies and shipped out where they were to be allotted, a horrendous amount of paperwork had to be constantly generated, sent out, and followed up with more.

Further tasks, also requiring much paperwork, were the procuring of *podvodi*—that is, wagons or sleds—and their drivers; of boats and rafts and their crews; and of other workmen; and the purchasing or hiring of horses. At least from Yakutsk on, cattle and their drivers were part of the convoy, too. Steller's lament in the "Description of Irkutsk" that he would be able to gather so much more valuable information if he did not have to spend so much time fighting for his pay expresses his frustration. He was even prompted to complain to Schumacher, the academy's librarian, that a "person doesn't need a tongue in these parts because everything is done in writing; I venture to say I could earn my living as a government clerk if I had to in the future" (*Quellen* 3:414).

All these memoranda, copies of memoranda, answers to memoranda, reminders, letters, and so on were of course handwritten, and each document painstakingly first repeated the contents of the document in response to which it was generated. And all that writing had to be done in cramped, occasionally sooty quarters, on board a boat amid chunks of ice, or by a campfire at night. In conjunction with the instructions, Steller was given 161 sheets of copied materials (document 26, *Quellen* 3:94–95). No wonder he needed an extra podvoda just to transport the books, papers, and instruments for his work (instruction 3). Since Steller's Russian was limited, the student Gorlanov served as his translator and scribe of the various memoranda to various local government offices as well as the official reports to the Academy of Sciences and the High Governing Senate, but Steller of course first had to generate them.

These logistical challenges were on a par with those posed by the environment and the people. But because he was most in his element in nature, he seems not to have resented her challenges. Though a rudimentary system of trails and way stations, zimovia, had been established even on that most challenging section between Yakutsk and Okhotsk, horses still got irretrievably stuck in bogs, and at least twice Steller found himself lost in the forest. In the face of rivers choked with ice, seemingly bottomless bogs, steep mountains, bloodthirsty insects, incompetent helpers, and extreme weather, he almost always kept his cool and his good spirits. Although suffering diarrhea after another dunking in a raging river, he could still appreciate his good stomach and observe that he remained diligent and merry (143).

It should be clear from the wealth of information Steller gathered about the country and its people that he more than fulfilled his obligations to the state as outlined in the instructions he was given. While the state that employed him may not have benefited fully from his findings, these findings established a baseline for the research of later academicians and scholars, and they should still be of considerable interest to present-day scholars and to lay readers as well. It is our hope that you who read this find it so.

Notes

1. *Cossacks*, term applied to a great variety of men—adventurers, outcasts, restless misfits, homeless men—all of whom served either on horse or foot to supplement the streltsy. Pushkarev.

2. Originally a small fort in Russia and Siberia, encircled by twelve- to fifteen-foot-high palisades made from sharpened tree trunks, with a garrison. Later many of these forts developed into towns and cities.

3. Established in 1637 as a *prikaz*. In 1711 Peter the Great transferred many of its functions to the Office of the Guberniya of Siberia, in 1730 Empress Anna reestablished some of its powers, and in 1763 Catherine II abolished this office for good. Dmytryshyn, Crownhart-Vaughan, and Vaughan, 18–19.

4. All native men of Siberia and northern Asia between the ages of eighteen and fifty except the crippled, the blind, and converts to Russian Orthodox Christianity were required to take the oath of allegiance to the czar and to pay an annual yasak in furs. The amount varied depending on availability. Early in the seventeenth century, when sables were still abundant, the assessed quota was twenty-two sables per man per year. Dmytryshyn in Wood, 31. As the supply of fur became exhausted, yasak began to be paid in cash. Collection was often taken by force and marked by violence. "In 1695, the Siberian Office [again] instructed officials not to 'execute or torture natives' and noted that many had been killed, whipped to death or tortured, that bribes had been demanded from them and livestock stolen, leading to the 'ruin of many tribute-paying people.'" Hartley, 38–39. Before Cossacks and hunters began to colonize Siberia, it was the form of levy the Mongol Tartars imposed on subject people. Czars were simply following the practice that existed in lands under Mongol rule. Hartley, 37–39.

5. Chief administrator of a district with far-reaching legal, economic, administrative, and police powers; term is old Slavic, originally meaning military commander, leader of warriors.

INSTRUCTIONS FOR GEORG WILHELM STELLER FROM FEBRUARY 18, 1739, FROM YENISEYSK

Johann Georg Gmelin and Gerhard Friedrich Müller

IN THE HANDWRITING OF ALEKSEI GORLANOV, SIGNED BY Johann Georg Gmelin and Gerhard Friedrich Müller; in *Quellen* 3:71–93 (translated from the Russian)

Instructions

Provided by the professors of the Academy of Sciences, Gerhard Friedrich Müller and Johann Georg Gmelin, to the adjunct of the Academy of Sciences, Georg Wilhelm Steller:

> In accordance with Her Imperial Majesty's ukase from the High Governing Senate and the decision of the Academy of Sciences, you were assigned to the Kamchatka Expedition. By that Academy of Sciences, you were issued instructions signed by Her Imperial Majesty's *Kammerherr*[1] and president of the Academy of Sciences, Baron von Korff, in which you were ordered to describe all things pertaining to natural history, to assist us in all matters after you arrived here, and to be guided by our determinations in everything. For these reasons we have decided to send you to Okhotsk and to Kamchatka and to issue you these instructions you are to follow unconditionally.
>
> 1. From here you will travel with your present party via Irkutsk, Yakutsk, and Okhotsk to Kamchatka and will investigate and describe—en route as well as on Kamchatka—everything concerning natural as well as political history, and in all places where it seems appropriate you will carry out meteorological observations and those concerning the nature of the earth. All this is recorded in our instructions, copies of which were provided to you on your departure from St. Petersburg. You will always act as befits a faithful servant of Her Imperial Majesty.

2. To your party will be assigned the painter Johann Christian Berckhan to draw and paint everything noteworthy in natural and political history; the student Aleksei Gorlanov to assist you with your observations, especially with those concerning geography and political history, and with the correspondence with the government offices; the prospector Grigorei Samoilov to look for ores; the huntsman Dmitrei Giliashev to shoot animals and birds [for the scientific collections]; and the Yakutsk sluzhiv Fedot Klimovskoi to interpret in the Yakut language and communicate with other native peoples and interview them about their faith, customs, and way of life, for which Klimovskoi has the necessary skills, having gained several years' experience. He is also to pay the *progon* money [Russian (R), money collected per kilometer traveled].

3. You will receive from the Yeniseysk Provincial Administration the progon money—from here to Irkutsk via Taseevskoi Ostrog, Kanskoi Ostrog, and Udinskoi Ostrog—for eleven podvodi [R, for-hire, government-sponsored wagons with horses or, in winter, sleds pulled by horses or dogs], namely, four podvodi for you, three for the painter, one for the student, one for the prospector and his instruments, one for the huntsman and the Yakutsk sluzhiv, and one for the books, instruments, and materials belonging to the Crown. The Yakutsk sluzhiv Fedot Klimovskoi shall enter the progon money into the Schnurbuch [literally, string book, a ledger with a registered number of pages through which a string has been drawn and its ends sealed, issued by government offices to travelers on official business to record expenses and receipts; WH, Glossar; *Quellen* 1:331], which the Yeniseysk Provincial Administration will hand over together with the progon money. The book and what is left of the money shall be delivered to the Irkutsk Provincial Administration when you arrive in Irkutsk.

4. You shall make great haste traveling to Irkutsk so that you can still use the winter route. You shall order the student Gorlanov to describe the geography along the route you are traveling.

5. Once you arrive in Irkutsk, you will inform the Irkutsk Provincial Administration in writing about your plans for carrying out the assigned journey and demand assistance in making it all happen. You are going to demand that pay authorized by Her Imperial Majesty be set aside for you and your party up to the beginning of the coming year, 1740. For this year, 1739, you have received your pay until August 8, so you are to receive it for five more months. The other members of your party received only a third of their pay here in Yeniseysk and thus have yet to receive two-thirds in Irkutsk. The prospector Samoilov was allotted a food allowance equal to a soldier's ration. He received that until March of this year. The huntsman Giliashev and the Yakutsk sluzhiv were each authorized sluzhivs' rations. But they have not received theirs for this year 1739, so their rations have to be requisitioned in Irkutsk.

6. From the Irkutsk Provincial Administration, you will requisition three Irkutsk sluzhivs as escorts to assist you with the necessary shipments and with everything else necessary for your assigned observations. You will incorporate these sluzhivs into your party. You will also demand that the Irkutsk Provincial Administration issue a ukase in the name of Her Imperial Majesty authorizing the exchange of these sluzhivs in Yakutsk and Okhotsk for sluzhivs from there.
7. To shoot birds and animals, you will be given nine pounds of the Crown's gunpowder from the amount we received in Irkutsk in 1735. You will demand eighteen pounds of lead from the Irkutsk Provincial Administration since we do not have any to spare. When you leave for Okhotsk, you may add some of both gunpowder and lead from the supply we left in Yakutsk together with other Crown supplies. But you will not hand over all the gunpowder and lead to your huntsman but will give him what he needs in each instance depending on whether he uses the flintlock musket or the rifle, so that the supply is controlled and he does not use gunpowder or lead unnecessarily.
8. You will demand that the Irkutsk Provincial Administration provide information about the provisions they promised to set aside for us and our retinue in Okhotsk, and that the administration order as many of those provisions as needed to be handed over to you and your party. A ukase of Her Imperial Majesty, issued on February 13, 1733, by the High Governing Senate, states that if our and our retinue's personal supply of provisions somewhere should not be sufficient and there were none to be purchased, then if foodstuffs belonging to the Crown were available from local warehouses, they should, as long as necessary, be issued at cost. Concerning this we have repeatedly written to the High Governing Senate, requesting that the provisions in Okhotsk and Kamchatka be sold to us at cost and the transportation be paid out of Crown funds. Since we were quite confident that a favorable decision would be forthcoming, we demanded that the Irkutsk Provincial Administration see to it that the provisions required by us and our retinue are made ready for us in Okhotsk and sold to us at cost. In case the Irkutsk Provincial Administration has already begun to transport these provisions, you will see to it that everything is carried out carefully and speedily according to the ukases and decrees. In Okhotsk you will then accept as many provisions as needed by you and your party. If, however, the transport of those provisions has not yet occurred, then you must demand that at least as many provisions as needed by you and your party for two and a half years be transported immediately to Okhotsk; the amount is to be calculated so that each person receives 864 pounds per year. You will receive exact copies of the entire correspondence up to now so that you know what exactly we wrote to the Irkutsk Provincial Administration concerning the transport of provisions and what response we received from that administration.

9. In 1737 the student Stepan Krasheninnikov was dispatched by us to Kamchatka to carry out a variety of investigations and to collect all kinds of oddities. On his departure from Yakutsk, he took with him provisions for two years, 1737 and 1738. Last year, in 1738, according to our request and the decision of the Irkutsk Provincial Administration, the student should have been sent provisions for the current year, 1739. Up until your departure for Kamchatka, you are to make sure that he is annually sent the necessary provisions and that provisions for him for two and a half years are added to those required by you and your party. You will especially see to it that this year, 1739, the student Krasheninnikov is sent provisions for the year 1740, since according to a report sent by him from Kamchatka, a significant part of the provisions he took with him was jettisoned during the voyage. To keep you informed to the fullest extent, exact copies of the relevant request submitted to the Irkutsk Provincial Administration and of the ukases sent to Yakutsk and Okhotsk are attached. [According to document 26, following these instructions in *Quellen* 3:94–95, Steller received a total of 161 sheets of document copies—no wonder he needed an extra podvoda to transport all the papers, books, and materials.]
10. During your stay in Irkutsk, you will take a look at the instruments for meteorological observations that we left behind to see if they are still in good condition. And you will ascertain if the sluzhiv Nikita Kanaev, who was charged with keeping a written record of those observations, is properly fulfilling his duties. In case those instruments have been damaged in some way, you will restore them to their original condition. In case that sluzhiv is negligent in the performance of his duties, you will inform the Irkutsk Provincial Administration and demand that the administration hold him to fulfilling his duties in every respect.
11. In Irkutsk you will inquire about the health of the assistant miner Michailo Mel'nikov, whom we had to leave behind because of illness. When we left Irkutsk, we demanded that the Irkutsk Provincial Administration return Mel'nikov to our command when he recovered. We received word from the caravan physician who had been staying in town at the time and to whose care we had entrusted Mel'nikov that after our departure he was feeling considerably better and would shortly be fully recovered from this disease. Subsequently we have, however, not received another word from him. For this reason, if you should see that Mel'nikov can be sent on his journey, you will send him to us as quickly as possible and require the Irkutsk Provincial Administration, in accordance with our earlier request, to give Mel'nikov a podvoda and the progon money for it.
12. For the journey from Irkutsk to Yakutsk, you will demand that the Irkutsk Provincial Administration outfit you at the docks of the upper Lena with a *doshchenik* [R, flat-bottomed, single-decked, one-masted cargo vessel, rowed with up to ten long oars; term retained.] with the necessary rigging,

provisions, and crew. But if, contrary to expectations, the Irkutsk Provincial Administration refuses because, they say, there are no doshcheniks at the docks on the upper Lena, then you will travel either on *kaiuki* [R, cargo boats on Siberian rivers, small doshcheniks; WH, Glossar; *Quellen* 2:442] or on rafts to Kirenskoi Ostrog. Before leaving Irkutsk, you need to insist that the Irkutsk Provincial Administration send a ukase of Her Imperial Majesty's to the *prikazchik* [R, chief administrator of a village or of a district consisting of more widely scattered ostrogs or settlements; WH, Glossar; *Quellen* 3:444], or whoever is in command in Kirenskoi Ostrog, ordering that the best of the three doshcheniks we left behind in that ostrog be repaired and made ready for your journey.

13. So that in the future you and the members of your party will have no problems receiving Her Imperial Majesty's pay in Yakutsk, in Okhotsk, or on Kamchatka, you shall demand that the Irkutsk Provincial Administration issue a ukase of Her Imperial Majesty's to the Yakutsk Administration and the commander of Okhotsk. In that ukase the amount of pay is to be listed separately for you and each member of your party so that orders may be issued to set aside that amount of pay at the beginning of each year. It shall also be indicated from which income the pay is to be taken so that everything is clear. To ensure reliability you should personally receive such a ukase from the Irkutsk Provincial Administration and take it with you unsealed, or you should demand the Irkutsk Provincial Administration give you a duplicate or an exact copy.

14. You will demand that the Irkutsk Provincial Administration issue you a *Geleitukase* [literally, escort pass; a sample found in *Quellen* 3:278–79] of Her Imperial Majesty's to all commanders, ordering that you unconditionally be given everything you demand for carrying out the investigations you have been charged with. In case you need workers or artisans for these investigations, they are to be given you. Promyshlenniks and *inozemtsy*[2] from whom you may need to gather certain information shall likewise be found and sent to you, and wherever you demand it, interpreters of the languages spoken by those people shall be sent to you. In that ukase it shall also be stated that the Yakutsk sluzhiv Fedot Klimovskoi, whom we are assigning to you, is to remain with you during the entire journey to Kamchatka and back to Yakutsk to serve as interpreter of the Yakut language as well as to assist you in gathering oral information from various peoples since he has experience in these things.

    You are to be granted help everywhere in securing what is needed to expedite, assist, and assure the safety of your journey. In case you want to travel somewhere on the water, you are to be provided with suitable vessels including all the rigging and provisions as well as workers; if traveling on land, you are to be given podvodi as well as progon money for them: four podvodi for you, three podvodi for the painter Berckhan, one podvoda for the student Gorlanov, one for the prospector, and one for the huntsman Giliashev and the sluzhiv Klimovskoi to share. For the journey from Yakutsk to Okhotsk, however, each may be given his own podvoda, and then an additional one for the books, instruments, and Crown materials, as well as one podvoda for the three sluzhivs assigned as escorts and expediters. Both on land and water, you are to be provided with knowledgeable people as guides and, if the route traverses dangerous areas, a sufficient number of guards.

On the strength of Her Imperial Majesty's ukase and in accordance with the rules of the Academy of Sciences, the pay is to be handed out in advance at the beginning of each year: 660 rubles to you, 500 rubles to the painter Berckhan, 100 rubles to the student Gorlanov, to the prospector Samoilov 36 rubles as well as the allotted provisions equal to a soldier's ration, to the huntsman Giliashev 5 rubles, to the sluzhiv Klimovskoi 7 rubles, and to the three sluzhivs assigned as escorts the appropriate amounts as well as the provisions as indicated above. In Okhotsk you and your party are to be given the necessary provisions at cost, and you and your party are to be assigned quarters suitable for your investigations. Your reports directed to the High Governing Senate, the Academy of Sciences, or to us are to be accepted for expediting, and together with these reports all kinds of materials are to be shipped. You are to receive receipts for those. Shipments addressed to you are to be forwarded to you dependably and without delay from wherever they are received.

15. The student Stepan Krasheninnikov told us in his report of November 14, 1737, that on the sea voyage from Okhotsk to Kamchatka, together with other things, gray paper ["indispensable for the drying of plants," Steller's letter to von Korff, *Quellen* 3:271], part of the Crown things he had with him, was lost at sea so that he had only five books left. One thermometer broke, and a variety of vegetable seeds were lost at sea too. That is why we are now sending a thermometer, twenty books of gray paper, and a variety of vegetable seeds with you for that student. If you are confident that you will be able to depart from Irkutsk this spring and that there will not be any delays on the journey to Okhotsk, you will take these things you are now receiving with you to Kamchatka. If, however, you cannot expect to depart from Irkutsk soon or you have doubts about leaving from Yakutsk for Okhotsk in good time, then you must take these things to the Irkutsk Provincial Administration to be shipped right after you arrive in Irkutsk. Since it is necessary to get these things to Kamchatka quickly, you will demand that the administration, via ukase, stress the urgency of this shipment to the Yakutsk voevod's administration.

16. If you are sent out from Irkutsk as outlined above, you will travel to the Lena River and demand that the Irkutsk Provincial Administration give you the required number of podvodi as well as the progon money for them.

To keep a record of that money, you will demand a Schnurbuch ledger [see sample in appendix B] with the seal of the Irkutsk Provincial Administration in which the expenses will be entered and receipts recorded. In accordance with previous practice, it will be convenient to delegate these tasks to the sluzhiv Klimovskoi.

17. If, on the Lena, everything should be prepared for your trip on the river and you can be confident that there will be no disturbances or delay in transporting provisions for you and your party, then you are to travel to Yakutsk at once without stopping along the way so that you can use most of the summer for botanical observations in Yakutsk since that region has not yet been exhaustively investigated. If the opposite is the case, you will spend most of the summer in the region on the upper Lena to conduct similar investigations. You will then travel to Yakutsk in the fall and describe that region during the following summer. To carry this out in the best way, you are receiving descriptions of plants, birds, and animals on the Lena as well as lists of all the plants, animals, and birds of which we had drawings made and of those of which no drawings could reasonably be made for lack of time or other reasons. So that you are informed about what we have carried out and what you have to pay more attention to, we also added a list of some investigations we began but were unable to finish.

18. While you are traveling from Irkutsk to the Lena, you will describe the way of life, religious practices, and manners as well as anything regarding the political history of the Buryats living along the way. But if, because of other investigations, you should be unable to describe these things yourself, you will assign this task to the student Gorlanov. You will order the painter to make some drawings of the Buryat way of life—for example, a Buryat family in their [traditional] dress and their yurts, their kitchen utensils and other household items, the shamans, healing practices, and other remarkable things that should be represented in drawings. You will make an effort to do likewise with the Tungus on the Lena, especially in Yakutsk. You will order drawings made of any and all Tungus and Yakut dress, shamans, and sacrifices since up to now nothing about the Yakuts has been depicted in drawings.

19. After your arrival in Yakutsk, you will write to Captain Commander Bering and to the Okhotsk administration to demand information on when a seagoing vessel can be expected to depart from Okhotsk for Kamchatka. In the meantime you will promptly let the Yakutsk voevod know what you require for your impending journey so that, when the news arrives from Okhotsk that a seagoing vessel will depart from Okhotsk for Kamchatka in the summer or fall of 1740 and there will be no obstacles to transporting the provisions needed by you and your party, you will finally be able to travel to Okhotsk in the spring of the year 1740 and cross over to Kamchatka in the same year.

20. However, if against expectations you receive the news that no vessel will leave Okhotsk for Kamchatka in 1740 or that there are no provisions because none were delivered, you will, in the spring of 1740, travel to the lower Lena, either as far as the mouth of the Lena or only so far that you will be able to return to Yakutsk by fall of that year so that you will not have to spend the winter in those areas downriver, enduring much hardship. You will describe the areas through which you travel on the river in great detail and will compile a geographic list describing the banks, along with the ores and minerals found on them; the trees, plants, animals, and other things; and the peoples living there. You will make an effort to obtain a living Arctic fox [*Vulpes lagopus*] and a living small field mouse that Arctic foxes feed on and have them sketched. You will make an especially great effort to visit two or three places where either rotten or well-preserved mammoth bones are found in the ground. You will issue orders to dig for those from the top down so that no bones are moved out of place. You will describe the various sand, stone, and clay strata located above these bones, and you will indicate the depth of these strata and sequence in which these strata lie one on top of the other and whether they are horizontal, vertical, or slanted, and if slanted, their approximate angle and to which side they incline from top to bottom. When the soil above the bones has been completely removed so all the bones are visible, you are to describe, in detail, their position in the ground. At one of these places, you are to order the painter to make an exact drawing of the position of those bones. If you manage to gather a complete skeleton, you will take it with you to Yakutsk and ship it to St. Petersburg to be preserved in Her Imperial Majesty's *Kunstkammer*.[3] But if a lot of the bones necessary for a complete skeleton cannot be found, you will collect only the most notable and ship them to St. Petersburg. After these bones have been removed from the ground, you will describe the soil in which they were lying and dig up as much of the soil from the place underneath as you can without too much difficulty and describe that, too.
21. According to information sent to us by Professor de l'Isle de la Croyère, all kinds of investigations were conducted by him in the regions along the lower Lena. A student was sent by him to the mouth of both the Lena and the Olenek River, where he was ordered to collect all the curiosities found there and to bring them with him to Yakutsk. So that you may know ahead of time where you should concentrate your efforts, you will ask the professor for copies of the written information generated by him concerning the natural and political history, and you will look at the curiosities the student brought back. If among them you find some particularly unusual objects, you will select these and ask Professor la Croyère [*sic*] to have them shipped to St. Petersburg.
22. To complement information we had received before our stay in Yakutsk, we demanded that the Yakutsk voevod's office provide us with more details

Instructions for Steller from February from Yeniseysk | 17

about the geography and history of the Yakutsk district. We also requested that various Yakut clothing items be purchased for Her Imperial Majesty's Kunstkammer, a request that was given added weight by a ukase from the Irkutsk Provincial Administration. To date we have, however, not received either news or articles of clothing from Yakutsk. You will therefore repeat our earlier demands to the Yakutsk administration and report to us what was done.

23. In accordance with Her Imperial Majesty's ukase issued on June 19, 1732, by the High Governing Senate to the Academy of Sciences, it was ordered that the assay master Gardebol be assigned to our retinue. According to a letter Captain Commander Bering sent us on June 18 [actually January 18; WH, Anm. 35] of last year, 1738, Gardebol was apparently assigned in the summer of 1738 to accompany Captain Spangberg on a sea voyage. During your stay in Yakutsk, you will request Her Imperial Majesty's pay for Gardebol. In the letter mentioned above, the captain commander informed us that the pay for Gardebol had been requested from the Yakutsk voevod's office to the end of 1738, and that he was not obligated to further request pay for Gardebol since he had been assigned to our command. We replied to the captain commander that we would tend to Gardebol's pay but would not be able to do anything just then since we were too far away. For this reason you will inquire of the Yakutsk voevod's office for which years they had requested the pay for Gardebol and had paid him, and for which years, beginning with 1739, the captain commander did not request pay for Gardebol. You will request pay for Gardebol up to the year in which you depart from Okhotsk, and you will also take care of it until he is under your command.

24. We left some books and Crown materials in Yakutsk and charged the surveyor Krasil'nikov with looking after them. You will need some of those for your assignments. You have permission to use whichever ones you deem necessary but need to provide a receipt for them. You are being given an exact copy of the list of items in Krasil'nikov's care.

25. We left a variety of mining tools in Yakutsk entrusted to the Yakutsk voevod's office—for example, a large rock drill, a small rock drill, threaded shafts, hammers, mattocks, pick axes, shovels, hoes, drills, and other stuff, as well as a 360-pound supply of iron rods. Petr Bobrov, storehouse manager of the Yakutsk voevod's office, gave us a receipt for these tools and the iron. You may take whichever of these tools you deem necessary. A list of these tools is appended to these instructions.

26. To transport the papers and books from Yakutsk to Okhotsk, you may take some of the Crown crates mentioned above in which the Crown things are stored. In case you need leather saddlebags tanned white to transport any kind of Crown things, you may demand those from whoever is in charge of them with the Kamchatka Expedition since—according to a letter written on April 10, 1735, and sent us by Captain Commander Bering—two

hundred pairs of saddlebags were set aside for our retinue. When he left Yakutsk for Okhotsk, the student Krasheninnikov received twelve pairs of these for transporting his provisions.

27. When everything required for your journey to Okhotsk and Kamchatka has been prepared and you have received the news from Okhotsk that a sufficient supply of provisions has been transported to Okhotsk and that a seagoing vessel will be departing Okhotsk for Kamchatka, then you will, at the first opportunity, travel to Okhotsk with your party in the spring of the year in which the boat is leaving for Kamchatka. You will receive four horses for each podvoda for that journey in accordance with Her Imperial Majesty's Geleitukase given us by the Siberian Government Administration, of which a copy has been made in the Yakutsk voevod's office. Since this journey will take a long time, you will have the opportunity to diligently investigate everything concerning the geography, natural history, and political history of that region.

28. Until you can depart for Kamchatka, you will remain in Okhotsk. In the meantime you will devote your diligence to describing the natural history of the local area, especially the plants and trees, birds, animals, fishes, whales, all kinds of insects, shellfish, and crabs. This includes comparing the marine plants, birds, animals, fishes, insects, shellfish, and crabs to those plants, birds, and other creatures found in the rivers and on land, as well as to those living in both the sea and the rivers. As for the fish swimming from the sea into the rivers, you will describe precisely when they do so and how far up the rivers they go and at what time they return to the sea. You will describe which birds stay all year in the area around Okhotsk and which ones only temporarily, including which countries the latter come from and when and to which countries they return.

29. After you arrive in Okhotsk, you will demand that the administration of Okhotsk order the Koryaks to hunt a whale and bring it to Okhotsk. It is also possible that during your stay in Okhotsk a whale will be beached on the shore. You will describe such a whale and find out if there are other species of whales in that sea. You will dissect that whale and specifically describe it according to the special instructions given you as part of these.

30. You will also endeavor to find out if the medication called spermaceti may be extracted from that whale's brain. The abovementioned special instructions describe how this medication is extracted from Greenland whales. If this medication can be prepared, you will send us a certain amount of it. You will, together with the medication, send us half a pound of a fresh whale brain in a glass or pot, securely caulked and with seal affixed, so that we can find out for certain ourselves by conducting our own experiment.

31. After you arrive in Okhotsk, you will—according to point 23 of these instructions—accept the assay master Gardebol into your party and demand that he provide you reports. You will order him to describe in

detail what his investigations during his stay in Okhotsk consisted of, what he did on the sea voyage with Captain Spangberg, which places he explored, and what resulted from those explorations. As long as he belongs to your party, you will assign tasks to Gardebol and demand that he carry out investigations in line with his reports.

32. While you are in Okhotsk, you will find out everything about the religious beliefs of the local Lamut and Koryak peoples; about their customs, their way of life, their hunting and fishing practices; and about their weddings, burials, birth and rearing of children, oaths and vows, dispositions, virtues and vices, and anything else concerning them. If there happen to be any Tungus from Udskoi Ostrog in Okhotsk, you will find out from them whatever you can about the Gilyaks living around the mouth of the Amur River.
33. While in Okhotsk you will find out to the best of your ability the rivers and streams south and north of the Okhota River that flow into the Sea of Okhotsk, describing the width, depth, and flow rate of each, as well as the condition of their banks, the trees and brush, and the animals and birds found along their banks and the fish in their waters.
34. For the above-outlined investigations to be carried out in Okhotsk, you will, after your arrival, demand interpreters of the Lamut and Koryak languages from the administration of Okhotsk as well as a huntsman from among the local sluzhivs. When you leave Okhotsk, you will return all of them to that administration.
35. To provide you ahead of time with pertinent information about all kinds of animals, birds, fish, plants, and trees found in the Okhotsk region, you will receive exact copies of the lists the student Stepan Krasheninnikov made of the animals, birds, trees, and plants there, as well as of the descriptions Krasheninnikov made of some fish, birds, and sponges. Odds and ends of information concerning the natural history along the route from Yakutsk to Okhotsk have also been added.
36. If a seagoing vessel should depart for Kamchatka, stop your investigations in Okhotsk, leaving any unfinished ones behind for when you return from Kamchatka. Together with your party, take that ship to Kamchatka and go to Bol'sheretskoi Ostrog, where we sent the student Stepan Krasheninnikov and ordered him to stay.
37. After you arrive in Bol'sheretskoi Ostrog, you will take the student Krasheninnikov into your command and look over all the observations and investigations he has conducted since arriving in Kamchatka. Following our written directives, you will then correct any of his observations you consider questionable so no uncertainty remains. Then you will decide which future investigations are to be undertaken. As for the observations not yet carried out, you will carry those out as a supplement so that everything concerning natural and political history on Kamchatka shall have been described completely. You will write a general description of the land's

topography—namely, its mountains, grasslands, bogs, and forests as well as rocky, clayey, muddy, and sandy places, and the geologic structures. In this respect you should pay special attention to the location and inclination of the strata, which can be best observed in the mountains. Further, [you should describe the following:] the rivers and streams—where they originate and where they flow to; the season, time, and reasons for their maximum and minimum flows; the springs and lakes and their location; possible differences in size between the trees and plants growing there and those growing in Siberia, Russia, and other countries; and where in comparison to other regions the ground is elevated and the tallest mountains are located, for which barometric observations have to be made. You should also include a detailed description of the volcanoes and of the radical upheavals [earthquakes] occurring from time to time in the country—for example, that there used to be mountains, lakes, and bays where none now exist—and the creation of new mountains, lakes, and bays, as well as plague epidemics among the people, epidemics among the animals, and more.

38. To assure the best possible execution of the tasks you are asked to carry out on the journey from Yakutsk to Okhotsk, in Okhotsk, and on Kamchatka, you are provided an exact copy of the instructions we gave the student Krasheninnikov. In them all the duties relating to the natural and political history are laid out in detail. They also contain everything we have been told about those lands and particularly what is yet to be investigated. Also included is a geographical and political description of Kamchatka and the surrounding areas that you should scrutinize while on Kamchatka and, if necessary, correct and supplement.

39. Suitable help for your investigations is also provided by exact copies of questions concerning the natural and political history sent to the student Krasheninnikov at various times, as well as lists of animals, birds, fish, trees, and plants with their Russian names [see document 26, Quellen 3:94–95]. With this help you will be able to ask questions about all kinds of things. You will specifically order the painter to make drawings of whatever relates to the various native peoples' way of life and their faith based on idolatry.

40. When you have carried out everything you were ordered to do on Kamchatka, you will return to Okhotsk with your party. If you and the student Krasheninnikov had not been able to complete your investigations in Okhotsk earlier for lack of time, you will carry those out after you return. Then you will travel back to Yakutsk, where, according to our suggestion, you will receive a decision made by the High Governing Senate or the Academy of Sciences about the route you are to travel on the way back from there to St. Petersburg.

41. Before you depart from Kamchatka or Okhotsk, you will return the assay master Gardebol to the command from which he came since we have no information whatsoever where he has been ordered to go after completing his assignments under our supervision.

42. So that we may always be informed about your investigations, you will send us regular reports about your observations and investigations every three months during your entire journey, and once a year while on Kamchatka. With those reports you will include catalogs of plants and trees, animals, birds, fish, and insects you found, as well as of all the ores and minerals. You will, in particular, send extensive descriptions and drawings of things never described before as well as historical reports you collect about the native peoples and geographical descriptions of all the places you visit. In all your investigations, you will distinguish between what you have seen with your own eyes and what you gathered from what others told you.

43. Additionally, you will endeavor to preserve in any way possible one or two specimens of the unknown plants, animals, birds, fish, insects, crabs, and shellfish, and to collect samples of all the noteworthy ores and minerals. You will put together skeletons of the large animals, making sure to have the fat removed. You will send these things to be preserved in Her Imperial Majesty's Kunstkammer, together with your reports to us. Furthermore, with respect to the unknown plants and trees, you will very carefully gather their ripe seeds and roots dug up at a suitable time; you will ship them at the first opportunity. You will personally bring the roots and seeds you gather during your last year on Kamchatka with you to Okhotsk and send them off as quickly as possible to St. Petersburg so that attempts at propagating them can be undertaken.

44. Along with the abovementioned reports on your observations, you will also report on all the circumstances of the progress of your journey and on your priorities, where and when and coming from where you intend to spend some time, and when and where you are encountering the biggest obstacles, possibly causing interruptions in your investigations. You must therefore keep a daily journal in which to record everything that happens during your travels. When you correspond with government offices or other parties about your journey or investigations, you will diligently collect and save all letters, including those you receive, and order that they be bound into a book. With respect to things needed, you will send us copies of that correspondence.

45. In ukases of Her Imperial Majesty sent at various times during 1733 from the High Governing Senate to the Academy of Sciences, it was ordered that the students of the Slavic-Latin School attached to our retinue were to receive instruction and their pay through us, and we were to see to it that they would always have enough clothes and food, that they would not spend money foolishly, and that they would spend their time in a meaningful way. Therefore, you will definitely act in accordance with these ukases.

46. During the entire journey there and back, you will enter all the progon money and all the Crown moneys you spend into a Schnurbuch ledger,

which you will request of the Irkutsk Provincial Administration. You will have receipts for those expenses entered into that ledger, and you will also enter the expenses from your personal funds you use to purchase materials for your investigations.

47. When you send off your reports, it is permissible to accept letters from all persons with you and others belonging to the Kamchatka Expedition and send them by mail free of charge. However, in their envelopes you must not include private mail from foreign merchants or people of other ranks or include anything in packages since that has been prohibited under threat of legal prosecution by ukase of the Governing Senate.

48. If secrecy is to be maintained about some of the Crown things, you must absolutely not write about them to anybody in your private letters, and you can write in official reports only to those who have sent you on your way. But if anyone should hinder you in any way, you are free to write to whomever you wish. Name the matter you have been tasked with and who or what is responsible for this hindrance. You are equally at liberty to write to someone you trust, if an irregularity subject to secrecy occurs and it is impossible to voice a suspicion in reports to the offices or persons that have given you your assignments. However, you must—under threat of penalty through Crown ukases—not write about your actual assignments.

49. Furthermore, the Irkutsk Provincial Administration was thoroughly informed in a memorandum about every aspect of the assignments we gave you; a copy of it is attached. To keep him informed, we also wrote Captain Commander Bering in Okhotsk about them.

50. In support of your investigations, you are now provided with some books and Crown materials listed in the following catalog; according to instruction 24 above, you may add to these books and Crown materials whatever you deem necessary from those located in Yakutsk.

Catalog

Caspari Bauhini *Pinax* [Caspar Bauhin's *Catalog of Plants*]

Tournefortii *Institutiones Rei Herbariae cum Corollaria Institutionum Rei Herbariae* in II Volumine [Tournefort's *Elements of Botany with an Addendum (to the 2nd vol. after his travels in Armenia), in two volumes*]

Thomae Willis *opera omnia* [*Complete Works* of Thomas Willis]

Ioannis Raii *Methodus emendata et aucta editus* 1710 [John Ray's *Methodically Arranged Plant Survey*, improved and enlarged edition, 1710]

Eiusdem *De variis plantarum methodis dissertatio* [Ray's *Catalog of Different Plant Taxa*]

Eiusdem *Stirpium Europaearum extra Britannias nascentium sylloge* [Ray's *Catalog of European Plant Taxa Growing Outside of Britain*]

Eiusdem *Synopsis methodica animalium Quadrupedum et serpentini generis* [Ray's *Methodical Synopsis of Four-Footed and of Serpent Animal Genera*]

Instructions for Steller from February from Yeniseysk

Nine pounds of gunpowder
Two and a quarter pounds of quicksilver
Nine pounds of cotton
Five reams of stationery paper
Three books of thin stationery paper
Six books of gray paper
Twelve small pots for samples
Twenty pounds of Moscow clay from which to make such pots
One barometric glass tube with scale board
For the anatomical observations:
One hamulus [small surgical hook]
Four different-size needles
Five knives
Three lancets

The student Gorlanov was given the following Crown books:

Physicae modernae sanioris compendium Erotematicum Johannis Christophori Sturmii [Johann Christoph Sturm's *Love-Themed Compendium of Curative Modern Physics*]
C. Sallustii *opera* [Sallust's *Works*]
Juvenalis et Persii *Satyrae* [*Satyr Plays* of Juvenal and Persius]
Plinii Junioris *Epistolae* [Pliny the Younger's *Letters*]
Grammatica Germano-Russica [*German-Russian Grammar*]

The prospector Grigorei Samoilov received:

Two hammers
Two pickaxes
One hoe
One shovel
Eight mattocks
One hatchet

The huntsman Giliashev was issued his rifle.

Notes

1. Title and function likely corresponding to an English councillor's.
2. Literally, foreigners; at the time, usually foreigners in Russian service, but *iasachnye inozemtsy* meant yasak-paying Siberian tribes. WH, Glossar. Gmelin and Müller use the term to refer to the indigenous peoples.
3. German (G), collection established by Peter the Great in St. Petersburg and completed in 1727, dedicated to preserving natural and human curiosities and rarities.

PART I

DESCRIPTION OF IRKUTSK AND ITS SURROUNDINGS

1

ABOUT IRKUTSK AND ITS SURROUNDINGS

In describing the town of Irkutsk and its surroundings, I can be brief, since I am well aware that Professor Müller's incredible diligence and skill have omitted nothing concerning the region, the public buildings, the number of private dwellings, the founding and growth of the place, the inhabitants' trade and character, and the income of the province and town. I also know that the town's location together with the advantages a kind Nature has bestowed on it have been described in such a way that to write more about it is quite unnecessary. Strictly for order's sake, I shall limit my observations to the shortest review of some information received, in order to proceed to a more thorough description of Lake Baikal.

The town of Irkutsk was built at 52°12′ northern latitude on the western bank of the Angara River, in the middle of three rivers: the Angara; the Irkut, which flows into the Angara's eastern bank above the town; and the Ushakovka, a small stream that joins the Angara's western bank directly below the town. I shall write more about it below.

This town got its start as well as its name about sixty years ago with the construction of a zimov'e[1] on the Irkut River. Because of its location, which is pleasant and convenient for trade, in a short time it became so popular with the Russians that due to its many advantages it can now rival the fame of Tobolsk, the capital [of Siberia since 1709]. Although the town has now left its original location, having moved from the bank of the Irkut to the west bank of the Angara, it has nevertheless retained its original name of Irkutsk.

Its location is undeniably one of the healthiest and most pleasant places in all of Siberia. From the south to the north, the Angara River flows past it,

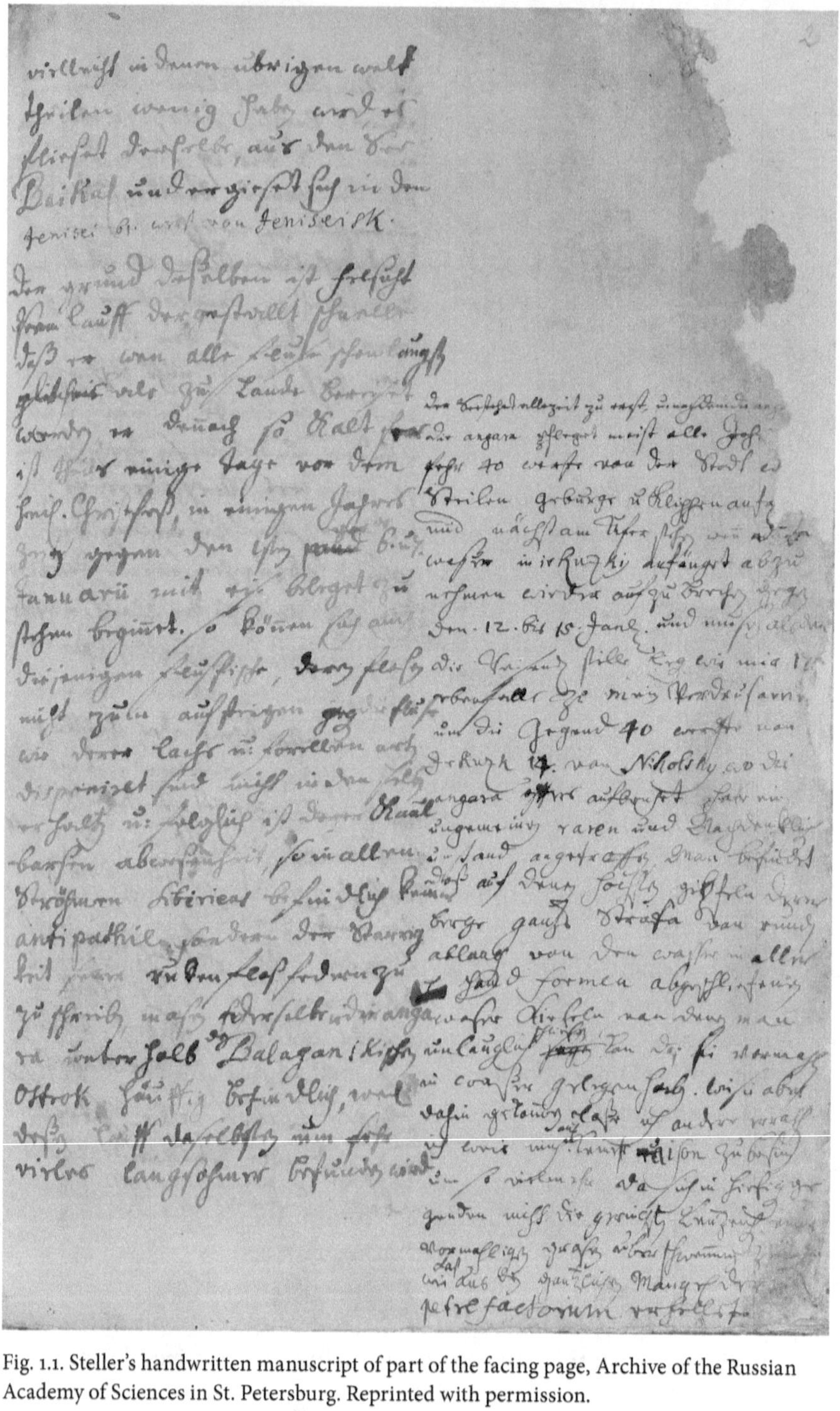

Fig. 1.1. Steller's handwritten manuscript of part of the facing page, Archive of the Russian Academy of Sciences in St. Petersburg. Reprinted with permission.

which is so clear and fast it likely has no equal in all of Russia and Siberia—few, if any, in the rest of the world. It flows from Lake Baikal, emptying sixty-one kilometers from Yeniseysk into the Yenisey.

The Angara's bottom is rocky, its current so fast that though the water is very cold, it does not begin to freeze up until a few days before Christmas, some years as late as the first or even the sixth or seventh of January. By then, all the other rivers in the country can already be used as ice roads. The lake always freezes first and afterward the Angara . . . [omission in MS.]. About forty kilometers [in text, *verst*, R, equals 1.067 kilometers; consistently translated as kilometers] from town, where the steep mountains and cliffs begin and hug the bank, the Angara tends to break up again almost every year around January 12 to 15 when the water flowing past Irkutsk begins to recede, forcing travelers to stay put, which happened to me, too, in 1740, much to my vexation. In the area forty kilometers from Irkutsk and fourteen from Nikolski, where the Angara often opens up, I came upon an extremely rare circumstance, emphatically worth mentioning. On the highest mountain summits, you find whole layers of round or oval gravel, waterworn in many ways; you can undeniably conclude that they had previously lain in water. I'll let others guess how they got there. I cannot think of a reason, especially since there are no indications whatsoever of a previous great flood in these parts, which is evident from the complete lack of petrifications.[2] Unlike the species of salmon and trout, those river fish whose fins are not suitable for swimming upriver against the current cannot sustain themselves in the Angara River. Consequently, the absence of the Eurasian ruffe [*Gymnocephalus cernua*] that occurs in all Siberian rivers is due not to antipathy but to the rigidity of its dorsal fins [not a valid scientific explanation. Arkadii Vladimirovich Balushkin, in WH, Anm. 16]. For these fish are found in the Angara far below the Balaganskoi Ostrog where the current is considerably slower. This river's water is extraordinarily clean, light, and clear so that for thirty-five or forty-two, even up to eighty-six feet, you can clearly see the stones on the bottom and even distinguish their colors. The local residents have also noted that, no matter how much you drink, this water does not weigh down your body, nor cause any harm, though it is unsuitable for washing wounds since it would prevent their healing.

Usually the Angara breaks up in the beginning of April; in 1739, for example, it went out the night of April 5. Both when it freezes and when it breaks up, two phenomena occur that constitute the biggest part of spring or fall weather. Before the river opens, Irkutsk is such a filthy place that you cannot proceed on foot without getting horribly dirty and at every step running the risk of losing shoes or boots. As soon as the river breaks up, all the streets dry up and then remain clean.

The severest cold happens between Christmas and about the twentieth of January. After that, it is uncommonly warm and pleasant as long as ice is drifting in the river, but as soon as the Irkut freezes up, Irkutsk is invariably shrouded in fog, especially above the Angara, so that it keeps you from clearly seeing the other side of the river, sometimes for weeks. Yet you do not hear that this thick, foggy, damp air makes people especially susceptible to disease. As soon as the river [not clear whether Steller means the Angara or the Irkut] freezes up, it is uncommonly pleasant and without a hint of fog. The cold immediately lets up, from which you should guess that the seasonal cold of a place is caused not only by its latitude, mountains, or north winds but also by fast river currents and evaporation. You notice that the wind coming across the Angara feels colder than when it blows directly from the north.

This river's name, Angara, is a proper name in the language of the Buryat and Tungus, and until now I have not been able to ascertain what it actually means or why it is applied to large rivers. One Angara River flows into one end of Lake Baikal in a delta with three arms; the other flows from the lake's other end and past Irkutsk. This latter Angara does not, like other rivers, flood in spring but instead floods in the fall even though the weather is the most constant then. As wet as the spring is, the fall is dry—entirely free of rain; so heavy rains cannot, as in other places, cause the strong increase in water flow. Rather, it is due to the Angara's gradually freezing and ceasing to flow. For two hundred kilometers below Irkutsk, near Balaganskoi Ostrog, it freezes a month earlier than at Irkutsk, and as the ice gradually sets up, freezing closer to the town, the water backs up more and more because the ice downstream impedes the current. As soon as the river freezes solid in Irkutsk, the water gradually disappears. This year it rose so high that it was level with the streets and flooded the basements. Eventually the water recedes and returns to the river. Also, this river does not freeze for good at once but within twenty-four hours sometimes breaks up again six to ten times. This year, the Angara resembled a boggy meadow more than a river, the great flood having inundated all the pastures and fields. When the water reached its highest level close to freeze-up, it swept up whole fields and deposited them in front of the town so that the river indeed looked more like a boggy meadow.

Fig. 1.2. Traveling on the Lena with rafts and doshcheniks. (Ann Arnold adapted this and the other drawings from her book *Sea Cows, Shamans, and Scurvy: Alaska's First Naturalist—Georg Wilhelm Steller* [New York: Frances Foster Books, 2008] and granted us permission to use them.)

As soon as the Angara is frozen solid, Lake Baikal is, too, but like the Angara it often freezes only to be torn open again by the winds. On the lake and on the Angara, the doshcheniks go to the Selenga River and the Posolsky Monastery and from there regularly to Irkutsk with goods for sale until the middle of December, which deserves to be noted as something special in this region. Yet the trips in late fall are not without danger, because sometimes the vessels drift with the ice around and around for six to seven weeks, not being able to sail either into the Selenga or to the other shore, suffering distress and deprivation in the process. The distance between where the Angara flows out of the lake and Irkutsk is over one hundred kilometers by water but only ninety-six by land. The river flows so rapidly that, with little rowing, you can drift from Nikolski to Irkutsk in four to five hours. Pulling a boat upriver, however, requires close to four full days and the great effort of many workers. The river has rapids, here called *shiveri*, that you have to pay close attention to going up- or downriver. The Angara also divides into *protoki* or channels, forming big and small islands here and there.

Both Lake Baikal and the Angara are surrounded by tall, rugged cliffs, decreasing in height and ruggedness as they approach Irkutsk; just before Irkutsk they become lower on both sides, constituting the most pleasant landscape you can imagine. In this respect, the Siberian Cossacks' natural intelligence shown by their sensible choice of this place—as well as of

Yeniseysk and Tomsk—has to be admired. You almost come to believe that they had all the necessary architectural, mathematical, and physical reasons for establishing a town on a list before their eyes and followed them. To be sure, from Nikolskaya Zastava to Irkutsk—that is, a hundred kilometers downriver, on either side of the Angara—there is no place as suitable a location for a town as the one where it was built. For immediately above Irkutsk, at the place called Krest[3] not far from the church built in honor of the Trinity, the mountains on both sides of the Angara hug the banks, leaving—much to the regret of the town's residents—no suitable room for grain fields or a pretty village or estate. If the Angara's dammed-up waters had not turned the few level places into bogs as well as calm lakes, the residents feel that the trip to Nikolski would be ever so much more pleasant and the area would have been better cultivated. As it is, there are only huts built of necessity and named after the merchants who built them. Still, the ample scenery and images inspire the viewers to utmost delight.

The region around the outlet[4] of the Angara is above all worth noting. Around Listvenishnoe Zimov'e, seven kilometers from where the Angara flows out of the lake, tall, forested mountains form a semicircle like an amphitheater. In the middle before the outfall, an imposing rock rises out of the water, thirteen feet tall and twenty-one feet wide, called *Shamanski kamen*, Shaman's Rock, which the Buryats and Tungus venerate, even considering it divine, and they habitually swear on it and are afraid of it as if it were God himself. They will rather admit any guilt than go there to kiss it. It is less respected by the gulls, who have completely painted it white with their excrement. At that point, the river is very fast and the noise so overpowering [In text, *prächtig*, dazzling; we assume Steller meant *mächtig*, mighty.] that nobody is able to understand another's word. It is also dangerous to get there and then only possible in small boats. Among the rocks are field stones, pieces of wood, and rags that the natives [In text, *heathens*; replaced with *natives* where appropriate] have thrown there as offerings. The rock itself is a coarse, blackish-gray sandstone mixed with spar. I am sending a piece of this nature-made idol to the Kunstkammer as a testament to heathen foolishness, though I do not know which of the god's members it resembles.

To the right side of the Angara's source above the lake, approximately forty kilometers from Nikolski, the eternally snow-covered Tunkinski Range is visible, with the tallest mountains on the whole lake and among those I've ever seen anywhere. They are visible though only in clear weather not far from Tulun, the first place in the Irkutsk district, three hundred kilometers from town. From the middle of the area opposite Medvedev's Church, you can see between the mountains toward the source of the Angara and the Tunkinski Range for over a hundred kilometers, which reveals that Irkutsk was built in a direct line from the source of the Angara though the river has many bends. Below Ilimsk where the Ilim River flows into the Angara from the left, the Angara loses its name and becomes the Tunguska; from then on till it flows into the Yenisey, sixty-seven kilometers from the town of Yeniseysk at Tunginskoi Ostrog, it is known as the Tunguska. Downriver, the Tunguska has many *porogi* or rapids that cause considerable dangers and costs for the merchants. These rapids are clearly formed by the cliffs that extend underwater into the river. Nine of these are especially big and dangerous. The first is called *Strelovskoi Porog*, seventy-one kilometers from the town of Yeniseysk, ten before the Tunguska joins the Yenisey; the second is *Murskoi Porog*; the third *Kasina Shivera* [waterfall]; the fourth *Aplinskoi Porog*; the fifth, *Shamanskoi Porog*, is called that because a shaman fell in there and broke his neck. The sixth is called *Dolgoi Porog*, the seventh *Padunskoi Porog* because it is very steep and precipitous. The eighth, *Pianoi Porog* [the Drunken One; WH, Anm. 58], has its name from a plant that makes people drunk, of which Dr. Gmelin will give extensive information; the ninth is called *Pochmel'noi Porog* [R, Hangover Rapids], and I could say more about it if I didn't know that Professor Müller has described all you need to know in the greatest of detail. While the water around Irkutsk is very clean, it gradually becomes less so, mixed with diverse kinds of pollution the closer it gets to the Yenisey.

The fish in the Angara are as follows: common sturgeon [R, *oseter*; *Acipenser sturio*], sterlet [*Acipenser ruthenus*][5] and starry sturgeon [In text, *Schebriga*; best guess *Acipenser stellatus*; WH, Anm. 65]. But these fish are never caught below Bratskoi Ostrog where the Ilim flows into the Irkut even though they are numerous in Lake Baikal because they are used to swimming upstream and not downstream. Siberian taimen [*Hucho taimen*] and sig [common whitefish] sometimes swim up the Irkut into Lake Baikal, but as soon as the Irkut freezes up, not a single one of these fish is to be seen because the sig in Lake Baikal [Baikal Lake sig, *Coregonus lavaretus baicalensis*, best guess] do not swim downstream in the Irkut. Sharp-snouted lenok [*Brachymystax lenok*], grayling [*Thymallus thymallus*, "Siberian Fish," or *T. arcticus*; Bond, pers. comm., May 1991], Eurasian dace [R, *elets*, *Leuciscus leuciscus*, best guess, "Siberian Fish"], species of roach [in text, *sorogi*], *plotva* [R, common roach, *Rutilus rutilus*, "Siberian Fish"], *pizda ryba*; bullhead, best guess; WH, Anm. 75], northern pike [*Esox lucius* L.; WH, Anm. 76; see ch. 5], and omul [Lake Baikal omul, *Caregonus migratorius*, of which there are four to five subpopulations in Lake Baikal; since 2004 listed as endangered; "Fishes: Baikal Omul," Baikal.ru] are sometimes caught around the solstice. The omul is native only to Lake Baikal, being occasionally swept out of the lake with the current. Below Balaganskoi Ostrog in the upper regions of the Angara and in Lake Baikal, there are no burbot [*Lota lota*], perch [species of *Perca*], or Eurasian ruffe, the reason for which I have given above.

Most of the fishing in the Angara takes place in spring and fall; in winter people make do with frozen or salted fish. It is almost a hallmark of Irkutsk that in the morning or evening you almost always see people in the street carrying a string of Arctic grayling in their hand. In spring, the fish are full of worms and lice, which I have extensively described in my *Catalogus insectorum*. In some places, like below the Voznesenski Monastery, this river is bottomless and never freezes. Elsewhere I will describe the kind of villages, landed estates, and farms—in this country called *zaimki* [small settlements in Siberia with just a few houses; translated as village when not used as part of a proper name; WH, Glossar]—as well as the zimovia or single huts found on the road on both sides of the Angara. The Irkut, the other river that flows into the Angara across from the city, is almost as wide as the Angara; in addition, it is very deep and rather muddy in some places. I shall describe its course, as well as its banks and the rivers flowing into it and the settlements built on it, in a special treatise [No proof such a document exists; WH, Anm. 85].

The Ushakovka, or Ida River, which originates close to Lake Baikal between mountains not far from the source of the Golousnaya, is no more than 70 to 105 feet wide and flows into the Angara, approximately fifty kilometers from its source, close to and below the town—that is, between the town and Monastery Village, which is located on a hill and contains a nuns' convent. The Ushakovka is named after the man Ivashka Ushakov, who first built a mill on its bank. These days this mill belongs to the widow of Ivan Pivovarov and generates an annual income of five hundred rubles. The Ushakovka's bottom is rocky, the gravel in it red and ferrous. Iron used to be smelted from bogs along this river. Nowadays this iron is left lying by the wayside since it is friable due to all the sand. Ten kilometers from the mill on a hill surrounded by boggy areas, Pivovarov's widow has built an estate

Fig. 1.3. Carrying home a string of grayling in Irkutsk (Arnold).

or zaimka, and about forty or fifty kilometers from town live promyshlenniks who hunt Siberian stags or *iziubri* [*Cervus elaphus*; WH, Anm. 94; common name is red deer], moose [*Alces alces*], and deer either by means of pits or with guns. About eighty years ago, this area was famous for hunting sable, but for many years now not a single one has been seen here. Many springs and small streams that flow into the Ushakovka are too insignificant to have names. The fish in this river are the Arctic grayling, the sharp-snouted lenok, lake minnows [*mundi, Rhynchocypris percnurus*], Eurasian dace, a species of roach [in text, *sorogi*], and burbot.

The nicest hayfields, belonging to the Demientievs, are found along this river. The woods are mostly young trees because, being so close to town, the trees are constantly being felled and transported to town for firewood. Many of the springs flowing into the Ushakovka never freeze, and that is where the water ouzels, or dippers, called *vodianie vorob'i* [most likely the Eurasian dipper, *Cinclus cinclus*; Springer, pers. comm., August 24, 2016], are found.

It is no mere flattery to say that this place, Irkutsk, has all the qualities of a well-positioned trade center and on top of that is endowed with many amenities that no European could imagine exist in Siberia. The air is healthy, the fall more pleasant than in all other areas of Russia or Siberia; the weather is constant, the river teeming with fish and navigable, except for a few shallow places that take a lot of effort to get around. The area is wonderfully scenic. Mountains rise above the Angara, if not on both sides, at least on one. Where the town is located, these mountains are about seven kilometers apart, gradually becoming a plain. One end of this valley is called Krest; the other is the Monastery Village, where the mountains gradually begin again, extending along the Angara. They are studded with the most beautiful forest of Dahurian larch [*Larix dahurica* Turcz. subsp. *cajanderi* (Mayr) Dylis; Jäger], Siberian spruce [*Picea obovata* Ledeb.; Jäger], Scots pine [*Pinus sylvestris* L.; Jäger], Japanese white birch [*Betula platyphylla* Sukaczev; Jäger], and a few Siberian pine [*Pinus sibirica* Du Tour; Jäger].

On this plain between both mountain ranges, the Ushakovka flows through forests and meadows, providing the most pleasurable strolls. Across from town, the left bank of the Angara is flat, with the most delightful meadows full of the most beautiful, colorful, and unusual flowers, which convince even the exiles that their lives are not utterly wretched.

You can see across this plain for about twenty kilometers. As the Voznesenski Monastery adds to the charm of Monastery Village, so this village and Zhilkina Village, in which the archbishop has built an uncommonly beautiful building, enhance the appearance of Irkutsk. Although the villages are about two kilometers apart, the people in town do not seem to perceive the space between them, judging them to be one and the same. Upriver from town, across the Angara, on the side of the Irkut, are pleasant forested hills that look like a rampart. Various estates and farms have been built there. A boat trip across the river to the monastery takes a little less than half an hour. The *slobodas*,[6] located for eighteen to twenty kilometers across the mountains of the Angara in the nicest bottom lands, are endowed with the best soil, perfectly suitable for growing grain. You can buy the *pud*, thirty-six pounds [consistently converted] of rye flour firsthand from the farmer for six or eight kopeks, at the bazaar for ten or twelve, wheat flour for fifteen. As the rivers teem with fish—as I have related extensively in my separate "Description of Fish"[7]—the forests and meadows are full of the most enjoyable songbirds, as are the rivers with waterbirds. Whole sleds full of various species of ducks, geese, capercaillies [*Tetrao urogallus*], and black grouse, hazel grouse, and Daurian partridge [*Tetrao tetrix*, *Tetrestes bonasia*, and *Perdix dauurica*; Springer, pers. comm., August 24, 2016] are daily brought to town for sale by both Russians and Buryats, so that even a spoiled palate cannot complain of a lack of delicacies.

In town the Angara's banks are full of boats, called doshcheniks, that transport goods from Russia here and to the Chinese border as well as returning from there across Lake Baikal to continue on down the Angara. At the bazaar as well as in the *gostinii dvor*,[8] you can buy a lot of Russian and Chinese goods for reasonable prices. Every year more goods become available; some things can be bought at the same price or for little more than in Moscow—for example, German, Dutch, and English cloth, hats, linen, and sugar.

Notes

1. *Zimov'e*, R, literally winter hut, used by hunters and travelers primarily in winter; by the time of the expedition, used as way station; consistently translated except when part of a name.

2. Steller is right about the water-worn gravel having once been in the water; flooding or glaciation are possibilities. Robin Beebee, hydrologist, USGS, personal communication.

3. Krest, R, meaning *cross*. Traditionally, a cross was erected at the beginning of important routes for travelers to offer prayers; this is the route to Lake Baikal. WH, Anm. 34.

4. In text, *Mündung* or mouth; consistently replaced with source or outlet, where that is obviously meant.

5. A relatively small species of sturgeon from Eurasia, also native to rivers in Siberia as far east as the Yenisey, has excellent flesh and makes very good caviar; listed as threatened. "Siberian Fish," www.sibrybalka.ru/ryby.

6. *Sloboda*, derived from the Slavic word for freedom. "Large communal villages settled by voluntary colonists with government assistance." Gibson, 156; term retained.

7. In a letter to Baron von Korff, dated December 23, 1739, Steller promises to send his *Historia piscium Angarae et Lacus Baikali cum iconibus* [History of fish in the Angara River and Lake Baikal, with pictures] by April 1740. No such work has been found, but Steller's descriptions of fish from 1739 are found in other places. WH, Anm. 121.

8. *Gostinii dvor*, prerevolutionary arcade, in towns and forts usually built out of stone. WH, Glossar; term retained.

2

ABOUT IRKUTSK ITSELF

As mentioned above, the town got its name from the Irkut River, which in turn is probably derived from the Buryat word *Byrrkuth* or *Burkuth*, meaning eagle, because the birds are said to be found in greater numbers in the high mountains sixty kilometers upriver than elsewhere. Two species are often to be seen not far from town—namely, *Haliaetum* and *Naeviam*.[1] I leave this judgment to others [unclear what is being judged]. The town itself is, for the most part, built in the round with the number of buildings increasing from year to year. It would, in a short time, be built up as far as the mountains toward Krest and along the Ushakovka, by thousands of houses even to Malaya Rozvodnaya five kilometers from town, if the promyshlenniks arriving from Russia were allowed to get married, settle down, and build houses here. Various ukases prohibit that, however, because most of these people would then forget their home and parents and ruin them because the parents would have to pay the head taxes for them. Many a Russian landowner would also thereby lose his subjects. However, that could be prevented if only Her Majesty's subjects were allowed to settle and the parents were freed of this tax burden through an edict made known in everyone's home. Then these settlers would pay their head taxes here or ask the nobles whose subjects they are to let them buy their freedom in a certain number of years, since there are very few such promyshlenniks anyway.

On the land side, the town is surrounded by palisades, a small moat, and chevaux-de-frise. But the Church of the Holy Trinity and about forty houses on an arm of the Angara toward Krest are outside the palisades, and in the last two years some people have built about twenty houses outside the Monastery Gate. There they live as neighbors of the Buryats who have set up five or six yurts, which is also said to be the knacker's yard. But on the water side along the Angara the town is open, a necessity for trade—loading and unloading the doshcheniks as well as pulling them to shore by tow ropes. It is estimated that there are altogether 1,500 houses. Public buildings are, first, the fort, containing the provincial government's office building made of stone with warehouses for storing Russian as well as Chinese goods underneath. The Russian goods come through customs into the Cassa, the government coffers, and are resold, the customs office being supervised by a merchant. The Crown has a monopoly on Chinese trade goods like rhubarb[2] and Chinese tobacco. In other storage sheds, the furs brought in through the yasak from the local area are stored and checked; then they are sent either to Russia or via the caravan[3] for trading in China.

The fort itself has four gates, the largest and most imposing of which faces the gostinii dvor, below which stand four bronze and ten iron cannons that are fired off for defense as well as on high holy days. The second gate stands beside the Church of Christ the Savior, opposite the government office building; the third, through which you go to the river, is beside this building. You go through the fourth gate to the vice-governor's old and new houses.

The whole side of the fort next to the gostinii dvor and the main church is lined above and below with storage spaces. [Precise location and arrangement unclear.] To the left of the first gate is the main guardhouse, in which prisoners are also housed. In the center of the fort, a stone building with a vault has been built for storing gunpowder. Directly across from the government office building stands a stone church of peculiar architecture, dedicated to the Icon of Christ the Savior, every day more inclined [Steller's pun] to fall down. Cellars underneath the church are rented to the merchants; they pay the church half a ruble every month. The government office used to have only one secretary, but since the Kamchatka Expedition has added to its obligations, it now has two; it also has a recordkeeper, a government official, a subofficial, and seven scribes, seated at seven tables in three rooms, each having their own records to take care of and copy.[4]

Then there is the customs house, always supervised by a Siberian nobleman. Formerly, these were ennobled by the vice-governors, but that practice ceased with Pleshcheev [Irkutsk vice-governor, 1734–1737], and the honor has once again been entrusted to the Siberian Office[5] alone. The customs official's function is to check all incoming and outgoing goods, allotting a tenth of them to the government coffers. He has several scribes under him. Next to this customs station is the *podval* [literally, cellar], a special station for brandy distribution and taxation watched over by the town official who oversees trade and taxation. He sells the brandy to the taverns or to the merchants leasing them. A *vedro*, a 3.2-gallon bucket, of double brandy sells for six rubles, a 3.2-gallon bucket of regular for three rubles ten kopeks. The third administrator is the mayor, elected for three years by the *posadski* [inhabitants—artisans, merchants, traders, farmers—who live outside the town center and fort, i.e., the *posad*; terms retained] and whose area of operation is the city hall. He oversees the posad and has the right to question people under torture, but generally he volunteers to cede this right to the provincial government. In addition to these public buildings and offices, there's the gostinii dvor, which is made of lumber and looks quite modest although trade is important. The suggestion to build one out of stone and with underground vaults and cellars was made years ago. It might happen if it had to be moved in order to build the archbishop's residence in that location. The town is presently quarreling with His Eminence, the archbishop, over this. Besides the gostinii dvor, in which the merchants of Irkutsk as well as the ones from Russia have their booths, some other trade venues have been built in the square. Next to the Church of Christ the Savior is the grain market, and not far from it the hay market. The middle of the square is always filled with peddlers selling their goods carried in their arms or on their shoulders. In this locale everybody is more into trading than working. Behind the gostinii dvor, which is built in a square, is the meat market, and behind the meat market the fish market.

There are altogether seven churches in town. [We have supplied the numbers.] The first is the main or bishop's church, Church of Christ the Savior [After the Icon of the Savior "not made by hands," which is the face of Jesus Christ on a cloth or towel; in the West known as Veronica's Veil; Fr. Oleksa, email, March 3, 2016], a well-built, expansive stone structure. Its newly installed iconostasis shows that its architecture and the artistry of its sculptures and paintings are in no way inferior to those in the best churches of Moscow and St. Petersburg. It is located half inside and half outside the fort. This church has an archpriest, two priests, deacons, and a sacristan or *trapeznik* and is attended by nobility, foreign merchants [possibly foreigners and merchants], promyshlenniks, and people new in town. [This sentence moved up from Transbaikalia section.]

The second church is named after the Vladimir Icon of the Virgin Mary, built by a posadski, Daniil, and improved and furnished with vestments, iconostasis, bells, windows, and a huge candelabra by Mitrofan Granin [inhabitant of Irkutsk]. It is located not far from the Trans-Baikal

Street. The third church, named for the Tikhvin Icon of the Virgin Mary, is located in the very same street. The fourth, the Two Holy Fools of Ustiug Church, stands on the banks of the Angara River. The fifth, the Trinity or Medvedev's Church, was built by a once very wealthy merchant who is now totally impoverished. The sixth, St. Michael's Church, has only recently been built and very well at that. It contains a winter and a summer church, the one below, the other above with two beautiful towers. The lower church is dedicated to the martyr St. Charalampios. The seventh, the Holy Church of the Cross, outside of town, is located where there used to be a chapel. But because Peter the Great prohibited chapels in cities [WH, Anm. 1880], this church was built here on a lovely and charming hill at the edge of town.

The street leading from the Trans-Lake Gate along the Angara is called Main Street, but the lower part, which has only recently been built below Medvedev's Church to its end, is called *Poteriakha*, meaning loss, because when it was still a forest, a man was murdered here. [Others say the name derived from cattle frequently getting lost here; WH, Anm. 195]. In the past, murder was an extraordinary thing, but nowadays it is no longer a rarity. The remaining streets, though there are many, have no names. When you ask for directions, the person asked will tell you with reference to the churches or the dwellings of rich or well-known people how many houses your destination is from one or the other. By the way, the town has three main gates, but you do not have to pass through any of them to get into the town. The first is the Trans-Lake Gate, through which you go to Krest, Rozvodnaya, and Lake Baikal; the second is the Mill Gate, where you go to the mill on the Ushakovka; and the third is the Monastery Gate, where you go to the convent and Convent Village.

Besides these abovementioned offices, there is the police headed by the Cossack leader, also called *polkovnik*, colonel, or chief of police, the one in office now not having much sense. Any sluzhiv or Cossack[6] who has good friends in Irkutsk or the Siberian Office in Moscow can get this position. This official has some scribes under him. The police had its beginnings under the voevod Ivan Ivanovich Poluekhtov, and the officers' duties are as follows:

1. In every way to safeguard the security of the town, hence to catch the thieves. The chief of police can interrogate them under threat of the cat-o'-nine-tails but afterward has to report to the vice-governor and hand over important prisoners. It has been observed, however, that with the establishment of the police, thievery, too, began in Irkutsk.

2. To see to it that nobody does forbidden work or trades in smuggled goods—that is, distills and sells brandy or trades in Chinese tobacco, wine, or rhubarb. It nevertheless happens.
3. To take care that nobody builds in a dangerous [presumably from fire] or unhealthy manner. People observe the first; the houses are built far enough from each other because until now there was enough space. But the many secret chambers [an ironic euphemism for toilets] emptying into the street and the many dead dogs, cats, and pigs lying about everywhere attest to the fact that the latter point is not observed.
4. To maintain the Christian order by diligently catching the whores, punishing them, and convincing them to refrain from their activities in the future. But this point suffers the same fate as the first one above. It is believed that approximately twenty years ago prostitution became ever more common, and since the Kamchatka Expedition it is practiced without shame or sin. As proof, I myself own several such "Siberian love offers" advertising whores' professional services. It is assumed that this situation stems from the following causes:
   1. Many wives do not get to see their husbands for many years while they are away as traders or as members of the expedition or in Moscow on government business, often not having lived as husband and wife for more than a week or a month.
   2. There are many exiled women in this area without husbands and men without wives who, in hopes of going back someday, cannot marry, nor do they want to.
   3. With the Kamchatka Expedition and the Swedish imprisonment,[7] all kinds of questionable characters and other undesirables came into the country.
   4. The promyshlenniks are not allowed to marry; therefore, they seek the benefits of marriage clandestinely.
   5. The Russian merchants, some being yet unmarried, some living here without wives, pay well for their pleasure.
   6. Siberian indolence wants to earn its keep by easy means.
   7. Gluttony and drunkenness and the resulting poverty open the door to all vices.

For these very reasons, Siberia has already been somewhat weakened; care should be taken that its people not be totally ruined, which might happen if both the men by wasting their virility and the women by using all kinds of birth control become incapable of procreating. For in Siberia the blessings of large numbers of children encountered in every Russian village are sadly lacking, their numbers being much smaller. It could also be said that the French disease [syphilis] has, so to speak, become naturalized and domesticated, and it would be no lie to say that a third of the population has the French affliction. This evil has spread to such an extent that the smallest children get condyloma [wartlike growths on skin, usually on or around the genitals], if not in the uterus, then shortly after birth through the unclean nourishment suckled from French breasts.[8] While you see many faces with slit noses due to crime [a common punishment under the czars; WH, Anm. 226], venereal disease also deprives many of theirs. In Siberia, having intact noses might soon become as unfashionable as tails were for Aesop's foxes. This deserves to be mentioned especially because among many Russian experiments and heroic Venus remedies, none is yet known to cure the evil completely; most merely slow its course, making it ineffective for a time, but weakening people's general health, destroying their fertility, and ultimately having the most desperate consequences, frequently leading to the body's rotting away while still alive. To date, nothing protects these unfortunate people but the northern climate that slows the spread of this venomous seed. I wanted to present this problem thoroughly because Her Majesty's great interest demands that this evil be gradually alleviated, partly by insisting that people marry under supervision of the priests as well as through medical assistance and remedies. This much is certain: that, because of the locals' devil-may-care attitude, many will die early rather than allowing this evil to be eliminated unless treatment in hospitals under public supervision is instituted.

With regard to private buildings, everybody builds according to his own understanding, imagination, and purse, and it cannot be denied that this place has many well-built private residences—the large windows of *sliuda* or mica[9] from the Lena or Yakutsk, which have recently become the popular thing, really enhance their looks. Especially praiseworthy is that there is no house in Irkutsk—be it ever so modest—without a deep, water-rich well. That is why, even though fires are frequent here, the rules concerning prevention poor, the police indifferent, the local inhabitants lazy and in such emergencies uncaring toward others, it is rare that more than two houses burn down because the ample supply of well water makes it possible to extinguish the fire in the first house.

Notes

1. Unclear which two species Steller meant; *haliaetus* nowadays refers to the white-tailed sea eagle, *H. albicilla*, which is what Steller likely meant. Springer, pers. comm., August 24, 2016. *Naevia/us* is Latin for birthmark or spot. According to J. Slaght, *Clanga naevia* is an old

name for the greater spotted eagle, and Slaght is fairly certain this is the eagle Steller meant, now named *Clanga clanga* and found in the Irkutsk area. Pers. comm., July and September 2018.

2. Rhubarb root was one of the most significant items exported from China through Siberia to Europe. It was believed to be useful in treating digestive ailments, asthma, fevers, and problems with the nervous system, purging the body without causing any harmful side effects. It could be used by itself or mixed with other herbs. It was prized by doctors in Europe and was of enormous monetary value. "Russian rhubarb" was considered the best quality and therefore brought the best price, although it was not actually grown in Russia but transported across Russia from China and then to western Europe, in particular Amsterdam—the center for rhubarb trade. In 1652 the Russian government declared rhubarb a state monopoly, though it was not possible to stop private trade. Hartley, 31–32.

3. "Following loading, the pack horses were dispatched in 'caravans' or 'convoys' of 100 to 150 horses (including 5 to 8 spares), grouped in 'strings' or 'bunches,' each of which included 5 (or less) to 13 but usually 10 to 12 horses, with a Yakut conductor astride the lead horse." Gibson, 95.

4. Literally seven table scribes seated in three rooms. Unclear if this denotes a category of scribe.

5. In text, Siberian prikaz, the Moscow office responsible for Siberian affairs. Stejneger, 134.

6. Cossacks originated from fugitives and refugees who fled the steppes of southern European Russia in the late fifteenth and early sixteenth centuries and were eventually employed by Moscow as frontier guards in return for certain privileges; they were largely responsible for the conquest of Siberia. Gibson, 4.

7. When, during the Nordic War (1700–1721), the Swedes lost the Battle of Poltava in 1709, some of the Swedish prisoners of war were deported to Siberia. WH, Anm. 216.

8. "There is no evidence of transmission via human milk itself; a nursing mother with primary or secondary syphilis with breast involvement can infect the infant through the contact of the lesions with the mucous membranes." Joel A. Lamounier, Zeina S. Moulin, and César C. Xavier, "Recommendations for Breastfeeding during Maternal Infections," *Jornal de pediatria* 80, no. 5 (2004).

9. In text, *Marienglas*, a selenite or satin spar, varieties of gypsum, used in place of glass (e.g., to protect icons or images of the Virgin Mary); hence the name in German. WH, Anm. 234.

3

ABOUT THE PUBLIC OFFICES

As the town's public buildings have increased in number and improved in appearance, the prestige of government and church personnel in Irkutsk has increased over the years. In the beginning, the town stood under the jurisdiction of Ilimskoi Ostrog, which nowadays in return receives its voevod from Irkutsk. Later, when Irkutsk received voevods, it was directly under Tobolsk but indirectly still under Ilimsk. But since then Irkutsk has been administered by vice-governors, of which there have been three before the present one, *Staatsrat*[1] Aleksei Yur'evich Bibikov. Mr. von Bibikov is the first to whom the administration of this far-flung province has been entrusted without being answerable to the governor of Tobolsk. Everything that is now considered part of the Irkutsk province previously was under the voevod of the Yeniseysk province. That province encompassed all the Russian places, towns, villages, settlements, and yurts from Tulun, Krasnoyarsk, and Yeniseysk in the west to Yakutsk in the east and from the mouths of the Lena and Olenek Rivers in the north as well as the whole area around Lake Baikal south to the Chinese border to the Kyakhta River and Nerchinsk. There are now the following voevods: the one of Yakutsk, the one of Selenginsk, and the one of Nerchinsk, which in addition to Irkutsk are the three capitals of this province. The voevods as well as the administrator or commander of Okhotsk and Kamchatka are sometimes appointed by the Siberian Office in Moscow or sometimes by the Cabinet or High Senate. But the other secular officials—commanders, administrators, chiefs of police—are all appointed to their offices by the vice-governor's office.

Since its founding, Irkutsk has had the following voevods, first within Idinskoi Ostrog, afterward within Ilimskoi Ostrog:

Ivan Maksimovich Perfil'ev
Ivan Petrovich Gagarin, in Nerchinsk [1692–1695; WH, Anm. 651]

Stepan Vasil'evich Rakitin [commander of Irkutsk, February 1719 to February 1722; WH, Anm. 652]

Ermolai Prokop'evich Liubavskij [commander, voevod? 1716–1717? WH, Anm. 653]

Lavrentij Rodionovich Rakitin (lost his head)

Fëdor Rupichev, a Siberian nobleman [1711–1714; WH, Anm. 655]

Michail Petrovich Izmailov [1724–1731; WH, Anm. 656]

Ivan Ivanovich Poluekhtov

Larion Akimovich Sinyavin

Yurii Fëdorovich Shishkin

This province gets its income from the following:

1. The head taxes, amounting approximately to . . . [no amount given].
2. The yasak paid by the Buryats; the Tungus from along the Verchnaya and Angara Rivers, from Barguzin, Nerchinsk, and the area around Tunkinskoi Ostrog; the Yakuts; the Lamuts, who are also Tungus; the Kamchadals; and the native peoples living east of the Lena's mouth on the Yana, Kolyma, Alazeya, and Anadyr Rivers. This yasak partly finances the trading caravan with China and is partly sent to the Siberian Office in Moscow.
3. The brandy, which is distilled in two kinds of *kastaks*, distilleries, or *savods*, factories. The former are Her Majesty's distilleries that deliver brandy to the government cellar, of which there are three, *starii kastak*, the old one; *serednii kastak*, the middle one; and *Karluskoi kastak*. But because these Crown distilleries cannot deliver enough brandy for the province, some merchants operate distilleries on lease, which are supposed to distribute brandy at a specified price to specified towns, slobodas, and ostrogs. However, they usually do so for half the price for which it is sold from the government coffers, regular brandy selling for three rubles ten kopeks, double brandy for six rubles. But the distributors take one ruble sixty kopeks for the regular and three rubles for the double brandy. Although this arrangement is meant to be of advantage to the government, it is the opposite for the following reasons:
    1. The distributors first buy up the grain needed at a low price, through all kinds of scams inflicting economic ruin on the country folk; Her Majesty then buys it back at a much inflated price.
    2. The distributors do not only deliver brandy wholesale to the government warehouse. Since it is impossible to supervise them closely, they secretly retail it in towns and villages, and because they sell it more cheaply, the government brandy remains unsold, and to top it off, the government loses a large sum of money.
    [Steller omitted point 3; we have renumbered.]
    3. Because the merchants get each and every thing on lease, the promyshlenniks who, in turn, have to lease their hunting or fishing permits

from the merchants need to go to work for the suppliers in order to pay the merchants for their permits. The rest, however, who want to earn their living in service to Her Majesty, demand higher wages when they hire themselves out.

4. Thus, people are driven into poverty, first, by the grain buyers and the high price of the brandy nobody wants to do without. The more so since the tavern keepers, who in turn have leased the taverns at a high price, dilute the brandy with water in order to cover their costs and make a profit. Second, people do not plant more grain than they absolutely have to for their own consumption and sale because more work does not benefit them; rather, it does them harm because the grain would become ever cheaper while the brandy stays at the same high price. If they are unlucky and have even one bad year—as happened on the Lena in 1739 when the grain froze—they are suddenly left without anything at all to eat, no matter how rich and fertile the land. Unfortunately, distant places like Yakutsk and Okhotsk, which cannot grow grain due to the climate and therefore are dependent on importing provisions, suffer greatly then. Consequently, thirty-six pounds of flour that normally are sold for fifteen to twenty kopeks cost sixty to seventy kopeks as is now being reported from Yakutsk.

Her Majesty's interest suffers then, too, as the high prices paid by the Kamchatka Expedition illustrate. But if Professor Müller's suggestions were followed and everybody were allowed to distill brandy, a tax could be collected according to the amount of brandy produced and consumed, just as head taxes are levied according to the number of persons in each household. Some merchants would not have as high an income, but the country as a whole would benefit, and people would not have to fear such poverty. They would then like their work better if they themselves were to benefit from it, and the sums raised might well be doubled. It is also to be assumed that drinking too much brandy would become less common if the brandy did not appear so enticing because of its high price. In addition to the distilleries around Irkutsk, Afanasii Dementi'ev and Ivan Vorosilov have built more sixty kilometers from town on the way to Vercholensk. These deliver brandy to Yakutsk, Okhotsk, and the mouth of the Lena. [Between this and the next sentence, Steller mentions the names of Maksim Glazunov, Shcherbakov, Zverev, and Popov, possibly as other suppliers of brandy.]

Another damaging consequence of these distilleries is that brandy is delivered from Irkutsk to everywhere in the province while the grain for its production comes from the few slobodas around Irkutsk. Then the brandy is delivered to Nerchinsk, where grain is cheaper than in Irkutsk, and the progon, the transport tax, for every pail is lost. That at least would not happen if not everything were concentrated here in order to enrich Irkutsk. If I were not more concerned with what drives natural history than politics and economics because the former is less dangerous and hateful, I could easily report a few more consequences and the conclusions to be drawn from them.

The duties levied on Russian as well as Chinese wares are the fifth source of income; they amount in this province to . . . [no amount listed].

The rhubarb trade is the sixth source. It could be debated whether it is more profitable to have it bought up and sorted by Her Majesty's employees or whether certain merchants should be allowed to do so if, under penalty of death, they were to deliver it only to the government warehouses in Moscow or Petersburg, according to the weight established at the duty station. For these merchants understand the grading every bit as well as the most knowledgeable consumer, and the resulting moneys would stay in the government coffers.

[In the following, Steller is presumably discussing the advantages of turning the rhubarb trade over to the merchants. According to WH, Anm. 283, the lower third of the manuscript page is blank.]

[Steller lists no point 1.]

2. The costs of construction and maintenance of so many buildings, which amount to . . . [no amount given], would be saved.
3. The merchants would be better able to sell their own Russian wares.
4. The best rhubarb, which becomes expensive because of the progon and all the other costs until it reaches St. Petersburg, would cost the government only half what it costs now.
5. There is no need to fear any embezzlement because private merchants concerned for their own interests would also take the best care of Her Majesty's. Some years ago a ukase prohibited using the word *rhubarb* or *reven* [R] but wanted it called *kazna* [obsolete Russian for treasury; WH, Sachregister], and I suspect that the reason—none is given—must have been that European merchants would not find out how much rhubarb arrived, to avoid lowering the price. If the merchants, hoping for more profitable times, kept the rhubarb in storage for a while, much of it would rot and the government would suffer loss. Yet there may be other, lesser reasons hidden in the ukase.
6. The caravan would not lose trade. Now, however, since the trader Simon Il'ich Svin'in, who is interested in all kinds of far-flung projects, has been allowed to trade for rhubarb with just the things with which the caravan to

China trades, the caravan will lose profit and may end up being considered unnecessary, and the trade with China itself could by and by be discontinued. [Part of sentence missing; presumably the disadvantages of trade being monopolized by one merchant.] Importing Chinese tobacco is now limited to the said Svin'in. In my opinion, this monopolized trade does not benefit the government for the following reasons:

1. Tobacco goes to waste in the government warehouse or 36 pounds are bought on pretense in order to get 720 other pounds through duty free.
2. The private merchants and the customs agents enrich themselves through this trade while Her Majesty does not receive the duty. Among the merchants, this smuggled tobacco is called *krasnoi chai* [R], red tea.
3. As a consequence the native people, who cannot be without Chinese tobacco, would be ruined through the price set at the discretion of the private merchants. But if the trade were free or restricted to a number of merchants, and not just one, provided they paid a certain duty and agreed to a price set according to the distances transported, neither the government nor the native peoples would be disadvantaged. But if the trade is given to one person alone without restrictive levies, all the above disadvantages are to be feared.

Another source of income is the Karluk [a small tributary of the Angara] sturgeon glue, which is highly prized and taken by caravan to China. The merchants [omission in the manuscript, "... te," presumably *Kaufleute*] and promyshlenniks transport it to Irkutsk, but they are obligated to register at the customs station, where it is sold and then transported by caravan to China.

Another source of income is a tenth of all the iron smelted around Lake Baikal and along the Angara, the Irkut, and the Belaya Rivers by promyshlenniks as well as posadski and sold by the government. Yet it must be noted that even though there is a lot of iron around here, not enough is smelted to meet the needs of Irkutsk and the towns, ostrogs, and villages across the lake. Through special orders consumers should be encouraged to produce more and pay their tax. For iron is very profitable, especially around Lake Baikal because everything is transported across it except for that which the inhabitants of Nerchinsk bring in from China on the sly. It would also be a good idea to encourage prospecting for such ores on the other side of the lake; the promyshlenniks from Ust'iug and Sol'vychegodsk would soon prove to be good smelters and smiths, and this would in due time prove to be quite useful.

And then there are the silver mines, the operation of which, however, costs more than they bring in. If the silver mines ceased operation and the people working there were encouraged to work in the fields, ten times as much silver could be purchased at the border.

Finally, there is the trade with salt, amounting to . . . annually [no amount given]. The following places containing salt flats in this province are worth mentioning. [But none are mentioned.]

Note

1. Like Kammerherr (see instructions), *Staatsrat* is a frequently encountered title in the eighteenth century, but the functions of the position are not clear. It was likely comparable to the British privy councillor. Today it applies to ministers without portfolio.

4

ABOUT THE CLERGY

As far as the vice-governor's power extends concerning things political, the archbishop's supervision extends equally far concerning things clerical. The present one, Innocent II [archbishop of Irkutsk and Nerchinsk from 1733 to 1747; WH, Anm. 304], is from Ukraine; he is the third in the position and the first to have his own, separate diocese since 1730 [the correct year is 1727; WH, Anm. 307]. Unlike his predecessors, he is not under the authority of the Tobolsk metropolitan. He supervises all the clergy and monasteries as far as Kamchatka and the mouth of the Lena. He appoints clergy, promotes or demotes them, and punishes them for their misdeeds. He has an office staff and deals with the Irkutsk provincial government office through memoranda. His base salary amounts to 600 rubles, but he may take in 3,000 to 4,000 rubles altogether. If he is on good terms with the merchants, he may get twice that. This archbishop's first order of business was to assign each parish church a certain number of households, for example 250, which is incredibly helpful in maintaining good order. He also established a seminary to train Buryat and Mongol priests, who are to teach their people about the Christian religion and to translate the Mongolian written material he is gathering up everywhere he can. If this keeps up, it will eventually contribute greatly to explaining the history of these people. For now, the archbishop had a fine house built in the village of Zhilkina, eight kilometers from town on the left bank of the Angara; he will live there until a proper residence is built beside the bishop's or the main church. At the moment, he is fighting with the town about that because the gostinii dvor would have to be moved to a different location first.

5

ABOUT THE CHINESE TRADE AND CHINESE TRADE GOODS

[This title comes at the end of this section on an otherwise blank page; Steller titled this section "About the Trade."]

Concerning trade in these parts, the inhabitants distinguish the old or wild and the new, rational time. The wild years are called those from the beginning of trade with China to 1718, because then anyone could become a capitalist in a very short time. [They cite the following reasons for this distinction:]

1. Back then the Chinese were only too happy to trade with the Russians.
2. The Chinese did not cheat the Russians then but allowed themselves to be cheated in various sly ways.
3. There were more and better goods being traded and at lower prices.
4. Some imported goods had been traded against Chinese items at such high prices that you could have doubled your capital right away. [This is a very free translation of "so that one repeatedly had capital upon capital right away in that place."] Nowadays the Chinese do not even look at such things as glasses and mica [presumably drinking glasses and mica for window panes]. In the past, there was a lot of trade with gold, silver, gems, and damask, none of which can be sold at all now or only at a loss. Goods now being traded are said to be fakes or of poor quality. Nowadays, the locals think you have to be smarter if you want to get rich, and this is therefore the second period, the new, rational time, post-1718.

Care should be taken that trade is not further spoiled. The main trade spoilers are the Tomsk Tartars who disclosed the price of Russian goods to the Chinese. It takes just one of the large number of rich merchants trading with the Chinese to reduce his price out of greed to spoil the profit for everyone else. Then they add insult to injury by importing a slew of Russian goods, keeping them for three or four years as dead capital in order to tease the Chinese. Finally, the lazy Siberyaks are forced to accept the worst cloth because they have only the clothes they get from the Chinese, which would not happen if they were ordered to wear clothes made from wool and linen. Then they would immediately pass up bad Chinese goods with eyebrows raised contemptuously just as they regrettably do now with the Russian clothes, which would, in contrast, be highly esteemed.

On the other hand, now more than ever before, the Russians have taken a liking to curiosities—for example, all kinds of fine china. Everybody tries to compete with everybody else in buying and displaying such things; yet when these break at the least mishap, they naturally leave behind nothing but useless shards. Equally useless are all kinds of Chinese platters, plates, pictures, items made of stone, silk blouses, and little silk pictures. I firmly believe it is very detrimental to the empire if everybody owns a Chinese cabinet of curiosities. Things have gotten so bad now that the servant girls go about in silk, which not only impoverishes many people but further encourages their innate laziness. Around here, flax and hemp could grow as well as in Russia, but as it is, nobody cares about that. The large number of Bratsk and Tungus sheep would definitely provide wool for domestic clothing, but now it is left for the Buryats and Tungus to turn it into felt, and people prefer to buy stockings from Kazan at double the price.

The China trade continues to be very important just the same. First, because the Chinese take the worst sable pelts at a considerable price to dye, which would not be worth a third of that in Russia. Second, they pay such an exorbitant price for more precious pelts, such as Kamchatkan red foxes and beaver, which few in Petersburg and probably nobody in other parts of Europe would pay for them. Third, the Chinese buy some goods that would remain unused if they did not, like as many as a thousand *nerpa* or seal skins, which they dye a nice black, cut up, and then trim their fur coats with. The Siberyaks have so far found no use for them. Here trunks are not covered with them since everything is exported in bales, crates, and *chemodani* [R] travel bags.[1] It is not worth the trouble to take those skins to Russia.

There is also more sturgeon glue than needed in Siberia because things are more often nailed than glued here. But what Russia needs to trade abroad is obtained from the Caspian Sea and the Volga. [Apparently, Steller regrets that surplus glue made from Siberian sturgeon bladders is not exported to China.]

Saiga or antelope² [*Saiga tatarica*] horns have recently become very popular, partly because the Chinese carve them to carry as an antidote [unclear for what], partly because in its pulverized form it is given to women in labor as an unfailing aid to birth. It is also said that the Chinese recently invented a way to distill a spirit from it; it is to be feared that—in their usual bragging way—they will sometime soon claim that they, not the European chemists, invented hartshorn spirit [a source of ammonium carbonate]. They especially value the bloody horns taken off young animals killed. They also buy dried blood and offer to pay as much as demanded for a few live animals they want to import to China. It cannot be done, though, because this antelope—just like the musk deer—cannot be tamed but will starve itself to death in captivity because of its natural wildness. The instigator of this horn trade is a merchant from Tomsk who, when he bought up a whole doshchenik full of saiga horns, was jeered by everybody like Aesop when he assumed the heaviest load.³ Nowadays everybody wants to take part in this trade, but fortune will not smile upon them because this trade is not valued as it used to be. For the Chinese are now apt to deal with the Russians with restraint and sarcasm. The Russians, however, who are not inclined to be patient, cannot stand their hesitation and give tit for tat. It would be advisable to limit the amount to be traded and to set the bottom price. Thus, each item would retain its value, and the Chinese could indeed be sold a bill of goods. [In text, *Hörner aufsetzen*, a play on the word *horn*, be cuckolded.]

Cow hides were previously imported from Russia but are now prepared in factories in Irkutsk, Yeniseysk, and Tomsk. The Russians use them to pay back the Chinese for their poor-quality damasks that are no better than the ones previously classified as second-rate or worse because the Chinese seem to believe they are buying Russian cow hides though these Siberian ones are nowhere near the quality of the Russian ones.

Yard goods, German as well as Dutch or English ones, have not been much in demand in recent years. You can therefore have garments made for the same price as in Moscow. Russian as well as Silesian linen and lace were previously much in demand, but now the Chinese make them themselves and sell them under the name of *rupha* [possibly R *ruga* or *ruba*, meaning cheap linen clothes; WH, Anm. 344].

Locks from the village of Pavlovo Selo, scissors, and knives [unclear if scissors and knives are also from this village] were highly valued until quite recently. But now that trade has ceased, too, because the Chinese make these items themselves. I have actually noticed that the Chinese have copied many toys from Nuremberg and Augsburg and sold them to the Russians as their originals for twice the price you can buy them in Nuremberg. It is just that the local people are so enamored of these fakes that they do not want to believe the deception, thinking that such useless doodads would be beneath the Europeans. The presently-so-popular small teacups with painted heads [in text, *Knöpfen*, buttons; presumably Steller meant to write *Köpfen*, heads] or landscape scenes inside the cup are imitations of those from Dresden[4] that they bought for a lot of money from Count Sava Lukich Vladislavich-Raguzinsky and his entourage after they returned from China.[5] I would get rich quick if I could sell just two of every item sold at the Nuremberg Christmas Market, because the local people are very fond of novelties.

The porcelain snuffboxes are patterned after those that Peter Funk[6] had made, and in my childhood I used to play with those riders that mechanically move around a table by clockwork, but mine did not have flat Chinese faces or hairy beards. The Chinese now also make velvet, silk—known as *Gros de Tour*—woolen material for inner linings called *Kardies* in Germany, *Fries* or a coarse woolen cloth, Augsburg fustian [a coarse cloth made of wool and linen], German milk jugs, and little teapots with silk handles. They undoubtedly get these models for their imitations from the meddlesome Jesuits, who would surely be willing to become tannery apprentices in Yaroslavl in order to teach tanning to the Chinese and ruin the Russian trade. It would be good if some of the local people came up with their own new products instead of coveting such imitations and in addition took up silk dyeing. I have discovered a few things in my short time here, and I would surely succeed in finding out more if I had the good fortune after returning from my Kamchatkan trip to be sent on orders to China, not for my own profit but for the good of the public welfare and the sciences. You cannot be sufficiently concerned about those if you have to be focused day and night on the information needed to get paid, which is what I am getting used to doing more and more each day.[7]

The Chinese also buy horses, oxen, and camels from the Russians and the natives, mostly when they are at war with the Kalmyks. At that time, too, the leather and cloth trade thrives, which makes the local merchants very happy. The Chinese often allow the Kalmyks to take the camels they just bought from the Russians on the Kyakhta River away from them. In Tomsk the Russians then buy these camels back from the Kalmyks and at the border sell them a second time to the Chinese. But because the Chinese habitually brand the animals when they buy them, the owners will recognize their camels, and they will pay even more for them and consider themselves lucky if they can keep them in the future. I do not think they will be that fortunate, but I would consider it more fortunate if they had not bought them back. It is pathetic how often the Russians cheat the Chinese while trading horses, but I cannot resist sharing a funny bit of skullduggery. When buying horses, the Chinese are in the habit of opening the horses' mouths with an iron prod to examine their teeth, also beating the horses with it to find out if they are spirited. During the last encounter with the Kalmyks, a Russian horse trader bought over sixty horses, all of which were old and unfit for work. At the border, he tied them to trees here and there but spared the Chinese the trouble of having to open their mouths with the rod. He made the rod glowing hot. As soon as he approached the horses' mouths, the horses jumped with all their might. He had done this already the day before. He went from one to another with it. The horses, shying away from the rod, cut such capers that the Chinese bought them all at a pretty good price. Then the seller left them in the dust while the Chinese could not move their [wingless] Pegasi and, to avoid being further laughed at, had to get rid of them at a ruble or two each. But now they are paying the Russians back by not allowing them to open the packaging or look at the damasks or other yard goods but selling them uninspected. They also often sell a crate of the best green tea with only about ten tins of it on top, covering the rest consisting of the lowest quality, which is sold at the bazaar in Irkutsk at fifteen kopeks per pound.

In the past, the dogs were highly valued as well, because to the Chinese they are for pets and food. But now the Chinese do not look at the dogs especially because they have them bred right in China. Concerning this dog trade, the most underhanded tricks happened in Peking between the Russians and Chinese as well, but I do not want to talk about them.

Notes

1. Today, *chemodani* means suitcases; WH, Anm. 328 translates it as *Mantelsack*, *Felleisen*, both outdated. Current replacements would be *Reisetasche*, valise, and *Rucksack* or *Tornister*, backpack. Not clear what it was in Steller's day.

2. In text, *Steinbock*, a member of the goat family, which a saiga is not. Today, poaching saiga for Chinese markets has caused a dramatic population decline from about 1,500,000 animals in the early 1970s to an estimated 50,000 today. J. Slaght, pers. comm., July 2018.

3. Aesop's load of bread became lighter every day while the loads of his companions remained as heavy as they had been.

4. Steller is mistaken; European manufacturers copied the Chinese.

5. Count Raguzinsky, a Serb, served as Russia's trade and economics representative in the Balkans. In 1725–26 he was dispatched to China as Russia's special envoy to settle trade and border disputes. On his return in 1727, he signed two treaties with Chinese representatives at the border, settling the disputes. WH, Anm. 351.

6. There was no Peter Funk in Nuremberg, but there was a David Funck, an art and book seller who also issued faience wares [tin-glazed painted pottery]. WH, Anm. 355. Like the cups, the snuff boxes were likely copied from the Chinese.

7. The prodigious number of memoranda and requests to and from various government agencies reprinted in volumes 1 and 3 of the *Quellen* amply proves Steller's point.

6

ABOUT CUSTOMS AND LIFESTYLE IN IRKUTSK

WHILE THE NAMES OF THIS NORTHERN OR NORTHEASTERN part of Asia are general and vague, it would be absurd to assume that the inhabitants or their customs and traditions were all alike. Differing climates compel the customs and traditions to become different just as we find animals in one place to be more cunning and industrious than in another; they are more cunning where they have less food, and in order to appease their hunger they need to be more intelligent and hardworking. All the wild animals in these parts—the antlered ones as well as bears, wolves, and foxes—prepare themselves for the winter. Dogs are particularly adaptable. The further north they live and the harder they work in place of horses, the more alert they are during the hunt and the better they remember distances. You could write down a complete history of dogs based on all they have been used for and what has happened to them—the more so since certain tales of the Asian post dogs[1] still utterly amaze the European nobles.[2]

In addition to the climate, the social environment affects a lot of things, and dealings with foreigners—which is also the purpose of traveling to cultured countries—trade, and imported goods make a people more or less proud or frivolous. The Siberians themselves know this; thus, the inhabitants of almost every provincial town or place also were, by the others, given a nickname based on their distinguishing characteristic. For example, people from Tomsk are called *bulygi*, oafs [WH, Anm. 379], because of the crude peasant pride travelers passing through ascribe to them. The people from Yeniseysk are called *gwosniki* or cunning ones, and those from Irkutsk are called *Ivani* because of their clever and worldly-wise ways in contrast to the people from Tomsk. There is no place in Siberia you pass through that does not have its own particular nickname. And so the lifestyles along with the customs noticeably differ according to whether you are in Tobolsk or Tomsk or Yeniseysk or Irkutsk, and those of the latter I shall now deal with.

In the same way as periodic changes in the acculturation of European countries can be observed, so here in Asia: the harder it is to get people to give up their old beliefs and customs, the more they overdo when association rather than brute force makes them do it. This town, which grew from the seeds of the rigid streltsy, has not only truly taken to German dress, food, and drink but blended them with Chinese high spirits to boot. While this town is built where two rivers flow together into a third—one of these rivers, the Angara, flowing out of a big lake and the second, the Irkut, draining a mountainous wilderness—it is the third, insignificant one, the Ushakovka, its name given to it by a miller, that best illustrates the birth and growth of the place. It started out as a winter hut of Cossacks living in the wilderness and grew into a village. Those who were exiled from Moscow and the entire country speedily built it into a town. The old inhabitants, the Buryats, a major subgroup of the Mongols in Siberia, who live in a few yurts outside of town, hardly count anymore. Today Irkutsk has three types of inhabitants: Siberians, the exiles or new Russians, and the Buryats. However, the promyshlenniks also could be added to these. Even though they have arrived from the poorest places in Russia in order to seek their fortune and return home with it, many of them have settled down here as permanent residents. The old Yeniseysk and Krasnoyarsk Cossacks probably number the fewest now because most moved, when the town prospered, to the ostrogs around Lake Baikal as well as across the lake—for example, to Barguzin and Donsk. For they were no longer needed locally to guard the many exiles.

The smallest number of families are those of the Russian merchants who have settled here of their own free will, such as Miliutin and Brechalov [merchant families]. The exiles are now the most numerous as well as the wealthiest people, and they would not dream of disobedience but get embarrassed at the mere mention and recollection of the streltsy. So I will not mention them either since their names come up often in this description anyway. Primarily, these people live in the suburb along with Cossacks, now called sluzhivs, who are employed in Her Majesty's service in war and peace. However, they prefer to be employed where there is commerce and wheeling and dealing. They are paid in money as well as provisions from the government coffers, which is dealt with in the following ways. Some accept neither money nor provisions but instead contribute in such a way that they are given the job of tax collector or are sent to Russia with the government coffers, enabling them to make additional profit as traders. The poorer ones accept the money and provisions and are sent to the most difficult posts, as now to Okhotsk and Kamchatka, or employed as construction workers and carpenters. Many get the government to allot them a piece of land where they build small villages with houses and farms, where they raise livestock and crops, trade with the Buryats, and live rather well. Merchants are also rewarded by the government with plots of land on which they build houses and farms, which over time grow into villages and finally slobodas. Most of the slobodas around Irkutsk began in this way, and eventually they pay property taxes to the government.

The third group of people, the promyshlenniks, have come from cities and towns all over Russia and Siberia, but since the trade in Arkhangelsk has stopped,[3] most of them have come from Arkhangelsk Province and its towns—Ustiug, Vologda, Sol'vychegodskaya, Yaransk, Pereyaslavl-Riazanskii, and Riazan. In Russia these people are called *burlaki*, seasonal workers [WH, Anm. 410], or *gulashchniki*, vagabonds [WH, Anm. 411], but here they have been given the misnomer of promyshlenniks, regardless of the work they do. Previously, this name was reserved only for those who, in groups, hunted sable, fox, beaver, wolverine, or Arctic fox; who fished; or who traded in whatever merchants wanted, such as mica and all kinds of other things.

There are two kinds of promyshlenniks. [Steller does not identify the second kind; perhaps they are conscripted promyshlenniks.] The first kind come here voluntarily with good intentions, wanting to improve their lot in life, later to return to and settle down in Russia, buy property, and live as honest people. They are either Her Majesty's peasants or various kinds of craftsmen. They are issued a three- to six-year official pass from their place of origin. This pass is signed as proof of good conduct by the voevod in all the places they work. They usually get here as workers on the merchants' means of transport. They may also be in service in one place and then use the money earned there to become peddlers, moving from place to place till they get here. In Irkutsk or any other town, they hand in their pass at the government office where it will also be signed, and if they are Crown peasants, they also register at the city hall. Then they go on the hunt, of which there is great variety here.

Some go fishing. They take doshcheniks to Lake Baikal, especially to the mouth of the Barguzin River—three doshcheniks usually go there a year—to the Chivirkui River, fifty kilometers from there; or to the Upper

Angara River. Nowadays, however, hardly anybody dares go there anymore because the local Tungus are more impudent than in other places, taking fish at will from the promyshlenniks and shooting them dead if they resist, as has happened several times. But before the promyshlenniks take off, fourteen or fifteen of them get together, consult with each other, and pool their money—usually fifty rubles per person—to buy a doshchenik that, together with sail, mast, ropes, and the *nebot*, the net, which is 300–350 yards long, costs 500 rubles. Then they go to the government office to request a permit attesting to their having cleared their fishing expedition at city hall, by paying their seven rubles per net. They make this request humbly, fearing to disturb the clerks at their work.

The government office then notifies the customs house where the promyshlenniks have been told to fish, because on their return they have to have their catch inspected at the border station to make sure that they are not smuggling goods in the name of fish, especially if they have been fishing at Selenginsk. They pay a tenth of the price at which the customs agent has valued their catch. Once they have cleared the bureaucratic hurdles, they buy salt, provisions, meat, and some housekeeping gear, and after St. Nicolas [probably May 9; WH, Anm. 424] they make their way up the Angara to Lake Baikal. They carry their barrels with them as staves, putting them together at the outlet of the river, where they build themselves a hut and a sauna, as well as a canopy under which they will salt their fish and repair their nets; they also erect a rack on which to hang the nets to dry. Leaving the doshchenik to lie at anchor, they take off in their two boats to go fishing.

The following tasks are divided up among the group. At the head is the leader, who does not pay a share. He has to know the way to the lake, all the anchorages and dangerous places, and the more level banks and the mouths of rivers suitable for fishing. Secondly, he must be knowledgeable about the net, how to cast it, fold it again, and repair it; he also tells them when to fish. The second person is the *bochar* or cooper, who makes the barrels all winter long and sets them up. He does not pay into the cooperative but receives only half a share. The other half goes to the cook, who prepares the meals at the prescribed time and according to regulation, brews kvass, bakes bread, and butchers and preserves the meat by salting, having first procured salt; he also brings the food to the table and dishes it up. He is the third person who does not pay into the cooperative, and he does not do any other work. The other eleven members who pay their fifty rubles into the cooperative share duties on board—for example, alternately standing at the rudder while the leader commands from the bow, *na prava*, to the right, *na leva*, to the left. On land they work together at whatever.

They live very peaceably with each other, amicably settle whatever disputes arise, and are friendly and polite with one another. Before eating they devotedly pray, but during the meal itself there is no talking; it is as quiet as in the dining hall of the orphanage in Halle.[4] At the end of the meal, they pray again and then go back to work. Hotheads are not taken into the co-op to begin with or are quickly expelled, because the promyshlenniks say that strife stands in the way of God's blessing. They eat and drink well and consider themselves fortunate to be their own masters and not to be ordered around by anybody else. Toward the end of August, they return, their boat loaded with sturgeon, Baikal Lake sig, and Baikal omul. Sturgeon are caught at any time, but especially at the Chivirkui before the omul begin to migrate upstream around the middle of August. Previously sturgeon were so numerous that the fishermen paid little attention to the omul and sig, but now sturgeon are very rare, and so the fishermen thank God for the omul. Around Ol'khon Island a single catch of sturgeon used to fill sixty barrels, but now a whole co-op barely fills seven barrels. Until the omul arrive, the fishermen catch sig, but once the omul come in, the fishermen get ten to thirteen barrels per net.

At the beginning of September, they usually return to Irkutsk with the following load: seven barrels of sturgeon worth 119 rubles, twenty-five barrels of sig worth 175 rubles, and one hundred barrels of omul worth 300 rubles. [Unclear why Steller here also mentions 2.5 pud, or 90 pounds, of salt for preserving the sturgeon and sig, and again for the omul. Another computation, $18 + 58 + 225 = 301$ pud, or 10,832 pounds, is also unclear.] A barrel holds 1,000 to 1,100 fish. A barrel of omul usually sells for three rubles, at least for two and a half; sig sell for seven, or at least five rubles per barrel; and sturgeon for seventeen, or at least thirteen. The total amounts to 594 rubles, or forty-two rubles per person [for fourteen persons].

Now account for the costs:

Taxes: 60 rubles
Office expenses on the way back with presents to various officials, including the governor: 10 rubles
Salt: 66 rubles
Provisions [grain]: 30 rubles
Meat: 20 rubles
Total: 186 rubles
That leaves exactly 29 rubles per person.

You may add that they make a profit of 20 rubles from the salt [unclear how] and an eighth share of the driver's wages [unclear what driver or how].

They spend the winter in a hut, and though they do not live as well as when they are working, they do not go hungry, and because they live in a group, their food costs for nine months are no more than five rubles. But there are downsides. Sometimes the doshcheniks are taken away in the service of Her Majesty to transport provisions or the like; in the marketplace they are often pushed from one place to another, and they themselves are also often conscripted as laborers without pay. All of this they patiently and uncomplainingly endure while the war is being fought [Austro-Turko-Russian War, 1735–39; WH, Anm. 444] and the ukase about sending them back to Russia is in effect. Previously, as long as they paid the tax per net, they were free to fish on the Selenga, at the *prorva* or isthmus at the Posolsky Monastery, on the Barguzin and Chivirkui, and everywhere else around Lake Baikal. Now, however, a ukase of the Irkutsk government, issued at the request of Brigadier Bukholts, prohibits them from catching omul in the Selenga, the reason given that the fish at the mouth would be either caught or driven away and could therefore not migrate up the Selenga, so the inhabitants there, deprived of their harvest, would suffer shortages. The promyshleninks were driven away from the isthmus by the Posolsky Monastery people because they claimed the fish there for themselves. Ol'khon Island was given up by the promyshlenniks themselves because for several years no sturgeon have been found there—they have moved into the Selenga, where the promyshlenniks catch them all year long. Some of these promyshlenniks work at other jobs during winter—for example, serving as temporary workers at monasteries or on farms.

The promyshlenniks' second occupation is hunting for seals, of which more below.

The third pursuit is for game, including sable, about which Dr. Gmelin has written extensively.

The fourth is "hunting" [in text, *promis*] for sliuda or mica all the way upriver on the Vitim. For that, all the official requirements are the same as for catching fish.

Some promyshlenniks are in business for themselves or become clerks for merchants. Several merchants, by now rich, made their fortunes this way. Others prospect for iron, smelt it, and pay a tenth into the government coffers, as is the case on the lower Angara, at Kamenka, and in the past on the Ushakovka, the Bogul'deicha, and the Anga Rivers; they have now been built into smelters and taken over by Afanasii Dement'ev and Lanin.

Yet others who do not know how to make a [business] deal work as laborers. They commonly earn twenty to twenty-four rubles per year, plus food. Others are hut caretakers, brew beer, cut hay, or sell bread and salted fish on the undeveloped roads like the ones to Yeniseysk or the Lena River. Some work at Her Majesty's brandy distilleries as woodcutters or distillers; many are craftsmen—actually, almost all the craftsmen in Irkutsk are promyshlenniks. At the moment you cannot really tell if you are in Moscow or Irkutsk. There are gold- and silversmiths here who create works by casting, hammering, embossing, and engraving. They even make scientific instruments like quadrants, astrolabes, and compasses you would think were made in England rather than by Russians in Siberia. Yet others are stone polishers; machinists working at a lathe on wood, iron, silver, horn, or bone; copper casters; wire drawers; button makers, who make not only gold or silver buttons but also buttons from silk, even though that is women's work; or blacksmiths, locksmiths, and makers of gunstocks. There are now both a cotton mill and a dye works on the Belaya [now called Khanda] and Telma Rivers as well as in Irkutsk. Furthermore, there are tailors who work in spite of the ones in St. Petersburg, cobblers, embroiderers, painters, sculptors who fashion and delineate the most beautiful French leaves, wheelwrights, harness makers, nail makers, recently also a wig maker, sword smiths, pewterers, makers of carding combs, and weavers of silks and damask.

It should be noted that there are many calling themselves promyshlenniks who neither have learned anything nor are willing to do any kind of work. They have escaped to Siberia because back home on the Volga they used to steal and kill and now are living here without passports. Because of the much-vaunted security of the cities, they are viewed with suspicion, so they do not dare go home or be seen publicly or work, for fear they could be asked about their passport that either is outdated or never existed. Let us hope that due to the ukases and sharp questioning when examining the passports, these vermin may shortly be eradicated.

To list the qualities of the promyshlenniks: first, they are very hardworking; it is a pleasure to watch with what dexterity and strength they tackle their work, making three moves before a lazy Siberyak makes one. Second, they consider themselves and their work valuable because everything costs double of what you would pay for in Moscow. Third, they feed, maintain, and protect Irkutsk because they are fishermen, farmers, craftsmen, and, at a moment's notice, good soldiers who up to now have been the Russian garrison. Fourth, they harm Irkutsk because—being forbidden to marry—they encourage whoring and increase the incidence of syphilis.

Notes

1. Apparently referring to the system of stations set up for the regular exchange of draft or pack horses or, in the Far North, dogs, as we gathered from Steller's observation in his "Travel Journal from Yeniseysk to Irkutsk, March 6, 1739, to May 2, 1793," *Quellen* 7:6.

2. In text, *Ritter*, knights, thus aristocrats, possibly an ironic reference to specific European nobles Steller knew.

3. Peter the Great issued several ukases to divert trade to his newly established city of St. Petersburg. WH, Anm. 403.

4. While a student at Halle University, Steller was a tutor at this orphanage of the Franckesche Stiftungen, founded in 1698 by August Hermann Francke.

7

ABOUT TRANSBAIKALIA

[From here the text contains many more lacunae, probably because the manuscript was damaged. Much of it records Steller's visit to the trans-Baikal area from late July to early September 1739 and in particular describes the lake's seals and how they are hunted, a topic on which more information was promised above. Some of the information in these pages was obviously intended to be incorporated into the preceding text, and where appropriate, we have done so. On the other hand, we have omitted information lacking any clear reference as well as some passages too fragmented to make sense. We have noted the latter omissions.]

These seals are so fearful because some may be shot at ten times before they are caught. Loudly shrieking gulls flying above them—perhaps intent on picking up the seals' filth—show where they gather in large herds during mating season. The seals often go up on the beach to sleep with no schedule at all. You find them in the morning, at noon, in the evening—at all times—in large numbers or small, sometimes just one. They are playful animals. They will turn around in the water like oars, or they will roll rocks back and forth; they will smack the water with their back flippers and spray each other with their front ones. While the male lies down on a rock to warm it, the female is apt to hit herself lightly with her front flippers like a caress. Then they bump each other playfully, or one pushes the other off the rock into the water, who in turn will hop around the rock. When they come on land or the beach, they walk with their front flippers but help themselves along by hopping with their back ones. Like a dog, the seal bites people and lunges after them. Seals also bite each other, so much so that sometimes their entire skin is scratched up. The seal has a bone in its tail like a common or harbor seal [*Phoca vitulina*, here being compared to the Baikal seal or nerpa, *Pusa sibirica*]. The pups make a very small sound like newborn whelps; the adults, however, do not bark but when swimming through the water snort more like horses. The seals have a lot of milk. The Tungus commonly milk it into bladders to give to their children to drink. In the past, there were a lot of these seals in the Baikal, but now they are very rare.

[The text breaks off here, followed by a section, partially written in Latin, with so many lacunae that we have omitted approximately fifteen lines, unable to even guess at Steller's meaning. After the section we omitted, a new paragraph starts with ". . . become, through the promyshlenniks as well as the Tungus." Perhaps this connects to the sentence above and Steller meant that while earlier there were many seals in the lake, their numbers have now been drastically reduced by these two groups of people—that is to say, they have become rare.]

Around the Upper Angara, there is said to be a different species of larger seal than in the lower areas of Lake Baikal. They are most often hunted in the spring. Toward fall, merchants as well as promyshlenniks visit the banks of Lake Baikal in boats equipped with sails to buy up the pelts from the *raznochintsi* [commoners—artisans or peasants—liable to taxation; WH, Glossar; term retained] as well as the Russian promyshlenniks in order to sell them to the Chinese. Formerly, one hundred whole pelts cost thirty to thirty-five rubles, but now the Russians cut them in two lengthwise, fifty nerpi making one hundred pelts, for which the Chinese now pay fifty rubles. Sometimes they are worth only twenty or thirty rubles if they are not highly valued by the Chinese. When the pelts were selling a hundred for sixty rubles, the promyshlenniks along the upper lake used to cut three pelts from one large nerpa, but they do not do that anymore.

Thirty-six pounds of seal blubber is sometimes sold for twenty and up to forty kopeks. If the catch is large, the blubber is even thrown away. Especially in the upper regions of the lake, you get thirty-six to seventy-two pounds from one seal, which is burned for lighting the winter huts. It is also bought by the tanners for greasing peasant shoes and by the millers for greasing their mills. However, the Tungus and Buryats eat it. Three years ago, thirty-six pounds cost one ruble in the region of the prorva, the breach in the dune, across from the Posolsky Monastery. When the Baikal seal hops onto a rock, you see the fat under the skin tremble like aspic [in text, *Sülze*, headcheese].

The Selenga, Barguzin, and Chiverkui are the only rivers left for open hunting; it is now allowed only on lease at all other places. [A Latin note in the margin, translated, reads, "The smaller seals, when suddenly disturbed, make a sound, behaving just like people. The larger ones sound like somebody vomiting. I got a good look at the milk receptacles and ducts." [Seal Catalog. WH, Anm. 507; no such document of Steller's seems to have been found.]

The local common seals are valued less than those . . . [in the upper lake?] since one hundred of the local pelts cost eight or nine rubles. Transport costs here amount to twenty rubles per twenty to twenty-five pounds, so there is still some profit. The Chinese and soldiers buy them to decorate their special clothes with the pelts. [Whole sentence a best guess since the text contains many lacunae.]

Andrei Granin [Irkutsk resident] had made the best offer to the officials to lease the right to hunt seals for three years; the money, however, goes into the government coffers. Then the promyshlenniks, in turn, lease the places like the one from Granin. His first section is from the Golousnaya River to the Ol'khonsky Sound, for which a seven-member hunters' cooperative pays fifty rubles. On Ol'khon Island another cooperative pays seventy to eighty rubles. A third cooperative of five promyshlenniks hunts from the Samarechka to the Ledenaya River; a fourth, consisting of five promyshlenniks, hunts on Buguchan Island for one hundred kilometers around the island and up to three kilometers from the lake shore. The island is about fifty kilometers from the mouth of the Upper Angara River—using a towrope you get there in two days. There are two cooperatives from the Upper Angara to the mouth of the Barguzin, a separate one at Ushany Island, and one at Cape Sviatoi that also pays fifty rubles. Only one promyshlennik leases the area from the mouth of the Barguzin to the Maximishka River and further to the mouth of the Listvenishnaya. On the southern shore, individuals lease parcels since the seals do not often go there.

Fishing cannot be suppressed because, if it were, people in Irkutsk would starve since the promyshlenniks would not go there to fish. The small rivers—except for the Golousnaya—are all banks [a truly wild guess hinging on the theory that the German-looking *vergass*, meaning forgot, which makes no sense in the context, is, instead, a Germanized plural of Russian *berega*, meaning shores or banks] of individual Cossacks who give up their wages in return, like on the Bogul'deicha.

The Breach belongs to the Posolsky Monastery. The locals fish on the Selenga, and the promyshlenniks buy the fish from them because for about five years the promyshlenniks have not been allowed to fish there because they would not let the fish swim into the Selenga, leaving the locals without fish. People get there with three or four doshcheniks or small boats.

And because of the long distance to Barguzin, they use only doshcheniks; three go there. One doshchenik goes to the Chivirkui. There are no more doshcheniks going to the Upper Angara because, on the one hand, they are afraid to be caught in the ice on their return, and on the other hand, Irkutsk being far away, the Tungus there have become more aggressive and taken their fish from them, which had led to brawls. The pine nuts, however, are free for everybody.

In past years, the sable hunters had to lease this hunt too, but this year they get it for free; they just need a government permit. The monastery doshcheniks fish above the Posolsky Monastery at the shore called Korga.

Some other islands are Aspen, which gets its name from the aspen growing on it and is one kilometer long and approximately half a one wide; Long Island, which is more than a kilometer long but very narrow; Round Island; and Broad Island, which is just a rock with a few bushes, but a lot of seals are caught here.

In Lake Baikal the promyshlenniks identify three different kinds of seals. The first and largest are found between Ol'khon Island and the Sviatoi Peninsula where the lake is widest and all the way up to the Upper Angara. The second kind, called *iganki*, are found from Ol'khon Island to where the Angara flows out of the lake. The third kind, called small-mouthed [in text, *maloi rot*, possibly *malorotnye*; WH, Anm. 551], are found across from the outlet of the Angara in the Kultuk, the southwestern part of the Baikal, as well as along the southwestern shore. The iganki have a very broad head, tapering to very thin hindquarters.

The larger kind of seal goes out onto the ice early and remains lying on it, which is why they also mate earlier. The smaller ones [we assume the lacuna in the text (k . . .) was meant to be *kleineren*] are less tolerant of cold weather; they go into the water when a wind comes up and therefore also mate later. The locals have no special terms for this kind of hunt, but not because they do not think it important.

The seals have only two breasts and therefore at most two pups, never more. If the mother is killed, the pups do not leave her. The promyshlenniks therefore approach them stealthily behind a sail and grab them alive. The seal cannot turn around, but when it bites somebody, the wound does not heal for a long time. You can kill them by a blow to the head with your fist; it takes a long time to kill them by striking their body with large clubs.

Across from Kot'elnikova, there is a hot spring close to shore, and even the water in the lake there is warm. The spring's water has an awful burnt smell and takes off tar and grease; it is so hot, it cooks meat. In 1739, after the big earthquake,[1] the spring ceased to exist. The promyshlenniks were sleeping on the ice when the quake struck, and they were unable to sit up. Big fissures appeared in the ice, and grayling[2] and other live fish were thrown onto the ice at the mouths of the Golousnaya and Suk Rivers.

When seals see a person, they all lift their heads, then dive into the water and swim away. Using the waves, the male propels himself onto the female and then forces her into the water with all fours. Seals are said to eat only the heads of fish; they do eat the small crustaceans under the shore pebbles. They die with difficulty. Their heads may have been ever so badly bashed in and the loss of blood ever so great, yet they will recover, and quickly at that. [We omitted the following three lines about the Chekovka River, which seem meaningless.]

Nobody knows how long seals live. They molt three times a year, the heaviest in the spring, and then again in fall and winter. In fall their pelts are best. A hundred pelts sell for thirty or even forty rubles; five years ago, they sold for sixty rubles. This year the Chinese are dyeing them, so somebody leased the right to hunt seals for just a ruble and a half.

From Kultuk, the southwestern shore, to the Angara's outlet and further to Pashkovo Landing, five people pay twenty-five rubles to hunt; from Pashkovo Landing to the Golousnaya, however, whoever wants to hunt hunts for free because nobody wants to buy a lease there. From the Golousnaya to Ol'khonsky Sound near Ol'khon Island, seven promyshlenniks pay fifty rubles; last year they paid sixty rubles. Around Ol'khon Island seven promyshlenniks pay seventy rubles. From Ol'khon Island to the Ledenaya River, a three-day trip with a boat, seven promyshlenniks pay fifteen rubles. From the Ledenaya to the Upper Angara, three people pay fifteen rubles; they are afraid of the Tungus.

At the mouth of the Bogul'deicha, five kilometers upriver, promyshlenniks smelted iron some years ago. It lies twelve feet deep under the steppe, breaks up as an iron-colored hard rock, is hard to smelt, and results in iron like for steel. The Buryats have since burned down the promyshlenniks' hut there.

On the Talovka, five kilometers from the previously mentioned place, the Dauren[3] smelted iron, too, as is still evident from the mining pits. On the Anga River are Lanin's ironworks. Two to three, maybe even seven kilometers up the Ushakovka, they are hacking iron out of the swamp, but the iron is not usable because too much sand is mixed with it. In Kamenka on the Angara, promyshlenniks also smelt iron. The iron across Lake Baikal costs fifty-five kopeks per thirty-six pounds.

Glistnik [*glist*, worm] is a fern found around Smolensk, a village on the Irkut River, and is especially good for getting rid of worms. [We omitted the following four incomprehensible lines.]

The clacking noise reindeer make when walking is just caused by their long feet, as one foot hits the other. These animals also lack a gallbladder, which, however, the Kuriles say they have in their feet.

Glazunov's mill is located on an arm of the Angara River. The village of Lesser Rozvodnaya is located on a delightful hill; it has just a few houses but quite a lot of agriculture.

Greater Rozvodnaya has a prikazchik; the village is situated on high ground surrounded by swampy brush. Because there are lots of ponds, the people of Irkutsk enjoy coming here to catch both carp [possibly crucian carp, *Carassius carassius* L.] and tench [*Tinca tinca*; in text, lini, also known as doctor fish]. Lots of lake minnows and sticklebacks [probably *Gasterosteus aculeatus*] are also found here. Melnikova Derevnya [consistently translated as village unless it is part of a proper name], across from Rozvodnaya, above the Angara, belongs to Petr Fedorovich.

Glazkova Zaimka, across from the church in Medvedev's village, has two houses. His village is located over the mountain, on a most delightful hill, but together with its owner, who twenty years ago was the biggest merchant and capitalist in all of Siberia, is now ruined. This village has good agriculture, including excellent hayfields, and a mill on the Kaya River, which flows into the Irkut. [What follows repeats information found in previous chapters; therefore, we have omitted it here.]

In winter, in the ponds and lakes around Yakutsk, the crucian carp, which are very fat at that time, lie dormant, piled up to half a man's height. The Yakuts pull them out with nets, taking only the big ones and releasing the small ones back into the lake. These fish start to move again with the spring thaw. But the lake minnows are active all year long. In addition, big pike are in the lakes on the Tatta and Aldan Rivers. Common sturgeon and belugas are caught in winter in the Yaik [now called Ural] River, and sheefish [*Stenodus nelma*] are caught all summer long. Carp are very sly, managing to avoid the nets in many ways. On the Lena, the nets are almost three thousand feet long.

In 1708, under voevod Shishkin, a ukase was sent to Anadyrsk to dispatch thirty sluzhivs to the springs of the Penzhina River in order to establish an ostrog there. It took them five days of travel only to discover the area lacked enough fish and game to be able to live there. They did hold out for ten weeks in a winter hut at the mouth of the Chernaya River, which flows into the Anadyr River, and then they went back. Like the Kolyma and Anadyr Rivers, the Penzhina flows out of the mountains. The Yakuts believe that in winter a mammoth pushes up the ice on the lakes from one end to the other even if the ice is almost ten feet thick. Some even claim to have seen this animal but believe it would cause their demise within a year.

In 1718 Peter Tatarinov [who had been sent to Anadyrskoi Ostrog earlier to reconnoiter a sea route from there to Kamchatka] sent Cossacks to build a vessel on the Penzhina and sail it to Kamchatka because at that time the rebellious Koryaks and Iukagirs would not let anybody travel from Anadyrsk to Kamchatka or back; they had also taken the government funds away from the prikazchiks, which the Anadyrsk sluzhivs had to buy back with pots, knives, and hatchets. In Anadyrsk the sluzhivs were to gather precise information about these events. They traveled downriver from Ust'Chernaya for nine days. The left bank of the river is rocky and studded with cliffs; on the right the Aklan River flows into it, above which the natives' Aklanskoi Ostrog and, not far from the mouth, Kamenskoi Ostrozhok are located. In the river, you find sheefish [in text, *nelma*], broad whitefish [*Coregonus nasus*; in text, *chiri*], and other fish swimming up from the Sea of Okhotsk. It took them three weeks of rowing and sailing to travel from the mouth of the Chernaya. The banks are lined with nothing but rocky cliffs. At Lesnaya and at the mouth of the Tigil River, there is a small sound.

Peter Antonov [Okhotsk sluzhiv] told me that on the Lena River, sixty kilometers downriver from Ust'Kutsk, there used to be a boggy lake, now dry, which one night around epiphany broke up and flowed into the Lena via a channel, breaking up the ice all the way across the Lena, and the Yakuts assume it came from the mammoth. Antonov also reported that not far from that former lake there had been a bottomless pit filled with water on the bank of the Lena. When a man let down a rock on a string, he found that now the spring is barely seven feet deep; it may have become plugged.

Notes

1. Irkutsk and the surrounding area were rocked by strong quakes on April 5 and 6, 1739, which Steller told Gmelin about in his letter of May 10. WH, Anm. 558.

2. In text, *sorius*, a trout species, but more likely *charius*. WH, Anm. 550. Conceivably Arctic or Baikal grayling.

3. In text, *Bogdoizi*; WH, Anm. 587, cites Georgi (1775) about the previous inhabitants of the Baikal region: "Legend calls the old inhabitants Bargutes; they are probably . . . the former residents called Dauren or Duchery in the oldest documents, or, even more often, Bogdani or Bogdochani, which are names for Manchurian tribes or the Manchurians in general."

8

REPORT FROM THE UDA RIVER

From Bol'sheretsk, Kamchatka, Shestakov's detachment reached the Gilyaks in sixty hours; thus, the width of the sea can be estimated to be not over four to six hundred German miles.¹ There they found an incredibly beautiful country with good grass and beautiful forests. The Gilyaks live together in villages, in log houses built like in Russia. Their storage sheds stand on posts, two to three feet high above the ground. The people are dressed in silk robes lined with Chinese fanza, a silken material. They have lots of tobacco, presumably also tea, the leaves of which may well come from the shrub from which the Tungus bring [sic; but maybe Steller meant *brechen*, break] finger-thick twigs, the shavings from which they spread onto wounds. The Russians compare it to spiraea shrubs. [Several species of these occur in Siberia, primarily in larch forests or in rocky locations; Jäger.] The Gilyaks have long arrows as well as beautiful bows and quivers with silver inlays. They are tall people and wear silver rings in their noses. In addition to a lot of sables, foxes, and moose, they shot twelve Russians to death. They say that, instead of making them pay yasak, the Chinese take all sorts of things from them: moose antlers, both good and bad sables, fox pelts, moose hides, and whatever else the land provides. They also have beautiful lakes on which Yakut refugees live and are tolerated, in defiance of the treaties between Russia and China.² Both the Tungus and the Yakuts trade with the Gilyaks, but secretly, because it is said that the Chinese border patrols check closely every year.

On the Uda River, the land is considerably more productive than around Okhotsk. There are foxes, excellent sables, striped marten [in text, *Igorken*, R, *chor'ki*. WH, Anm. 709], moose, reindeer, and hares, even black ones. With boats carrying 7,200 pounds, the Gilyaks travel to the river's mouth in half a day, returning in two and a half days, using tow ropes.

Fig. 8.1. The great effort of many workers pulling a boat upriver against the current (Arnold).

They catch whales and belugas in large numbers with nets made of beluga leather, but of anadromous fish only dog salmon [*Oncorhynchus keta*] and in the river a few Siberian taimen and sharp-snouted lenoks, and in the sea also large turtles, but people do not eat those. There is good wood: larch, fir, spruce, birch, Scots pine [*Pinus sylvestris* L.; Jäger], and Siberian dwarf pine. Among the birds Siberian grouse [*Falcipennis falcipennis*; in text, *dikushka*; WH, Anm. 717] are worth noting, which are very tame and said to closely resemble the black grouse.

On the Kolyma River and around Verkhoyansk, the northern lights are seen in the fall almost every night, but they cannot be seen in July and August because the sun keeps it too bright. The Yakuts attribute the northern lights to the marine fish and large marine mammals that, they say, emit this brilliance when they play. One night, when a Yakut at the mouth of the Lena happened to catch glowing fish in his net—sea stars [Asteroidea] and sea nettles [*Chrysaora melanaste*, northern sea nettle or brown jellyfish, best guess; Ricketts and Calvin, 228–29] may have been among them—he was so terrified thinking he had caught the devil that he cut his net to pieces and fled.

The Yakuts bury only the rich; the poor are flung into the snow or put out somewhere in the woods a few kilometers from the yurt. They throw away small children when they are too poor to raise them. Once two brothers would have buried their mother alive had the Russians not stopped them. Saying their mother was old and no longer useful, they had tied all her tools on her back and dragged her to the grave they had already dug. When people get too sick to walk, they put them on a sled and pull them out into the snow to freeze to death, not even turning around to take a last look. Or they leave them lying there in the yurt to starve to death while they build themselves a new one. Deformed babies are placed live in a lidded birch-bark basket and hung on trees to die there. In Yakutsk many people starved to death in 1739 and were simply thrown to the bottom of a hill. When the snow melted, a lot of corpses appeared, which the dogs dragged around until the voevod had the corpses dragged out onto the frozen Lena, so that when the river broke up, they were carried downriver with the flood.[3] In Bol'sheretsk a prostitute drowned three children in the Bol'shaya River with everybody's knowledge, and she still lives there without being condemned.

When beavers are attacked by a dog on the ice, the first beaver turns over on its back and the others all follow because in the water, like geese in the air, they move along in V formations. Their pelt is loosely attached; it can thus be pulled off very rapidly except on the head where it is more firmly attached. Therefore, when in a hurry, the Yakuts usually cut off the beavers' heads.

On Kamchatka, the Cossacks boil blueberries [*Vaccinium uliginosum* L.] mixed with alum into a thick juice, then put it on a rag to dye beaver and sable pelts black, a deception that is hard to detect because the dye does not wash off. But if you were to pull out a few hairs, you would notice the swindle because the roots are white. The dye also protects the skin of the pelt from moisture, something the Russians call *oprevat'*, ruining by sweat and moisture. People also dye bleached-out silk goods and fanza with this tincture.

The sea lions fall from rocks 87 to 258 feet down into the water without suffering injury, even though they are almost as heavy as bears.

Notes

1. One German mile equals 24,000 German feet, and one German foot equals 13.2 inches; thus, 400 to 600 German miles equals 1,800 to 2,700 miles. The actual distance between Bol'sheretsk and the mouth of the Uda River is closer to 880 miles. National Geographic Atlas.

2. In 1689 the Chinese-Russian Treaty of Nerchinsk was signed, in which the border between China and Russia along northeastern China to the Sea of Okhotsk was determined. Points 2 and 4 of this treaty specified that in the case of border violations, no asylum was to be granted to subjects by the other side; instead, they had to be returned to their own people for punishment. WH, Anm. 707.

3. Strahlenberg (1730, 377ff.) reported, "The Yakuts bury their dead in different ways. High-ranking people pick out a nice tree and say that is where they want to lie after death; they also are buried with some of their treasured objects. Other corpses are just put on a board placed up on four posts out in the forest and then covered over with an ox or horse hide. Some are buried in the ground. Most are just left in the yurt after they die; the relatives take the valuables, close the yurt tightly, and then take off. People who die in Yakutsk are left lying in the streets where the dogs usually come around and eat the corpses." Quoted in WH, Anm. 724.

PART II

TRAVEL JOURNAL FROM IRKUTSK TO KAMCHATKA

9

FROM IRKUTSK TO UST'ILGINSKAYA (3/4–3/13)

Tuesday, March 4. In the evening I sent off eight sleds with our gear from Irkutsk under the sluzhiv Aleksei's command.

Wednesday, March 5. It thawed all day. I said my goodbyes, and in the evening I too departed with four sleds, together with Mr. Berckhan, his servant, the student Gorlanov, the huntsman Nefedrov, and two sluzhivs. We were accompanied by Voevod [Steller's error, actually Vice-Governor] Bibikov, Mr. Henks [Carl Hencke, caravan physician in Kyakhta? WH, Personenregister], Mr. Beck, Sinyavinskii, Markov, and Protopopov's Ivan Ivanovich. Because of the miserable trail, it was ten at night when we reached the Kudinskaya Sloboda, right on the Kuta River, a tributary of the Angara River, located in excellent grain-growing country. In this sloboda five hundred people pay head taxes.[1] It is located in a well-watered level plain nineteen kilometers from Irkutsk, and the trail there leads through a beautiful forest. Her Majesty's brandy distillery, called Karlutskoi Kastak, is located seven kilometers from the sloboda, from which you travel across a broad steppe. To the left forested hills rise.

Thursday, March 6. A clear, mild day; it thawed, and nine kilometers further we came to Kranin's mill, after another ten kilometers to Turchenninov's Zaimka, which is, however, ruined and of little significance. Fifteen kilometers from Kuta and thirty-four from town, another large sloboda is located, and from here the podvodi go as far as Manzurskaya Sloboda, which is also located on the Kuta River; above it a small stream, Oyok, from which the Oyoskaya Sloboda got its name, flows into the Kuta. It is approximately twenty-six kilometers from Oyoskaya Sloboda to Aphonassii Dementiev's Zaimka and about twenty kilometers from the Posolsky Monastery's Village

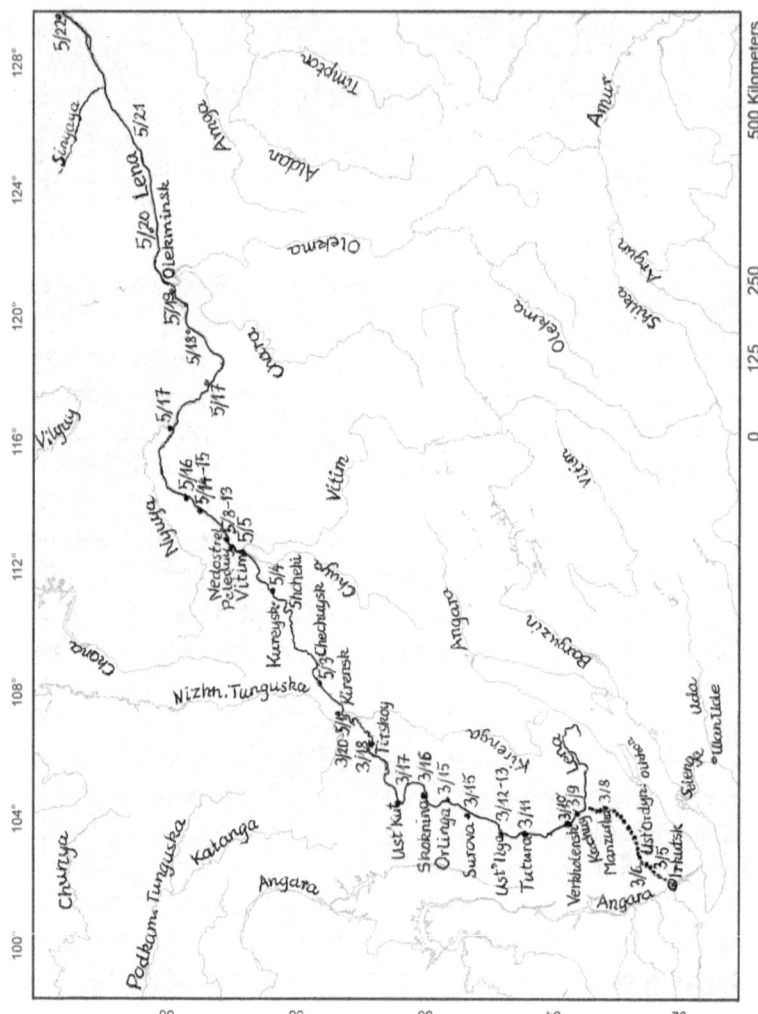

Map 9.1. Steller's route with stopovers from Irkutsk to the Pokrovsky Monastery, designed and labeled by Eckehart Jäger.

to Varasilov's Zaimka on the right. Fourteen kilometers from Oyok, on the road to Varasilov's Zaimka, is Monastery Zaimka, which still belongs to the Posolsky Monastery. All these places are very suitable for growing grain, but they are all located to the right, off the trail. The actual road to the Lena takes off to the left, and after traveling twenty kilometers from the Posolsky Monastery, you come to a mill on the Kuta. Approximately eleven kilometers further on this road, you reach the first zimov'e, wayside hut, called Ordinskoe Zimov'e, and the caretaker is a newly converted Swede, Stalberg, now called Michael Beklemishev. This hut is located on the banks of the Orda River, where it flows into the Kuta. This is where we stopped for the night. Five kilometers before you get to the hut, on the right, is Dementiev's mill, and parallel to the mill stream, forested mountains stretch along the road through the steppe. On both sides of the stream in the steppe are many wooden Buryat yurts.

Friday, March 7. In the morning we departed, and toward noon we came to Kokorino Zimov'e, thirty-eight kilometers from Ordinskoe Zimov'e. We left in the afternoon, and around ten at night we reached Listvenishnoe Zimov'e. It had been pleasant and clear all day long; toward morning it started to freeze.

Saturday, March 8. Toward noon today we reached Bol'shaya Manzurskaya Sloboda on the Manzurka River, 145 kilometers from Oyok, 179 from Irkutsk. More than sixty kilometers from its source in the area of the Bogul'deicha River near Lake Baikal, this river flows through the Kosaya or Sloping Steppe. And about five kilometers from Kachega on the left it flows into the Lena. From Manzurskaya Sloboda to the Kosaya Steppe is approximately forty kilometers. On the Kosaya Steppe are a tax collection station as well as some houses for sluzhivs who keep watch for prohibited goods and make sure other goods do not go via the control station at Bogul'deicha Zimov'e to the border or back without duty being paid. There is good grain-growing land around this sloboda and for about twenty kilometers of the surrounding steppe, but it lies fallow because of the Buryats' herding. We left here in the afternoon and, after covering five kilometers, came to the village of Raspashnina, which has two houses and is located one kilometer to the left of the road. Two kilometers further is the village of Paltusa, also with two houses. Two kilometers from here we crossed the Sukhaya River or the Little Dry Stream. Around dusk we reached Kudrina Zimov'e to the right of the road, twelve kilometers from the sloboda. Here the steppe between forested mountains is not more than five kilometers wide. During the night

Fig. 9.1. A zimov'e or wayside hut (Arnold).

we came to Malaya Manzurka, where we spent the night. The weather was just like yesterday. Three kilometers from Kachega, we passed a mill, and to the right of it, about half a kilometer away, are two more houses.

Sunday, March 9. In the morning we reached Kachega, the first settlement on the Lena, built above the river on the right bank. Here we met up with all our gear. A few years ago, construction of a church was begun in Kachega, but because the place was too small the bishop forbade it. Since construction had already progressed to the roof, the building now serves the state as a warehouse for provisions. The place consists of about five households, but from the fall of 1739 till this date in 1740 a rampant epidemic befell it and spread as far as Birulka, Kulinga, Anga, and down to Ust'Ilginskaya. The Buryats have not been affected by this epidemic, but they won't let any Russians into their yurts, or only grudgingly. The disease causes a high fever that cannot be broken by sweating. There are two different symptoms: either the patients are in a rage from severe headaches, without sweating at all until about the ninth day, or they are hot to the touch but internally feel very cold like with a high fever. This epidemic carried off mostly the young and able-bodied people between sixteen and thirty years old; few children or old folks died. I consider the cause to be the early and abrupt arrival of winter, which, from one day to the next, kept the people working in the fields from sweating. Bloodletting and a few grains of camphor could have done much good and kept many of them alive. But in this regard, too, no preventive measures were taken. In vain I offered my services in November to the Irkutsk government even when you could see how necessary a physician would be in these regions.

In addition to this epidemic, these people are afflicted by three other ills. The first is their previous poverty; many are pawning wife and children to be able to deliver their tribute. The second is the crop failure of 1739, when almost all the grain all along the Lena froze before it matured and what ripened couldn't be harvested because so many people were sick, so it stayed in the fields, and afterward they had to procure seed grain from three hundred kilometers away as far as the Urik, Oyok, and Kuta [Rivers]. The third is that many are ordered to work on the freight boats and provision rafts to Yakutsk. This year the inhabitants along the Anga[2] have been recruited as a special favor to the people along the Lena. Consequently, a lot of land lies fallow; nevertheless, the peasants have to deliver their tribute in grain just like every year. It is worth noting that the epidemic did not spread beyond the mountains along the Lena. Where there are open spaces and fields, the epidemic either did not come at all or was not bad and did not last long, a fact that confirms my first opinion.

At Kachega and down to Verkholensk, the Lena is not wide, but it does have many shallow places. Above Kachega on the right, the Big and the Little Anga—or according to Buryat pronunciation, *Agna*—flow into the Lena. To date, I have not been able to inquire about the meaning of it, or of Manzurka, Kachega, *Kulin Kaehn* in Buryat, or *Kulinga* in Russian. A reminder to myself: I must try to find out the meaning of the word *kuta* in the Buryat and Tungus languages, whether it is the generic word for river, which is exactly the meaning of Angara. *Ilga* also has to be a Tungus word. The Bratski or Buryat call the Lena *zsukaei*, and I do not know its etymology or who named the river Lena.

Close to the village of Kachega, the stream named Kachega flows into the Lena on the right, and that is where the *utesi* or steep cliff walls of red sandstone start. For three kilometers they stretch up to the place where a well-proportioned series of hills starts but with a different layout. For it looks as if there were many newly raised grave mounds, descending diagonally from the uppermost part down to the river, with valleys running between each of them. About five kilometers from Kachega, on the right, a low mountain range starts in three horizontal segments and continues for two kilometers. Its top is densely covered with tall larch [*Larix gmelinii* (Rupr.) Kuzen.; Jäger], Siberian spruce [*Picea obovata* Ledeb.; Jäger], Scots pine, and birch trees [*Betula platyphylla* Sukaczev, syn. of *B. pendula* subsp. *mandshurica* (Regel) Ashburner & Mc All.; Jäger], but the left bank of the Lena is flat throughout and also covered with dense forest.

Six kilometers from Kachega, the *pisani kameni* begin, these being rocks painted with hieroglyphic figures of birds, animals, and other characters (petroglyphs). They are found in various places up to Verkholensk. Professor Müller has published sketches and his thoughts on them in his *History of the Lena River*. It is my opinion that, under various circumstances, the natives carved these figures into the rock by order of the shamans, as a kind of vow. The right bank turns flat and wooded, the left one steep, rocky, and high. Darkness and sleep kept me from making further observations of what things look like till Verkholensk, but I shall make up for it when I return from Kamchatka.

Monday, March 10. We arrived in Verkholensk—that is, the night before. This is an ostrog, the oldest settlement on the Lena, and it has a commander and about eighty sluzhiv houses. It is located to the right side of the Lena on a hill, 263 kilometers from Irkutsk, 29 from Kachega, and it grows the least grain. Good gray and white woolen stockings are made here for sale at thirty kopeks a pair, and Russian cloth at thirty kopeks for twenty-eight inches.[3] Without this cottage industry, the poor people couldn't buy bread. In contrast, in the grain-rich places, people are much lazier, from which observation you can deduce the Russian womenfolk's economic sense. Birulka, a fine sloboda, grows good grain—Anginskaya Sloboda as well—and is famous for its hogs that are sent from here to Yakutsk, Okhotsk, and Kamchatka. From here I wrote to the governor about sending the two last memoranda of Dr. Gmelin's—see the copy in the Acta journal—to young Mr. Bibikov, Mr. Hencke, and Lapakov [secretary in the Irkutsk Provincial Office], to whom I sent the bottles Fedor had stolen as well as Stroganov's booty. Today was warm, clear, and calm though I noticed the air changed considerably on the eleventh, becoming colder than around Irkutsk and on the steppe up to the Lena.

In the afternoon we departed from Verkholensk. About three kilometers from there, we passed Mikhailo Kozlova Zaimka, which has only one house and is built on the left bank of the Lena right at the foot of the mountains. One kilometer further is Peter Popov's Zaimka, also one house on the left. Several kilometers further, about twelve from Verkholensk, is another Kozlova Zaimka with four houses, across from which there's a fifth house on the left. From there you get to Pulyaevsk, a Cossack's small village. Twenty-four kilometers from Verkholensk is Opushkina [fur-trimmed clothing] Derevnya, which is situated on the left of the river, has two houses, and grows good grain.

In this part of the country, the Cossacks and sluzhivs are compensated with villages instead of a salary, while the posadski have to pay for their dwellings with about 1,625 pounds of flour to the government coffers, the *pashennie krest'iane* or peasant farmers 542 pounds and a head tax of seventy kopeks. The peasants who do not work in the fields pay 110 kopeks. Sluzhivs, posadski, and peasant farmers augment their income from hunting in winter. A man may, for example, have three to four hundred, perhaps even one thousand traps. There are three types of squirrels in this area: gray ones, black ones with black tails, and black ones with reddish tails. The price for a winter squirrel's pelt here is twenty-four kopeks, occasionally even thirty. I noticed for the first time that these squirrels are plagued by a lot of fleas. There are also fairly large numbers of ermine.

I have found it necessary to remember two things here: first, that all villages and small settlements in these parts do not have permanent names but are renamed as often as they change owners, which causes a lot of confusion in descriptions and charts that could be alleviated by a ukase or statute. This place, Opushkina Derevnya, received its name as a joke because the previous owner had dressed himself and his family in hare pelts, just as the Cherepanov family, meaning potter, in Kirenga got theirs from shards, in Russian *cherep'e*, because their ancestors are said to have made the first pots in this area.

Second, I must remind myself that, as on the Irtysh and Ob Rivers, only those places are settled and used for agriculture that lie on high enough ground to escape flooding or that have enough level land between the mountains, which if not arable is at least suitable for growing hay. That's how it is on the Lena, too, because almost to its mouth it is surrounded on both sides by high mountains and steep rock faces stretching to the very edges of the river, and thus the land is not suitable for growing grain or hay.[4] But there are also places where the mountains stretch inland away from the river for one to three kilometers or where they gradually decrease in height and slope down to the river. These places—as has often and reliably been noted—have loamy or black soil and are mostly covered by birches. These are the places from Kachega to below Kirenga that the Russians have chosen as suitable for growing grain, and that's where they've built small settlements and larger villages. You could well say that, while elsewhere in Siberia many nice locations lie fallow, on the Lena not the smallest advantageous place has been overlooked or lies untilled. Nevertheless, some cleared land now does lie untilled because, partly due to the current epidemic and partly due to the ordered delivery of provisions for the Kamchatka Expedition, there are fewer people and the population has been decimated. Other than that, the residents on the Lena are well-satisfied and in good condition.

However, those places where formerly birches stood, which are called *berezniki* [R, airy birch forests] or *yelani* [R, forest glades], are especially popular because in a few years the birch roots rot, further improving the soil. And in the case where good soil and birch forests are found on the highest mountains, the local residents have made them into arable fields and seeded them, as is the case around Manzursk, Kachega [today Kachug], and Ust'Ilga. They do, however, take the precaution of leaving many trees all around, especially on the north side, as protection from the turbulent north wind. The larch forests are the least suitable for growing grain because their roots grow deep into the earth and do not decay for a long time. Places where willows or alders appear are condemned as totally unsuitable because they tend to receive and retain much moisture from the river, which causes the seed to rot; those places also can never be completely cleared and cleaned up. But as for why the steppes are not used for growing grain, the local inhabitants can give only one reason—namely, that the winds would tear out the plants, roots and all. I am of the opinion, however, that people just don't want to make the effort to relieve the barrenness by fertilizing. According to the inhabitants' observations, the fields on the Lena cannot be fertilized with animal or plant matter. I proposed they try fertilizing with the amply occurring bolaric earth [product of weathered iron silicate; WH, Anm. 159], which lies white between the clay layers of the mountains, just as people do in Hesse and Westphalia with the *lithomarga* [a clay mineral, kaolinite]. Rye is sown here at the beginning of August around Redeemer Day [in text, *Spasky*, of which there are three: August 1, 6, and 16; WH, Anm. 162], barley around Nicolni Day [probably May 9; WH, Anm. 163]. Ripening depends on the weather. Usually, rye flour costs twelve to fifteen kopeks per thirty-six pounds. It is, however, least expensive in December when the head taxes are due, selling for only six to ten kopeks. This year the ration sells for twenty kopeks in the upper regions of the Lena, in the central areas like Ust'Ilga for sixteen; in the lower parts around Kirenga, the inhabitants themselves have nothing to spare, hence to sell. Monday the weather was mild and clear all day.

Tuesday, March 11. In the morning we arrived in Mark Vorob'ev's Derevnya. Before that, nine kilometers from Opushkin's Derevnya, we had passed another pisani kamen—that is, a rock with petroglyphs. Sixteen kilometers from Opushkina, we had come to Sider Korkina Derevnya on the right side of the river, which has four peasant houses and is the first in the Ilimsk district. From there we had come to Mark Vorob'ev's Derevnya, which also has four peasant houses, good arable land, and good hayfields. Around six in the morning, we departed,[5] passing on both sides of the river many utesi or steep cliffs of red clay or sandstone that look from afar like old walls built of red brick. From Kachega to here, the rock is uniformly layered and cohesive—that is to say, partly reddish sandstone, partly gray or bluish with a red tint. The rocks are fused by red chalk of a poor and wild quality, lying for two to three inches between the strata, which are all horizontal in some slabs or rocks that also have foot-wide protruding ledges, lattice-like, fastened to the lower rocks. Among the crags, there are many nests of bank swallows [*Riparia riparia*],[6] owls, and other raptors. Twelve kilometers from Mark Vorob'ev's Derevnya, we came to another settlement with two houses, the name of which I forgot to inquire about; another two kilometers from that one is Pirogov's Derevnya on the left bank of the Lena. Nine kilometers further we came to another, called Vorobeva Derevnya, and seven kilometers from there to Kozma Rudov's Derevnya with two houses on the right bank of the river. At this point for several kilometers, the Lena plunges visibly downhill and is very fast in spring. But in summer it is shallow here and hard to navigate, in dry years at times even impassable. Seven kilometers from here we came to Ponomarev's Derevnya with two houses on the left bank of the Lena; two kilometers further on, also on the left, Buturin's Derevnya is located with two houses inhabited by peasants. Six kilometers further, on the right, is Golovnia Derevnya, which has three peasant houses. Two kilometers further is Rudia Derevnya with two peasant houses, and yet another two kilometers further is another Golovnya Derevnya with three peasant houses. Tuturskaya Sloboda, consisting of eight houses and a church with a priest, a prikazchik, and a *zakazchik* [administrative assistant to the prikazchik; WH, Anm. 220; term retained], is located on the Tutura River 95 kilometers from Verkholensk, 124 from Kachega. In this place the epidemic raged too. The inhabitants are raznochintsi and peasants. Around Zhigalova are good millstones. The river has its source across from Opushkina. This day was incredibly warm, pleasant, and clear.

Wednesday, March 12. The weather was like yesterday, pleasantly sunny and calm. But in the afternoon it turned very windy and cloudy, and it snowed. In the night we left Tutura and traveled the forty kilometers here, to Ust'Ilga, arriving in the morning. But before that we passed the following settlements: Kusnezov's Derevnya, Tichin's with four houses and located three kilometers from Tutura, and Zhigalov's Derevnya. From Kachega to here and far downriver on the Lena, no iron ore is to be found. In Ust'Ilga the people get it from Kamenka on the Angara, and thirty-six pounds cost 60 kopeks, occasionally even 120; an axe is seventy kopeks. The blacksmiths around here praise the iron from Yakutsk especially because it is soft and pliable like tin, and they say it creaks like tin when they bend it.

Thursday, March 13. We were stuck in Ust'Ilginskaya Sloboda waiting for the prikazchik to arrive from Ust'Ilginskoi Ostrog to direct him to have a raft built immediately. In the morning it was very cloudy and a bit windy. Immediately below Ust'Ilginskaya Sloboda, the Ilga River flows into the Lena from the right. It is shallow, has a rocky bottom, and is very small in the summer. In spring all the snow melting in the mountains creates the many streams in the valleys that cause the Ilga, like all the other tributaries, to rush into the Lena. But in summer these streams dry up and are therefore called *sochoi rechki*—that is, dry rivers—by the Russians; they do not deserve to be mentioned in descriptions. The Ilga flows fairly straight between the mountains until Ust'Ilginskoi Ostrog, located forty-four kilometers from Ust'Ilginskaya Sloboda, where priests live, in addition to the prikazchik, zakazchik, and several *bobyl'skie* [see below]. It also has two churches. One of these burned down several years ago but is being rebuilt this year. In this sloboda, which has fifteen houses, there is a church or rather a chapel [in text, *chasovnia*, a chapel without an altar but with icons and a lamp; WH, Anm. 222], but the priest lives in the ostrog. Bobyl'skie or *zakhrebetniki* don't have any farms and pay no head taxes but are hired as field hands. But around the ostrog there are many small peasant villages. The Ilga is not rich in fish, just like the Lena and its tributaries above Ust'Kutskoi Ostrog. Except for Arctic grayling, a few Siberian taimen, sharp-snouted lenok, round whitefish [*Prosopium cylindraceum*],[7] northern pike, burbot, perch, Eurasian ruffe, grayling, Eurasian dace, common whitefish, and gudgeon [*Gobio gobio*, best guess], it has no other fish.

Otherwise, this is one of the areas on the Lena most conducive to growing grain for bread even though it is surrounded by mountains, on the slopes of which the fields are located. In the mountains petrified shellfish are said to be found, but to locate those as Dr. Gmelin has requested is impossible due to all the snow. The epidemic raged here, too.

As a general rule about Siberia, it can be noted that the people in poor and bad places are much more industrious and of a better mind-set than in rich places and those of abundance. There is no house in these parts where hemp and burlap are not spun and woven for shirts and pants; young and old are intent on saving themselves from poverty as much as possible. Whereas in Irkutsk the womenfolk—as soon as the tea and cabbage soup have been prepared—can be found lying together on the stove like sausages in a frying pan, smoking their asses so they don't rot and fall apart from all the moving and whoring. You can also see how the inhabitants here, lacking hayfields, gather grass in the local forests in the German manner;[8] around the ostrog more fodder is available, and that's why more small villages are found there.

In this connection it occurs to me how necessary and useful it would be in the whole Russian empire and especially in Siberia to have an accurate description of all the places in every province and voevodship, listing the advantage of each over the others, its special natural advantages or flaws, and the inhabitants' wealth or poverty resulting from them. Also the population in each. With the frequent change and replacement of governors and voevods, each newcomer would—when extraordinary levies were imposed—immediately see on such a roster which place should proportionately be more or less imposed on. As it is now, all the inhabitants on the Angara and Lena have to deliver equal amounts of foodstuffs and hemp, namely fifteen pounds per person, even though in some places the people have no bread themselves, nor could they buy any if they had money to do so. On the other hand, right now, the residents of the slobodas on the Angara could easily give double the amount. Demanding the same from all is ruinous to the people. Some run away to work in small, out-of-the-way villages to avoid all future obligations, or, if they stay, they remain poor and in debt all their lives. For, from Viatka to Yakutsk, I have observed that the rich and well-to-do have the habit, in case of a crop failure, of loaning natives as well as Russians what they need to pay their yasak or foodstuffs and then every year making them pay back a third or even half that sum. But these loan sharks do not deduct these payments from the loan or provide an accounting; instead, they consider them to be interest and a gift. The loan remains forever the same. Consequently, in ten years such a usurer gets his loaned money back fivefold, but the one who borrowed it stays eternally in debt. The natives get very embittered about that and are moved to evil thoughts against this nation, which could easily be remedied through the publication of a ukase imposing heavy fines on the usurers and confiscating their capital.

Ust'Ilginskaya Pier—along with Biryul'skaya Sloboda and Ust'Kutsk Ostrog—is one of the *pristani* [shipyards] on the Lena where vessels are built.

Notes

1. Instigated by Peter the Great in 1724 as means of supporting the rapidly growing army; applied to all males who were subjected to taxes, e.g., farmers, merchants, and posadskie. WH, Glossar.

2. In text, *die Angarischen Anwohner*; suggests the inhabitants along the Angara River, which is much further away than the Big and Little Anga Rivers mentioned below.

3. In text, *arshin*, standardized by Peter the Great to measure twenty-eight inches; we have consistently converted *arshin* to inches.

4. Had Steller traveled to the mouth of the Lena as Dr. Gmelin instructed him to, he would have found himself on the Arctic plain and noticed the absence of mountains and cliffs and an environment not conducive to agriculture.

5. We are puzzled by their both arriving and leaving the same morning, very early at that.

6. In text, *Steinschwalben*, bank swallows (a best guess). Springer, pers. comm., August 24, 2016.

7. In text, *valki*, full Russian name *karilikoviy volyok*. Romanenko et al., 10.

8. It was customary for the poor to harvest grass in a clearing or gather branches from certain deciduous trees. Jäger.

10

FROM UST'ILGINSKAYA TO KIRENSK (3/14–5/1)

Friday, March 14. It was very windy, even stormy, and it snowed intermittently. We left Ust'Ilginsk in the afternoon and, after traveling twenty-one kilometers, came to the village of the Gruznye on the Lena's left bank. From there, after another twenty-one kilometers, in the first hour of the night, we reached Botovskaya Derevnya on the left bank. From Ust'Ilginsk to here you travel consistently downhill because the Lena drops, frequently so steeply that for two kilometers you can deduce from the height of the banks on both sides that the river must be 90 to 120 feet or more below the surrounding countryside. Eight kilometers from Botovskaya, we came to Shamanova Derevnya; after traveling another sixteen kilometers, we came to Golova Derevnya. Nine kilometers from this village, we reached Starcova on the right bank of the Lena, and from here we had another three kilometers to Tomshina Derevnya. Today was windy and cold.

Saturday, March 15. We reached Surova Derevnya on the left, thirteen kilometers from the previous place. From here, fourteen kilometers further, we reached Diadina Derevnya and four kilometers from there Zakobenina Derevnya, where we had our lunch at the place of a resident who was 116 years old. Fourteen kilometers from this place we came to the Basovys' village on the right bank of the Lena, and four kilometers from there to Dutkina Derevnya on the left bank of the Lena. Here I heard that on the Vitim River black mica is found through which light falls into the room, albeit a bit more darkly; from the room everything happening in the street can also be seen, but from the outside you cannot see what's happening in the room. It is eighteen kilometers from Dutkina Derevnya to Orlenskaya Sloboda. We arrived here in the evening. The day was cold and windy.

Orlenskaya Sloboda is situated on the right bank of the Lena at the confluence with the Orlenga River. Recently, during Lent, the church here had burned down. The place has a prikazchik. Around here people begin to become my countrymen because of the high incidence of goiters among them.[1] We departed in the night and, after four kilometers, reached Tarasova Derevnya. From the mountains around this community come the most beautiful whet- and millstones that are much harder and better than the ones around Michailova Zaimka. Four kilometers from Tarasova, we came to Sedunova Derevnya, which has two houses and is located to the left. Here we took fresh horses and immediately continued on. During the night we passed Skoknina Derevnya to the left, with two houses, seventeen kilometers from the previous village.

Sunday, March 16. It snowed all day long, after the previous night had been very cold, windy, and blustery. At nine in the morning, we left Skoknina, and after traveling twenty kilometers we came to the village of the Boyarskies on the right bank of the Lena, where we had lunch. After leaving and traveling twenty more kilometers, we came to Omolo'eva Zaimka with two peasant houses; six kilometers farther on, at dusk, we came to Sinyushkina. Both settlements are located on the left bank of the Lena. This latter place consists of nine houses, two of them for peasants; a bobilskoi [day laborer] lives in a third. Above the village, Kakara Creek flows into the Lena. We departed there at night, passing Rigina Derevnya on the right bank of the Lena with only one peasant house. Ten kilometers from Sinyushkina Derevnya lies Popova Zaimka, nowadays known as Shangin's Distillery, and fourteen kilometers from the previous zaimka on the right. Sixteen kilometers from the distillery, at nine in the morning, we came to Turukinskaya Derevnya with four houses and located on the right bank of the Lena fourteen kilometers from Ust'Kuth.

I've observed that on the Lena, households are much more blessed with children than around Irkutsk. From Orlenga to Ust'Kutsk, you find young people of both sexes who are good-looking. You also often notice that the women get girls or boys of eight to ten years to drive the wagons or sleds as *podvodchiki*, drivers, to allow the adults to do their housework or earn a living.

Monday, March 17. Aleksei Day ["the venerable Aleksei, the God-chosen prophet"; WH, Anm. 292]. The previous night was incredibly cold, and so was the day, as well as very bright and windy. In the afternoon we arrived in Ust'Kutsk on the Kuta River, where an ostrog, a church, and several houses for sluzhivs have been built. Four kilometers upriver from the ostrog is a saltworks. The salt is taken from a lake and only boiled in a pan. Still they can deliver 108,000 to 144,000 pounds per year. This salt is deemed very good both for seasoning and for preserving food. It is therefore exported on rafts upriver to Verkholensk as well as downriver to Yakutsk and from there to Okhotsk because the salt Nature herself provides on the Vilyuy is not suitable for salting fish or meat. The clay mountains continue to here, but further on the clay diminishes until the mountains become pure sandstone. The Kuta River can be navigated on rafts only in spring when the water rises considerably; in summer it becomes quite small and thus impassable. The ostrog lies on the left bank of the Lena. The fourth shipyard where vessels can be built is located here. We left in the evening and after traveling eighteen kilometers came to Yakurimovskaya Derevnya on Yakurim Creek, which flows into the Lena above the settlement, about fifty to sixty kilometers from its source. In the village four houses are occupied by peasants who together have about five and a half acres of land [in text, two *desiatini*; one *desiatina* equals 117,600 square feet].

Thirteen kilometers further a peasant lives in a house that's alternatively called a zaimka or a zimov'e. Thirteen kilometers further on and forty-four from the ostrog, we came to Podimakhinskaya Derevnya on the left bank of the Lena. Between the zaimka and Podimakhinskaya, a stream called Polovinnaya Rechka, Halfway Stream, because it constitutes the halfway point between Podimakhinskaya and the zaimka, flows into the Lena from the left; its source is approximately four kilometers from its mouth. The village gets its name from its builder. It has four peasant houses. Below the village two nameless streams flow into the Lena. The epidemic had raged here, too. I met a man of thirty-six who had suffered such a high fever that he had become blind from it, like with cataracts. I shall see what medical help I can render him.

Tuesday, March 18. Today was cold, bright, and a bit windy. Two kilometers from here, we passed the settlement of Kazarovskaya or Kazarkina on the left side of the Lena, which acquired its name in a charming manner. This settlement has two houses of raznochintsi and was built about thirty years ago. It began with the construction of a mill on a small, nameless stream—a mill run without wheels, called *mutovka* [the most primitive water mill with a rigid axle and horizontal blades; WH, Anm. 312] by the Russians. To help him with the carpentry, the builder used some Russian promyshlenniks in this region called *kazarki*, little geese. For, as the geese fly in winter from the ocean to southern lands for the sake of finding food, these people came here from Russia to make a profit and, having achieved their goal, they would return home. However, the mill builder's helpers had gotten into an argument with him when the mill was only half done, and they'd taken off. During the argument, the builder said to them [presumably sarcastically], *vy premilye kazarki*, "Nice geese you are!" and the name stuck to the place to this day. Two kilometers from here, forty-eight kilometers from Ust'Kutsk, to the right lies Borisovskaya Derevnya, and fifteen kilometers from it, we came to Kokuiskaya Derevnya, located under a cliff on the left bank of the Lena. Twenty kilometers further, we came to Tayurskaya Derevnya on the right bank. There are four peasant houses and one belonging to a raznochinets. Below the village the Tayura River flows between mountains into the Lena. This river has the reputation for the best-tasting fish, surpassing those from the Lena and other tributaries. Twelve and a half kilometers further, on the left side of the Lena, is Deveterikova Derevnya with three peasant houses.

Halfway between Kazarovskaya and Deveterikova is another little stream on the left. From Kazarovskaya almost till Kirensk, the forested mountains gradually become lower, but the Lena still drops, though not as noticeably as around Ust'Ilginskaya. But around Kirensk and Krivolutskaya Sloboda, it flows through a plain quietly like a lake, and because fish are more numerous there and you begin to find common sturgeon and sterlet, it becomes clear why there are fewer fish in the Lena above Kirensk: In the first place, the fish are swept along by the river rushing down from the mountains, and second, the fish wanting to swim upstream cannot do so because of the force of the current. Nor are there any round whitefish in the Tirskaya or Tira River. In the evening, we departed Deveterikova and after twenty-three kilometers came to Nazarovskaya Derevnya. Here again, halfway between the two, is a tributary, Polovinnaya Creek, flowing into the Lena on the left. We left at night and on the right bank of the Lena passed Markova Derevnya, which has forty-six peasant houses and is located eighteen kilometers from the previous village. Seventeen kilometers from Markova, we came to Tirskaya Derevnya, with five peasant houses on the right bank. Below the village the Tira flows into the Lena; it is approximately 120 feet wide and has a lot of shiveri or rocky places and not any round whitefish either.

Wednesday, March 19. It was cold, bright, and windy and pleasantly sunny and warm in the afternoon. We left Tirskaya and after seven and a half kilometers came to Ul'kanskaya Derevnya on the left, and after another ten kilometers to Kazimerovskaya Derevnya on the right bank with five peasant houses. Seven kilometers further we passed Krasnoyarovskaya Derevnya on the right. For the remaining places, see what follows.

Thursday, March 20. It was incredibly bright and calm but frosty. Around ten o'clock we arrived in Kirenskoi Ostrog, where we'll stay till the ice on the river breaks up.

Friday, March 21. The weather was like yesterday. We inspected the doshcheniks, and I ordered to have one made. To that end I had the carpenter Cholopov report to me what materials he would need and when he could be done. Cf. the *Acta*.[2]

Saturday, March 22. It was bright and windy in the morning. I inspected the doshcheniks and went to the Kirensk Monastery of the Trinity.

Sunday, March 23. The weather was like yesterday.

Monday, March 24. It thawed a lot; was now clear, now cloudy; and was very windy to boot. I sent a memo about the vessel together with a list of the needed materials to the local government office. I also hired my servant Yakov at thirty rubles for the year.

Tuesday, March 25. Feast of Mary's Ascension. It snowed all night and morning, was stormy, and thawed a lot.

Wednesday, March 26. It was clear and calm. It froze hard the night before, but at noon it started to really thaw.

Thursday, March 27. It was warm and thawed. I wrote to the doctor [undoubtedly Gmelin].

Friday, March 28. It was just as warm as yesterday. I continued to write to Dr. [Gmelin]—five pages.

Saturday, March 29. I wrote two pages to Professor Müller. In the morning the sun shone; in the afternoon it was windy.

Palm Sunday, March 30. [No entry—presumably the beginning of the journal reported burnt July 30; see chap. 15, p. 143.]

April 21. Today the Lena broke up.

April 24. There was high water. The Lena's breakup is very violent around here. The ice is smashed apart and dams up the Kirenga, causing the area to be totally and completely flooded. This year the water is higher than any time in the last fifteen years, and in the last twenty-six years, breakup has come as early only three times. Normally the river doesn't break up until the sixth, eighth, or ninth of May—that is, around St. Nicholas Day. On the last day of April, it rained heavily and for the first time thundered quite a bit.

May 1. It was cold, and it snowed.

Notes

1. Primarily caused by iodine deficiency; until iodized salt became common in the early twentieth century, many Europeans, especially in the Alps, suffered from it.
2. Steller's own catalog of his written work according to such categories as Journal, Letters, Economics, etc.; *Dokumente zu G. W. Steller 1740*; WH, Anm. 111.

11

FROM KIRENSK TO YAKUTSK (5/2–5/24)

May 2. The weather was clear and cold, and in the afternoon we left Kirensk on the water.

May 3. It was chilly and also snowed. In the morning we got to Chechuiskoi Ostrog, located on the left bank of the Lena—a poor and pitiful place. Toward noon we arrived in Sploshenskaya Sloboda, forty kilometers from Chechuiskoi Ostrog. All night long the north wind blew up a storm with almost unbearable cold.

Sunday morning, May 4. It was sunny and calm—very pleasant weather. We arrived toward noon in Ivanushkova Derevnya, which is the last village in the Ilimsk District and is on the left bank of the Lena. Below this village the rugged and barren rocky mountains become increasingly higher. Five kilometers below Ivanushkova on the left side is the Pine Cliff from which so many hares [presumably mountain hares, *Lepus timidus*] fell to their death a few years ago. In the afternoon it became very stormy and dreadfully cold because the wind blew right out of the north. Toward evening we arrived at the so-called *Shcheki*, the Cheeks, which are terrifyingly high, rugged, steep, and unclimbable cliffs, about four kilometers long.[1] Here the river is very narrow and therefore very fast and turns to flow straight north from having flowed mostly east. We came to Kureiskaya Derevnya with its one house.

Monday, May 5.[2] It was sunny and calm in the morning and rather tolerable. In the evening we arrived in Vitimskaya Sloboda on the left bank of the Lena. Opposite, on the right bank, the Vitim flows into the Lena in three channels. The lowest channel was free of ice, but the upper and middle channels were still frozen solid. In the afternoon we had a constant north wind and cool weather.

Tuesday, May 6. We left the Vitim and toward noon arrived in Peleduiskaya Sloboda on the left bank of the Lena where the Peledui River, which was already ice-free, flows into the Lena. Zaimkas are built on both sides of the Peledui, and I couldn't help but feel astonishment and pity for the devastation these poor people suffer from high water. Both sides of the riverbanks were piled high with eighteen to thirty-six feet of ice. Their dwellings were crushed, a lot of livestock drowned, and after having suffered from poor crops the previous year, they will do so again this year because fields up to one or even two kilometers from the river were filled with blocks of ice so that none of the fields could be worked. The winter seed has been almost totally torn out and washed away. Because of the cold, windy weather and ice, we had to spend the night. Here I discharged the helmsmen[3] from Kirensk and hired four men for ten rubles from Vitimskaya Sloboda and Peleduiskaya Sloboda. The cold obliged me to have a Tatar-style stove—made of adobe and cow dung—set up in my cabin, which gave off enough heat that we could move our hands[4] and finish writing the reports for the High Senate, the Academy, and the letters to the professors.

Wednesday, May 7. We advanced seventy kilometers from Peleduiskaya Sloboda. In the evening we had to tie up because the otherwise swift river had turned into a placid lake, and we believed that the river below was still frozen. The weather was pleasant in the morning but gloomy again in the afternoon with rain and snow.

Thursday, May 8. We got only twenty kilometers further when, eight kilometers upriver from Nedostrelova, we came to ice that still remained. And so we had to take a break, albeit impatiently. The day was warm with bright sunshine and no wind.

Friday, May 9. Nicholas Day. It was unusually windy with the wind coming from the north, and we had a tough time working our way through all the ice from the right bank to the left in order to go into a small stream for safety, which the north wind as well as the sheets of ice ultimately prevented us from doing. Here we met Yakuts on a sable hunt, returning from the Vitim and Mama Rivers, and I gathered some information from them and in return fed them.

Saturday, May 10. We broke camp in the morning and traveled nine kilometers, and one kilometer below Nedostrelova Derevnya we again came to such thick drifting ice that we couldn't reach shore but were forced to make fast to the ice blocks and keep close watch day and night. With Mr. Berckhan I ventured out on the ice to walk back to Nedostrelova in order to visit a 137-year-old man and his 70-year-old wife and to deliver greetings from the professors. He therefore enthusiastically received me, sat up in bed, and discussed all sorts of things with me very intelligently. Just two months ago he'd become so weak that he's no longer able to walk without assistance from others. He does, however, still have a lot of his teeth and still eats meat and fish and also bread, though not much, because now it nauseates him. Mostly he just drinks milk and on fast days *suslo*, a mush made with malt [WH, Anm. 408]. Two weeks ago his feet began to swell, and all his skin itches constantly. The skin all over his body has shrunk so much that on the palms of his hands and the soles of his feet the cracks in his skin have split open enough that you can see his flesh. He usually has two to three bowel movements a day and urinates frequently. His eyes are still pretty good though he has trouble hearing. His pulse is very weak and slow. When I left I presented him with brandy and gunpowder for his son, and he regretted that he can't shoot anymore. He died in 1741 [noted in the right margin of the manuscript]. When we returned, the ice on the bank was 120 feet high, which we traversed by putting wooden stakes on top. After we'd been back on the boat for half an hour, the "boardwalk" we'd made across the ice had drifted off.

Crepido alae: the Russians call it flamed scarred wood where the outer bark is split so that both sides are swollen into round, lengthwise bulges. [Description and context not clear.] The interior has a grain like nut or maple tree roots—very heavy, thick, and hard—and because of this hardness they make ax handles out of it. The day was warm and sunny with a south wind in the morning that moved the ice around. After midnight the wind switched from south to north.

Sunday, May 11. It was pleasant all day with lots of moving ice. In the morning we left Nedostrelova amid floating ice and toward midday were again stopped by ice four kilometers from Fedoseeva Derevnya. With Mr. Berckhan and the sluzhiv Aleksei, I risked jumping from ice floe to ice floe, and with a lot of effort we hiked to the village to meet Vasilei Ert, a German-Russian noncommissioned officer from the navy, who had been sent ahead by Captain Spangberg and to whom I also gave[5] the package for the professors with fourteen copied illustrations. Returning from the village, we again had to risk life and limb, dancing across ice floes, using sticks we'd carried along as pontoons, to get across the confluence with the Khamra River; from there we still had a kilometer of dry river channel to cross. We hadn't been back two hours and were just getting ready to eat

Fig. 11.1. Steller risks jumping from ice floe to ice floe across the Lena River during breakup (Arnold).

when the sluzhiv Aleksei raised the alarm that our raft with the provisions and all our belongings was drifting in the ice and would, without fail, be destroyed by a collapsing ice wall or the strong current. That scared the living daylights out of me—I could remember having been this terrified only one other time—but I kept my wits about me as much as possible and sent Aleksei with three other people pulling a small boat over the ice to help out on the raft. Thanks to divine help and due to strong rowing, the raft stopped on the right side under a cliff and was tied up there. Just when we were in the middle of a safe anchorage, we saw our doshchenik in trouble, drifting in the middle of the ice. But after much effort, by evening it too got to a safe place right between the bank and the ice, as good as in a harbor.

Monday, May 12. The weather was like yesterday with the wind from the south. Today we took our raft to the doshchenik, where I occupied myself with unpacking and packing some things for transport to Okhotsk.

Tuesday, May 13. It was pleasant all day; yet we continued to stay put.

Wednesday, May 14. The weather was like yesterday. We departed around 8:00 p.m., but having traveled only fifty kilometers we again came upon a *zapor* or ice jam; so we had to stop. I observed the rocks and red cliffs on the right and found some very peculiar vegetation from last year, which I shall remember to look for on my return.

Thursday, May 15. The weather was like yesterday. Once again the river was being cleared of ice for twenty kilometers, and we followed after it. But three hours later we again came upon an ice jam, which forced us to stop. Here we noticed that this year the water had risen to a height of 120 feet. Here I saw, for the first time, gaggles of wild geese with black-tipped wings [snow geese, *Anser caerulescens*; Springer, pers. comm., August 24, 2016.]

Friday, May 16. The wind was from the south, but it was still pretty cool. After twenty kilometers we again reached an ice jam and were stuck until noon. I gathered a meal's worth of greens from great burnet [*Sanguisorba officinalis* L.; Jäger], wild turnip or field mustard [Brassica rapa L. syn.: *Brassica campestris* L.; Jäger; agroatlas.ru calls it "a pernicious weed"], compact dock [*Rumex thyrsiflorus* Fingerh.; Jäger], clustered bellflower [most likely *Campanula glomerata* L.; Jäger], and a species of milkvetch [an *Astragalus*; *A. alpinus* L., *A. frigidus* (L.) A. Gray, and *A. mongholicus* Bunge, syn.: *A. membranaceus* Fisch. ex Bunge are all large-leaved species found in Yakutia; Jäger], which I prepared like spinach, topped off with oxeye daisies [*Leucanthemum vulgare* Lam. var. *ircutianum* (DC.) Krylov; Jäger], and found very good. I also made asparagus salad from the sprouts of common horsetail [probably *Equisetum arvense* L.; Jäger] and dried enough roots of Arctic sweetvetch [*Hedysarum arcticum* B. Fedtsch.] to test if they might be suitable for baking bread.[6] I also observed the first hibernating ground squirrels [*Citellus undulatus* Pallas; Jäger] here. In the afternoon we departed, again following the ice, and having drifted for two hours once again got stopped by an ice jam. Due to the meltwater's rapid runoff, very thick ice kept falling from the shore on both sides into the water, sounding exactly as if cannons were constantly being shot off. Toward noon we caught up with the vessels of two merchants from Arkhangel'sk, Verchoturov and Petrov.

Saturday, May 17. I received a letter from Mr. Nikolai Alekseevich Bibikov [the vice-governor's son] of Irkutsk via the government boat transporting 43,000 rubles to the Kamchatka Expedition in Yakutsk. During the night we passed the Nyuya River, which flows into the Lena from the left. The day was extremely pleasant and clear; at night we passed the *Guselnye gori*, the Goose Mountains.

Sunday, May 18. We drifted through nothing but ice under great danger, and by evening we were approximately thirty kilometers from Olekminskoi Ostrog. The day was very pleasant, warm, and clear.

Monday, May 19. In the morning we arrived at Olekminskoi Ostrog. Prikazchik Gabychev sent me a quarter ox, together with milk, bread, a goose, and a beautiful sable pelt. This place is located on the left bank of the Lena. Here we had rain almost the whole day and occasionally thunder. I collected a partially opened Northern Labrador tea [*Rhododendron tomentosum* Harmaja, syn.: *Ledum palustre* L.; Jäger] and a nice milkvetch [*Astragalus*, species unspecified; Jäger] and exchanged the helmsmen, paying them 480 kopeks. In the evening we departed, and by ten in the morning on May 20, we had covered 110 kilometers up to the river [presumably the Markha]. All day we had a favorable southerly wind, and with this new fashionable sail without mast or rigging we advanced so well that by evening we had covered half the distance of the 200 kilometers from Olekminskoi Ostrog. In this area there was still a lot of snow on the mountains, and hence it was rather cold, so we had to revive ourselves repeatedly in front of the fire in our fireplace [presumably the Tatar-style stove on board ship; see p. 100]. The whole day was dreary.

Wednesday, May 21. We again got an unfavorable headwind from the north and snow twice during the day. Now and then the sun sent us some beams, but mostly it was dreary.

Thursday, May 22. It was cold enough during the night to produce ice an inch thick. The Olekma River seems to have broken up yesterday, and so the Lena was once again covered with ice. The wind was strong and in our faces all day long; several times we had to land, and the rest of the time had to row constantly. Opposite three rock pillars, I encountered the beautiful marsh cinquefoil [*Comarum palustre* L., syn.: *Potentilla palustris* (L.) Scop.; Jäger], also the greater rock jasmine [*Androsace maxima* L.; Jäger] on the rocks opposite the island. During the night we drifted with the ice so fast in the main channel that by ten in the morning we had arrived at the Pokrovsky Monastery on the left.

Friday, May 23. I went botanizing along cliffs for about ten kilometers and discovered two large caves; in the rock I found veins of grayish-white marble, widening all the way to the foot of the mountain and stretching to the river's bank. The ice had polished the marble such that an artist could not have done a better job of it. However, it easily shatters into small pieces, and the layers are no more than two inches thick. Today I tried for the first time to cook red fireweed shoots [*Epilobium angustifolium* L.] like spinach and found them very good.[7] All day long we had headwind. The ice robbed me of my handy office [ironic reference to the place on the boat where Steller wrote], which upset me so much I busted my Chinese pipe on a helmsman. Toward evening we passed the Island of Mazarin, named for

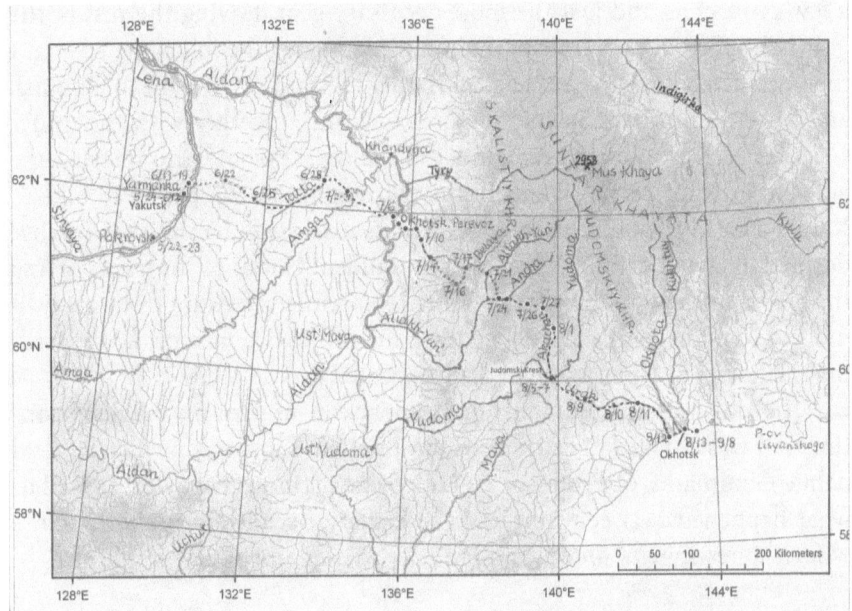

Map 11.1. Steller's route with stopovers from the Pokrovsky Monastery to Okhotsk, designed and labeled by Eckehart Jäger.

Chief Mazarin, who, when the Russians arrived in Siberia, was known as the Yakuts' Solomon and prophesied their subjugation. He was splendidly rewarded for that; because of his obstreperousness the Russians stuck his penis in his mouth.

Saturday, May 24. Before daybreak we arrived in Yakutsk. I immediately called on the voevod Aleksei Eremeevich Zaborovskoi and Captain Spangberg, whom the High Cabinet and Admiralty College had called back to St. Petersburg to report in person about his discovery of the Japanese and Yesso Land.[8] Both received me most cordially, and the voevod insisted I dine with him. In the afternoon I visited the wives of the lieutenants Waxell and Walton, who, together with the captain, paid me a return visit in the evening. To my great dismay, I learned of the effect of Dr. Gmelin's jealousy, who, via a deceitful and uncalled-for memorandum, had ruined my careful preparation for my departure for Kamchatka by presuming that I would head for the Arctic Ocean in the summer. Thus the podvodi as well as the hired horses had been canceled and no cattle purchased. However, I immediately decided not to give up my plans but to move ahead with only a few provisions and just the most necessary gear, leaving the rest of the gear behind to have it transported on hired horses the following spring. I then decided to take the Yakut sluzhiv Aleksei Danilov with me to Okhotsk and to send him back in the fall, ordering him, together with the miner Grigorei, to transport the remainder of the gear. I would also instruct the latter to look for certain items in the tripartite [natural] realm, to take to Kamchatka in the coming year. See *Senate acta 1740* in Yakutsk. I further decided to give the miner's horses to the student Gorlanov for transporting the provisions and in the spring to hire replacements for him from my own money. To manage this more speedily, I submitted two memoranda regarding the horses and pay and had them executed this very day.

The day was uncommonly pleasant, clear, and calm; breakup continued. I was amazed to learn from Mr. Brauner, subsurgeon with the Academic Command, of Professor de la Croyère's strange behavior, as well as what happened between him and the captain because of de la Croyère's wife. [Interestingly, *Captain* and *Frau* are written in Hebrew script.]

Notes

1. Ivan Gontcharov (1812–1891), a Russian novelist, wrote, "Last evening we passed the so-named Cheeks, a famous sight on the Lena—such mighty, majestic cliffs as I've seldom seen along a shoreline. They are so fissured and gloomy that you immediately breathe a sigh of relief when they are behind you," quoted by Kuschtewskaja, 38.

2. In text, Steller mistakenly repeated May 4, numbered the following days 5 to 9, omitted 10, and then continued with 11. Starting on this day, we renumbered sequentially 5 through 10, the way it was undoubtedly meant to be.

3. Helmsmen—in text, *podvodchiki*, literally drivers of podvodi, i.e., wagons or sleds. Consistently translated as helmsman/men when traveling on rivers.

4. In text, *die Hände ruhen*, rest our hands; presumably a slip of the pen for *rühren* since it is hard to write with your hands at rest.

5. In text, *schickte*, sent; presumably Steller meant to write, "gave to take or send to the professors."

6. *H. arcticum* grows in central and southern Yakutia; *H. alpinum*, or Eskimo potato, grows further north, but perhaps the roots of both species were used. Jäger.

7. *E. angustifolium* L. leaves are used for tea and rhizomes eaten raw by Siberian Eskimos. Jäger; Hultén and Fries.

8. According to a Dutch report from the seventeenth century, such a country was assumed to exist, which on some maps was the same as Kamchatka but stretching far to the south, possibly connected to Japan. In 1739 Spangberg reached the Japanese islands of Honshu and Hokkaido while searching for Yesso (WH, Anm. 489), thus reaching what was once the home of the indigenous Ezo.

12

IN YAKUTSK AND YARMANKA (5/25–6/19)

Sunday, May 25, Pentecost. The weather was like yesterday. I dined again at the voevod's, visited some good friends, and decided to live on the boat until my departure. But the painter Berckhan and the student Gorlanov moved into quarters. In the evening Mr. Soltner, a Swedish merchant and very well-mannered man, who at this time serves as minister to the expedition's German women,[1] paid me a visit.

Monday, May 26. The order concerning the acquisition of the horses reached the Cossack chief and the Yakut interpreter Gulyaev. The weather was very pleasant and calm all day; the river went down considerably. I visited Captain Spangberg, at whose place I met Ferdinand von Heidenreich, an exile who's in very bad shape emotionally; the surgeon of the fleet, Ginter; and the assayer Gardebol, who were already there. We discussed various things concerning the nature of the ocean and the Japanese Islands. In the evening I began to pack and described some plants.

Tuesday, May 27. I sent off Aleksei, my sluzhiv, and the Cossack chief's sluzhiv with instructions to procure additional horses and cattle. The weather was like yesterday. In the evening Secretary Daurkin and Major Pavlutskoi, who had commanded the skirmishes against the Chukchi, came to visit.[2]

Wednesday, May 28. The weather was like yesterday. I went botanizing and observed various flowering plants on the steppe that in the past year I had seen around Lake Baikal on the highest mountains, which attests to how analogy works in nature: since the elevation decreases the farther north you go and the rivers less visibly flow downhill, the plants likewise appear in lower-lying areas. And I was utterly amazed how fast everything grew. At this time of year, there is no night in Yakutsk, just a kind of dusk. But toward evening it is still pretty cool.

Thursday, May 29. The weather was like yesterday. I ordered new brandy bottles as well as leather saddlebags, around here called *sumi*, for transporting the provisions to Okhotsk. A pair costs fifty to sixty kopeks; in Okhotsk the price is back down to just five kopeks. One bag holds ninety pounds of provisions. Via a memorandum I also demanded thirty pairs of bags from the government coffers. In the evening I described some birds that had been caught in Zhigani.

Friday, May 30. The weather was like yesterday. From the Academy's supply depot, I took some necessary materials listed in the register that is a part of the *Senate Acta*, and I bought some things needed for the trip. The river dropped from 136 feet to 6 feet. Yakutsk has odd weather. From the middle of May to the beginning of July, there is almost no night, but in winter almost no day. If the Lena floods their islands, they have a bountiful year; otherwise, the grass doesn't grow much. In May, June, and July, little rain falls; toward the end of July when haying starts, it's often a deluge.[3] In winter it is foggy and so frighteningly cold it takes your breath away. And because the cold causes the smoke from the fireplaces to settle to the ground, it's so dark in the middle of the day that you can't recognize a person six feet away.

Saturday, May 31. The weather was like yesterday. Toward morning to my great joy the raft arrived with my people, the provisions, and the rest of the gear for me and my crew. Today we busied ourselves with unpacking und repacking various things. Captain Spangberg, Mr. Gardebol, the assayer, and the surgeon dined at my place. Toward evening the voevod paid me a visit. Shortly thereafter it started to rain and continued until midnight.

Sunday, Trinitatis, June 1. The voevod sent me his chaise to fetch me for dinner, where Lt. Colonel Merlin from Selenginsk and Major Pavlutskoi as well as Captain Spangberg were too.[4] We visited the captain in the afternoon. The weather, by the way, was clear, warm, and pleasant all day. I noticed that reddish flowers turn white in boggy places; in the future I'll have to check whether that's correct. I described the fish *munda* [lake minnow].

Monday, June 2. The weather was like yesterday. I busied myself with preparations for my trip.

Tuesday, June 3. The weather was like yesterday. I dined at Mr. Pavlutskoi's and learned from him that in place of the stuffed idols like other tribes, the Koryaks carry their shamans' bones with them wherever they go. In the yurts they put these at the head of where they sleep; while traveling they carry them on the best reindeer. When they embark on an undertaking, they lift up the bag with the bones. If it is heavy, they assume a favorable outcome. If the bag is light, they beat it with sticks and scold it by saying, "Why don't you want to help us instead of leaving us in the lurch?" If a shaman dies, they immediately cut the flesh off the bones. Mr. Pavlutskoi also reported that the Chukchi think their land is larger and more populated than Russia. They get the idea from the fact that Anadyrsk is thinly populated and yet in 1738 recruits were taken from there—it was unconscionable—to the Turkish Expedition [Austro-Turkish-Russian War, 1735–39; WH, Anm. 564]. The Chukchi would like to consider themselves too numerous to count and try to create that impression through all kinds of humbuggery.

When one of them meets another in the presence of Russians, they ask each other, "From which family are you anyhow?" When one gives a name, the other answers him, "I can't remember ever having heard this name," or at best, "Oh, yes, I do recall having heard this family or tribe mentioned." Major Pavlutskoi is certain that, in contradiction to those who would claim there are six to eight thousand or even ten thousand of them, they number hardly more than two thousand.[5] Their yurts are made of reindeer hide, sewn together from doubled skins to a length of sixty to seventy-two feet, with the hairy sides, slightly shorn, toward each other. In each large yurt are several smaller ones or separate compartments for families. They have no wood; therefore, they use moss to light their fish oil lamps. The Chukchi eat everything raw, but they are always pale-faced even though they are strong people. They don't harm the merchants at all but trade with them or at least let them pass through. But in 1735 the Koryaks killed seven Russian sluzhivs—that is, soldiers—because smallpox was rampant and the soldiers had come to them in spite of being told not to. The Koryaks also blame the Russians' arrival and their interactions with them for the disease.

Wednesday, June 4. The weather was like yesterday. I observed that in these parts the plants grow, so to speak, while you are watching. On May 26 an island opposite Yakutsk on which I had pitched my tent had still been underwater. Around June 1 I gathered compact dock for a dish of greens and found no trace of the flower stalks; on June 3 the stalk was already three feet high, and on June 4 it was flowering, from which you can get an idea of the sun's power in these parts. What grows on the islands prone to being flooded is comparable in size to plants in Germany and Russia; however, things growing in dry places reach hardly a third of their size. On June 4 a common chickweed, a buttercup, and a species of rockcress started to bloom.[6]

Thursday, June 5. The weather was like yesterday. I should mention, however, that at night it's rather cool. Today the new commander at Okhotsk, Anton Emmanuilovich Devier, arrived in Yakutsk from Turukhansk with a small dog, called Lastochka [literally swallow; WH, Anm. 580]. Passing by my island, he sent me greetings, so I invited him to my place for the evening. Yakutsk's German ladies of the navy [presumably the wives of navy officers] paid me a visit. In the evening the commander together with the voevod came by boat to my tent. Mr. Devier was so happy to see me that he actually jumped into the water before the boat could land, took three large steps,[7] hurried toward me, hugged me, and asked me to accept him as a friend since he had heard my praises sung everywhere and was happy to have a true servant of Her Majesty's and everybody's friend as his friend, which he expressed very well in German. He asked me to allow him to travel to Okhotsk with my party. He brought me greetings from the vice-governor, Aleksei Yurevich Bibikov, in Irkutsk and his son, Nikolai Alekseevich Bibikov, also a letter each from Mr. Beck and Mr. Hencke [who had accompanied Steller on his way out of Irkutsk; see p. 81], along with a teakettle and tobacco. We had a good time under my shelter by a night fire until two o'clock past midnight. Among other things Mr. Devier found it quite remarkable that in Turukhansk the *severnoe silanie* or northern lights were out every year in November and December, at certain times continuously, at others intermittently, and it was then pretty light. During that time the promyshlenniks would go out to check their traps and retrieve the white foxes, which I shall investigate thoroughly in the future. Mr. Devier also reported about the peace treaty with the Turks and that there would be no more trouble with the Swedes.[8]

Friday, June 6. I dined at the voevod's together with Mr. Devier and Mr. Pavlutskoi. After dinner a lieutenant came from Okhotsk who, among other things, reported that starting on March 23, at a mountain called Bear's Head near Okhotsk, it had snowed continually for eight days with the snow reaching a depth of seven feet, which shows how strange this climate is. The voevod sent me a saddle-horse as a present for the road. I rented forty horses for the coming year and paid 220 rubles to Shestakov [Yakutsk *syn boyarskoi*, a member of the nobility; see glossary]. I also learned that the best sable and squirrel pelts are to be found in rocky regions, the blackest in larch and Siberian pine forests [*Pinus sibirica* Du Tour; Jäger], and those of lesser quality in Scots pine, Siberian spruce, and Japanese white birch forests—on account of the food that these animals get from buds and cones. That's pretty much consistent with the areas around Barguzin and Vitim where the forests are mostly of larch and Siberian dwarf pine [*Pinus pumila* (Pall.) Regel; Jäger]. I noticed that from the last day in May on, insects were within eight days as numerous in these parts as at home in Russia in July. On May 1 and 2, I found large weevils [in text, *Rüsselkäfer*; unclear exactly what Steller found], lice [in text, *Feldwanzen*], and mosquitoes, which shows that the long days shorten their maturation dates by a lot.

Saturday, June 7. The weather was pleasantly warm in the morning, cloudy in the afternoon; it rained intermittently all night. I described the birds from Zhigani.

Sunday, June 8, was incredibly warm and clear, but for the brandy sellers from Irkutsk it was downright gloomy because, due to their workers' treachery, the lieutenants Ostyakov and Lebedev [both of the Yakutsk regiment] took two thousand rubles' worth of brandy from them, brought clandestinely on their doshcheniks. The Cossack chief visited me and brought me a blood-red carp [*Carassius carassius* L.]. I ascribe the color change to its age. During the conversation it was mentioned that there are very old pike on which mosslike material is said to grow. Grigorei Borisov [Yakutsk posadski] visited me with his mother, and the woman treated me to beef sandwiches. Aleksei Danilov brought the news that he had delivered his number of horses and had had their hooves sealed with pitch. In the evening I went to see honest old Kychkin [Moscow *dvoryanin*, a member of the nobility; see Glossary] and offered him 3,600 pounds of flour, asking him to replace it when the price was right and forward it to me on Kamchatka. I learned that the plant the Yakuts use to scarify the eyes is a leafless horsetail [*Equisetum hyemale* L. or *E. fluviatile* L.; Jäger] with which they scrape the eyes. Kychkin also told me that, when a Yakut's head has been cracked by a fall or a hit, they cut away the skin on the head with a knife and put a warm animal heart against it to soak up the blood. Then they wash out the wound with warm, sweet milk until the bone is cleansed of all blood. With a knife they scrape the bone until it is very thin. Then they break open the cranium, letting the effluent material, be it blood or puss, drain; they also take out the splinters. Then they position the sick person so that he [or she] is not lying on the wound so the skin over the wound can heal shut. The incision and the scraping of the skull occur exactly on the injured spot. They do not bleed people. But if someone has a headache, they cut open the skin on the head and let the blood drain out. They also scarify in the case of broken legs by cutting under the break. They reset the break and bind it with splints without using a poultice or other medication. They know nothing for treating venereal diseases.

Monday, June 9. The weather was like yesterday. Borisov, an inhabitant of Yakutsk, told me about four ways people cheat to secretly bring brandy on the Lena into Yakutsk. [Steller enumerates only three ways. His explanation is also very confusing. We are guessing that under point 2, he has actually combined two different tricks, and we have renumbered accordingly.] As a result, over several years, the people charged with selling the government brandy incurred debts of forty thousand rubles. This is a real problem, especially since every year they are expected to sell enough from the government supply to reach the erstwhile profit of eight thousand rubles. This did not happen, first, because the people selling it are usually drunkards, both themselves managing haphazardly and letting others do likewise, as well as neglecting the billing; second, because almost everybody with the Kamchatka Expedition distills not only for himself but also to transport and sell in Yakutsk, Yudoma Cross, Okhotsk, and Kamchatka. The cheaters engage in the following deception: they buy fifty buckets of government brandy, rectifying it together with their own three times and then mixing it with more water for sale locally, thus getting two or even three hundred buckets of brandy to sell—diluted and renamed. Their third trick is to change the fifty buckets of government brandy to five [presumably in record keeping], adding forty-five of their own as well as setting aside another thirty to fifty for their own consumption; they are, after all, allowed to resell what they buy from the government. Fourth [Steller's point 3], because the people in Irkutsk who have leased the brandy distillery and the delivery to Yakutsk secretly import as much as three times the agreed-upon quantity and sell the double brandy for four rubles when the diluted one from the government is sold for eight rubles. Consequently, it being cheaper and better, the secret double brandy is bought by the inhabitants as well as the members of the expedition while the government brandy does not sell. Thus, the proper sum cannot be delivered. The upshot of these practices is that the buyers in Irkutsk have been told this year, 1740, not to deliver the usual number of buckets to the *podryadchik*, the contracted supplier [WH, Glossar], because there is still so much old brandy in stock. The secretly distilled brandy is brought to Yakutsk in the following manner.

For one, they declare it to be delivered on demand of certain officers; then nobody wants to insult them because all the officials are aware of their own bad conscience. Second, they put the barrels in lakes in ostrogs close to Yakutsk, or bury them; and when they arrive in town, they send Yakuts with one of their men to these places to bring them in during a bright night. Third, they build rafts on top of the barrels and load them with lumber to avoid any suspicion. At an opportune time, the brandy is toted home, or they carry it home in buckets as if they had fetched water. The same inhabitant told me about water hemlock [*Cicuta virosa* L.] with a leaf like parsley, called *omeg* in Russian; that it does not harm the horses, but only the cows because they have no gallbladder, *quod idem oppido falsum* [which is surely totally false; WH, Anm. 642].

Tuesday, June 10. The weather was like yesterday. I heard from master assayer Gardebol that—contrary to previous opinion—copper and iron were found in Kamchatka, but nobody knew how to smelt them; he thought it was probably inadvisable to take up the work in the vicinity of the Yukagirs and Chukchi because against all prohibitions they would make not only household tools but also spears—that is, weapons—in order to trade them for profit to the rebellious peoples, who, anyway, would attack not merchants but only sluzhivs. Kychkin also told me that the white-winged scoters [in text, *turpany*; *Melanitta fusca*; Springer, pers. comm., August 24, 2016] nest in the mountains. Toward the end of May, the males go down to the sea, leaving the females behind to brood; the females in turn also fly off as soon as the ducklings can swim. But for every four or five nests, a single mother always remains to serve as guide. The Russians claim to know this from experience because with some twenty young ones they always just find one old one.

Wednesday, June 11. The weather was like yesterday, but the night so incredibly cool that a nice fur coat did feel good. A mail clerk told me that the Yakuts from the Tatta and Olekma Rivers go as far as the Amur River to hunt sable, in part catching the animals themselves, in part acquiring them from the Gilyaks whom they encounter hunting. The trade would be conducted as follows: they could not speak each other's language. Thus, when they became aware of each other, both sides would lay down their hunting spears, axes, and knives, gather around a fire, sit down, and show their wares to each other. Taking off in the fall, the Yakuts would ride their horses over rocky terrain and mountains. But the Gilyaks rode oxen. The Yakuts trade them tobacco, butter, and flour, a pound's worth for a yasak-destined sable worth at least five rubles. When the Yakuts go hunting, they charge the Russians three pounds of tobacco for three [in text, two] sables but bring them only two sables, keeping the third sable for their own yasak. When the Yakuts have eaten their horses, they switch to dog or reindeer sleds and return in spring to the places from which they set out. I am surprised by two things: first, that the Gilyaks have oxen, thus cattle and husbandry, yet do not know how to make butter, a sign of their stupidity; second, that they trade the tobacco from the Yakuts at such a high price, considering that they themselves are Chinese subjects. By the way, I must not forget to mention that those from whom we get this merchandise [tobacco] are—up to now—not subject to anyone [unclear who his suppliers are], from which one can see that the Chinese do not especially come to these places to trade or do not dare to.

Thursday, June 12. The weather was incredibly pleasant, warm, and clear. For us it was, however, a very wet day since we accompanied Captain Spangberg, who was returning to St. Petersburg with his family, and we gamely drank to his health along the way. Today I observed how the Yakuts bleed a person, using a spear tip like our smiths use when bleeding horses. The blood is wiped away by hand. Then they use a horn, first sucking out the air with their mouth; later plugging [the incision] with a little wet leather rag. The patient is lying on the ground. I also saw how they treated a shattered arm by first pressing the broken bones together, then splinting the break and bandaging it without using any medication. I also saw how they set a dislocated joint. The Yakuts are terribly infected with the Frenchmen [the French disease, syphilis]. Five kilometers from Yarmanka, I came upon a whole yurt full of this disease. They don't know any remedy for it at all, except what the Russians teach them, making them pay dearly. For example, they use a decoction made from jasmine [*Androsace*, species unknown; Jäger] for gonorrhea. During an examination when the man confessed to me in the presence of his *Hausehre* [literally, the house's honor; according to Grimm, a synonym for wife; WH, Anm. 673] that he had contracted the Frenchmen from another woman, I discovered that his wife was not the least bit jealous on account of it. The men, on the other hand, are said to be very jealous.

Friday, June 13. The weather was like yesterday. I bade farewell to all my good friends in Yakutsk, gave the raft to the voevod, and left after noon for Yarmanka. However, together with my servant Aleksei [Sofronov] I had the misfortune to be on a small boat so full of holes that we just barely escaped a watery grave.⁹ When we arrived in Yarmanka, twelve kilometers down the Lena River from Yakutsk, we set up our tents, unpacked, and began to arrange our gear the way we wanted to load it on the horses.

Saturday, June 14. The weather was like yesterday. I continued to arrange my things according to what is to be transported to Okhotsk this year, what is to remain in Yakutsk to be transported the coming year, and what is to remain in Yakutsk for good until my return. I also wrapped some things in leather and sent the boat back to Yakutsk. Sara Ivanovna Nilsen [presumably the wife of boatswain Nils Jansen; WH, Anm. 681] sent me a package of tea destined for her husband in Okhotsk, and I decided to return alone on the boat that brought the tea to look for my sluzhiv and my student, who had both stayed behind. I noticed that the Yakuts dig up silverweed roots [*Argentina anserina* (L.) Rydb., syn.: *Potentilla anserina* L.; Jäger] in spring and fall and eat the nut-shaped, fleshy growths on them. I found they tasted like *Rapünzchen*, lamb's lettuce [*Valerianella locusta* L.].

Sunday, June 15. The weather was like yesterday. I arrived in Yakutsk around noon, and I was still missing the horse Kychkin had made me a present of for the trip and that had caused the confusion until now. Toward evening, it was found again. Together with Mr. Endogurov [a lieutenant] I dined at the voevod's, and we visited the chief surgeon [Philipp Wilhelm] Butzkoffskii and Kychkin. I bought some more essentials and paid Mr. Soltner the hundred rubles he had loaned me and twenty-eight rubles to Daurkin for the five horses I had rented from him to travel to Okhotsk. Gardebol loaned me the remaining twelve horses. Before my departure I asked Mr. Soltner in a short note to see to it that Daurkin return these twelve horses to Gardebol. I also paid ten rubles to miner Samoilov for which, in the coming year, he is to make thirty pipe mouthpieces—at three kopeks a piece—and transport them together with a hundred Yakut flint and steel fire starters [presumably to Okhotsk]. That night I slept once more on my island.

Monday, June 16. It was pleasantly warm and sunny in the morning, the rest of the day stormy with a strong wind from the south. With Gorlanov I left Yakutsk in a boat in the middle of the storm, and luckily the bow reached a sandbank just as the stern, having sprung a leak, filled with water and immediately sank. I had it pulled onto the sand, unpacked, had it repaired, and took off again, reaching Yarmanka around three o'clock. But the wind kept the large boat with our horses from reaching the other bank of the Lena, drifting them so far downriver that we did not see them again until the nineteenth and only after much anxious waiting, fearing the boat had capsized.

Tuesday, June 17. The weather was like yesterday, the nights very cool. I once again sent Gorlanov together with Aleksei Danilov back to Yakutsk with an official request for five horses free of charge—which we received the next day—together with an order from the Cossack chief to Reshetnikov, a Yakutsk *sluzhiv*, to deliver them. After everything was ready for the trip, Mr. Berckhan painted a catchfly or campion, [may be *Silene uralensis* Bocquet; Jäger]. In the afternoon he and I amused ourselves with fishing, while my servant Yakov distilled brandy for the trip. I learned that, as I had originally guessed, the Verkhoyansk *sardana* is nothing but the roots of the artfully made *Hedysarum* with light yellow flowers I had dug up below Fedoseeva's Zaimka on the Lena and had found good to eat [see May 16]. The Yakuts also eat the roots of *Scorzonera* as Fedot Amosov, a soldier in the Yakut regiment, reported.[10]

Wednesday, June 18. The weather was like yesterday. For the first time, I watched shamanizing with a drum. I observed that the shaman pretended to faint three times and had fire struck above his head, and also that people shouted "guguk"[11] at him in order to make him remember once more where he was. In spite of my protests, he told me my fortune as follows: (1) that once at sea I almost had been lost with the ship; (2) that as a youth I had an injured leg; (3) that my wife, being my greatest enemy, had died; and (4) that, on Kamchatka, I would receive an order authorizing me to travel farther than Kamchatka and see unknown people whom nobody had yet seen and who were not yet subjects of Russia.

Walking back, I noticed a Siberian lily [*Lilium pensylvanicum* Ker Gawl.; Jäger],[12] which Dr. Gmelin had noticed on the Irtysh River and I had found among the dried plants Mr. Rosing, the pharmacist in Kyakhta, had collected around the Kyakhta River. I noticed about Yakut plants in general, first, that those found high up on the tallest mountains grow here in open fields and are much smaller and shorter; second, that the pungent and aromatic herbs emit a much more potent smell than in more temperate climes.

To everybody's joy Aleksei arrived with Gorlanov, the surveyor Ushakov, and our horses. I treated all who crossed my path to *vishnevka*, cherry brandy, that the vice-governor had sent me and had packs put on twenty-five horses. Mr. Berckhan had another twelve loaded, and Gorlanov six. I sent them off ahead that very evening to Tatta under the supervision of the sluzhivs Aleksei Danilov and Egor Popov. To see how I arranged everything and what things I sent off, see the *Economic Acta*.

Thursday, June 19. The weather was like yesterday. I spent all day very frustrated trying to put packs on horses, which they all too often threw off, running away. I couldn't get anybody to help me, nor find out from whom I should have expected help. I finally gave the station hand, a sluzhiv, a sound thrashing with the tent pole, as a result of which I caught on to the maxim that, when Pilate and Herod are friends, you need only catch one of them by the ear to learn from him everything about the other. In this way you hear a lot of things you would not learn otherwise. Thus I first learned for future use that my dispatch allowed me to claim the help of a syn boyarskoi[13] or somebody else to sort out horses, recruit people, and keep everybody doing his job. In that case I wouldn't have had any trouble. Second, I found out that Reshetnikov [a Yakutsk sluzhiv; WH, Anm. 749] and his employees—in addition to what the sluzhivs take—deduct forty kopeks of each ruble collected as progon. After a lot of aggravation, I finally got done toward evening. Mr. Berckhan left first, together with the student Gorlanov; I, together with the surveyor, left an hour later. Without a guide we lost our way among a confusing number of lakes. We would surely not have found the right trail had good fortune not led us to a yurt in which all the people understood Russian and provided us a guide. Before my departure I had let Yakov, my hired hand, go just as he was ready to mount his horse, surely hoping—what a ridiculous idea—he would be drinking my brandy with me in Kamchatka, but I did give him a ruble. I left behind Aleksei, my servant, with two horses and sent the miner to Yakutsk with an order. After my departure Ivan Andrich or Ivan Borisov Daurkin came, wanting to rent me five horses for forty rubles. But I had already left and didn't need them anymore. By the time we were on the right track, Mr. Berckhan had gotten as far as seven kilometers ahead when he made camp at midnight. However, I, the surveyor, and Peter, our guide, slept that night in the woods by a fire.

Notes

1. In text, *der . . . das Priesteramt bei der deutschen Frauenexpedition verrichtet*—who serves as minister to the German women expedition—an interesting but doubly misleading phrasing; undoubtedly Steller meant European (and Protestant) rather than strictly German women.

2. Afanasii Shestakov was killed in a battle against the rebellious Chukchi in 1730. As punishment, Pavlutskoi led numerous skirmishes against the Chuckchi during 1731, in which many Chukchi were killed. WH, Anm. 529.

3. Steller is only partially right. Most of the annual precipitation in Yakutsk (about eight inches total) falls in June, July, and August; December through March and May see less than an inch [Fiziko-geograficheski Atlas Mira; cited by Jäger, email, March 11, 2018].

4. Here the chaise is presumably a two-wheeled, horse-drawn vehicle; it could also be a sedan chair, which is what the women were transported in.

5. The entire Chukchi people numbered eight to nine thousand in the seventeenth century according to *Die Große Nordische Expedition*, 243.

6. *Stellaria media* (L.) Vill, or common chickweed; *Ranunculus*, buttercup; and a species of *Arabis*, rockcress, may be *Arabis lyrata* (L.) O'Kane & Al-Shebaz; Jäger. In text, *fing*; presumably Steller meant to write *fing zu blühen an*, started to bloom.

7. In text, "*sprang er dreifach vom Lande vor Freuden in das Wasser*"—literally, he jumped, for joy, triply from the land into the water; presumably, *vom Lande* is a slip of the pen for *vorm Landen*, and *dreifach* was then synonymous with *dreimal*, three times.

8. The Belgrade Peace Treaty of 1739 ended the Austro-Turkish-Russian War.

9. Literally translated, Steller says that they had the misfortune to just barely escape a watery grave, an example of either his black humor or his pen and mind not being in agreement.

10. *Scorzonera austriaca* Willd. in steppe plant communities and/or *S. radiata* Fisch. ex Ledeb. in larch forests, a genus of flowering plant in the dandelion tribe; roots of both species are edible. Jäger. In Hintzsche's Personenregister, Fedot Amasov is identified as a yasak collector; the Yakutsk soldier is identified as Dmitrei Amosov.

11. This may be literally what Steller heard; it could, however, also be a German translation of whatever was said—e.g., the equivalent of *guck, guck*, look, look, or Kuckuck, cuckoo, Steller often interchanging *g* and *k*.

12. In text, a wild-growing blood-red lily.

13. Literally, a boyar's son; the boyars were the lowest class of hereditary nobility but in Siberia might be conferred the rank for merit. WH, Glossar.

13

FROM YARMANKA TO THE AMGA RIVER (6/20–7/2)

FRIDAY, JUNE 20. THE WEATHER WAS PLEASANT ALL day, but the prior night was very cool. At noon I caught up with Mr. Berckhan on a brackish lake in a bog where we had bad water but a most enjoyable meal. Hours after us my [servant] Aleksei Sofronov arrived together with the surveyor Moisei Ushakov's hired hand. We departed toward evening, traveling through beautiful forests and grasslands with calm lakes, and toward morning we arrived at a yurt [likely Steller means a way-station] where we enjoyed tea, drained a cup of brandy, and lay down to sleep. In the mountains six kilometers from Yarmanka, I noticed a large number of Iceland poppies [*Papaver jacuticum* Peschkova][1] as well as Siberian phlox [likely *Phlox sibirica* L.; Jäger] with robust, bright reddening flowers and one that was white inside, northern coralroot [*Corallorhiza trifida* Chatel],[2] and a species of columbine [*Aquilegia parviflora* Ledeb., small-flowered columbine, the only species that grows in the region between Yakutsk and Tatta; Jäger].

I must not forget to mention that the area around Yakutsk is very pleasant. The town itself is located on a plateau on the left bank of the Lena, built quite irregularly without side streets. From afar it looks very attractive. Next to almost every house sits an earthen hut in which the animals and servants live together in good Yakut fashion. The town was first to have been built around the Pokrovsky Monastery. It has the disadvantage of being too far away from the water. In spring the inlet in front of town is filled with water; later all the water dries up so that you can walk—without getting your feet wet—to the island across from Yakutsk where I lived. However, this problem did not exist before the town was built because it wasn't until fifty years ago that the Lena changed its course more to the right side. The large island [Horse Island; WH, Anm. 781] across from town, therefore, did not exist until thirty years ago, which is why to this day only willows grow there. When the area around Yakutsk is not flooded in the spring, the inhabitants consider it a poor year. In view of the immense herds they had in the past, very few Yakuts lived in the area. But now, living alongside the Russians, they're just a remnant.

The inhabitants are very sly, untrustworthy, cunning, deceitful, lazy drunkards, and neither man nor woman cares that a bucket of brandy costs eight rubles. They also like variety in matters of love. The Yakuts, for the most part, live on calm lakes found here in large numbers and other larger ones downriver. Or they live on the numerous islands in the Lena where they have wonderful pastures and can catch fish and birds. There is little game here except for hares, which at certain times arrive like armies. People's food consists mostly of milk, *sosna* [R, literally Scots pine, but also flour made of ground-up Scots pine bark or flour mixed with bark; WH, Anm. 783], fish, and meat. From Yakutsk to Tatta, you encounter the most pleasant Scots pine, larch, and birch forests on scattered hills. The meadows between them are all interspersed with large ponds once teeming with pike, carp, lake minnows, and Eurasian dace. Now, however, the inhabitants seem to be totally deprived of this fish bounty, in the river as well as in the lakes, largely because the lack of cattle and grain forces them to eat more fish, and thus the lakes are quickly being depleted.

The calm lakes are full of insects like lice, among them *Pediculus arborescens* Swammerdami [some kind of small crustaceans, most likely copepods or water fleas (order Cladocera); Ilja Rochlin, email, March 2, 2016] and larvae of grasshoppers [most likely marsh treaders, Hydrometridae, or water skippers, Gerridae; Jäger], and on the shores grasshoppers in frightening numbers.

It is fifty-two kilometers from Yakutsk to the second station on a very good and pleasant trail. Having been burned off a lot, the forests are clean. The boggy ground around the meadows exudes a lot of white salt; it also breaks apart a lot and has many large fissures in which the cattle often break their legs. From Yarmanka to Tatta, the water is strictly standing water; consequently, the lack of potable water is the worst problem on this stretch because from the Lena River to Tatta there is only one little stream. Where the lakes are very big, the water is cleaner and better. The Yakuts catch lake minnows in *mordi*—that is, fish traps—and ducks they call *uranin* [Eurasian coot, *Fulica atra*; Springer, pers. comm., August 24, 2016] in snares set throughout whole lakes. You find such pleasant places that—considering the terrible climate and the short delight of summer—you cannot help but assume God had wanted to make amends for nature's malice by providing these ideal landscapes. In the lakes you find the most beautiful forested islands. The mountain ranges, stretching from north to south, are all forested and are separated from one another by five to seven kilometers of meadows and lakes.

We departed from the second station, where I described the Yakut smithy and for the first time tasted both kumis and raw mare's milk, and, having traversed ten kilometers, came to a large lake where we camped. We had the most delightful woods and weather—just a lot of flies and mosquitoes into the bargain. We traveled across some fields—six to seven kilometers long and two to three wide—overgrown with [wild] horseradish or dyers' woad and plume thistles (see my plant catalog).[3] You recognize the pastures on this route by the posts rammed into the ground to which intractable horses are tied while being packed.

Sunday, June 22. It was very hot. In the morning we covered thirty kilometers and camped in a charming landscape between a forested mountain and two lakes where we stayed until the next morning. I took note of a Eurasian coot, a liver leaf wintergreen [*Pyrola asarifolia* Michx.; Jäger], a special kind of columbine [small-flowered columbine; Jäger, see p. 119], and an alternate-leaved golden saxifrage [*Chrysoplenium alternifolium* L. subsp. *sibiricum* (Ser. et DC.) Hultén, syn. of *Ch. serreanum* Hand-Mazz., or *Ch. alternifolium* subsp. *tetrandrum* (N. Lund) Hultén, syn. of *Ch. tetrandrum* (N. Lund) Th. Fries; Jäger].

Monday, June 23. We covered twenty-five kilometers and had our noon meal at a lake. Unfortunately, one of my own horses ran away, so I had to leave my servant and my sluzhiv Gavrilo behind. Around six o'clock we departed again, and after ten kilometers on a good trail through totally delightful scenery we reached the third station. In the morning it rained a little; afterward it became very warm, cloudy, and muggy. Foreshadowing the rain, the mosquitoes had attacked us the whole night before, even flying into the smoke and the flames, usually the only means to keep them at bay. We camped by the station yurt and enjoyed a meal of crucian carp. I asked some questions about the people's history. Today I noticed an erect clematis with bluish as well as turning-purple flowers [*Clematis ochotensis* (Pall.) Poir.; Jäger].

Tuesday, June 24. The weather was first rather brisk and then warm. We stayed put expecting the people left behind would show up by noon.

Around Yakutsk the cuckoo starts to call at the beginning of June and continues to do so until July 10. This being St. John's and Mr. Berckhan's name day, we celebrated with kumis and butchered a calf. I continued with the people's history while we were waiting. In the afternoon it started to rain a little but afterward turned nice again. The Yakut stationmaster presented us with a calf.[4] Having gotten tired of waiting for our people, we finally departed at 11:00 p.m. Just then it started to rain heavily and continued until 2:00 a.m. The wetness caused our horses' belly straps to loosen and the packs to fall off. That hindered our progress quite a bit since we had to stop four to five times an hour.

Wednesday, June 25. Throughout the night until nine in the morning, we covered thirty kilometers through spruce forest glades and past lakes, finally arriving at Ivan Volodimerov's [Yakutsk sluzhiv] yurt, which is located 150 kilometers from Yakutsk. That's where we stayed. With the Yakut chiefs providing exalted company, we treated them and ourselves to tobacco and kumis. It was cloudy, cold, and windy all day.

Thursday, June 26. It was very pleasant in the morning, warm and clear. I learned another, very plausible reason for the scarcity of fish in the lakes several years ago, namely that these were very dry years, causing many lakes to go completely dry, others to have very little water in them. I sent my new driver—the former one had run away—to look after our gear. In the afternoon my people arrived and announced that they had been unable to find my horse; it had undoubtedly run back to Yarmanka. Ivan Volodimerov gave me another, promising to look for mine. He made me a present of a horse and a cow and gave me another horse in exchange for an injured one. I made an agreement with him to send forty horses to Okhotsk next year and paid him 230 rubles. We departed in the afternoon and camped by a pond twenty kilometers further on. Mr. Berckhan shot a female duck, a merganser [*Mergus serrator*, red-breasted merganser, or *M. merganser*, common merganser; Springer, pers. comm., August 24, 2016], and I had him make a drawing of it. I also described it. I found *Onobrychis* with white, red, and flesh-colored flowers.[5]

Friday, June 27. The weather was like yesterday. My people traveled thirty kilometers to Aleksei Posikov's station while I wandered all day until about midnight through the woods, unable to find a trail or yurt because the shy Yakuts have moved too deeply into the forests. Around midnight I heard a shaman's drumming. Knowing that such drums can be heard from twenty kilometers away, I followed the sound and came to a poverty-stricken Yakut's yurt. He was sitting by the fire with his wives and children, and they were eating lake minnows and drinking *undak* [a drink made by beating sour milk together with cold water; WH, Anm. 856]. I exchanged a few Yakut words with them; the rest I communicated with hands, feet, and gestures, and they caught on that I was lost. Pointing with their fingers, they asked if I had fallen off my horse, because I had covered almost fifty kilometers on foot. However, I understood them to ask if I was looking for love and wanted to sleep with a Yakut woman. I therefore answered, "No." Finally, when I had drunk some undak and my dog had eaten grass—he was that hungry—I signaled the Yakut I would reward him well if he were to take me to the station. Together we then went five kilometers into the forest and came upon more yurts. In exchange for tobacco, I contracted a podvodchik and a horse and departed. Toward morning, in the company of my naked Yakut, I lay down to sleep by a night fire. Lacking tobacco I'd smoked the fuzz of arctic sage [*Artemisia frigida* Willd., or *A. jacutia* Drobow; Jäger] with the leaf of *Tanacetum*.[6] The Yakuts liked that so well that they immediately imitated me and told me that they really liked my way of compensating for my lack of tobacco.

Saturday, June 28. The weather was like yesterday. When day broke I took off and toward nine o'clock met up with Mr. Berckhan and my whole crew. My servant, however, was away with three others, looking for me. Today I had them do the Yakut *chokania*—that is, we celebrated the big summer festival with a banquet. I described the ceremonies of this festival in all its aspects.

Sunday, June 29, Peter-and-Paul Saints' Day. We had to stay put all day because the wagons had not yet arrived. A Yakut chief presented me with a cow for the road. I described the chokania. I had my first taste of a roasted stork, which I found palatable and not much different from swan.

Monday, June 30. The weather was like yesterday. I baptized my Yakut guide's daughter, and Aleksei Posikov adopted her. The girl's mother made me a present of a cow and butter. We were busy all day exchanging the podvodi [horse and wagon teams].

Tuesday, July 1. There was thunder around noon, and it was very hot all day. I was given *uentshuelue* [a water lily] rhizome and experimented with it by making it into a Yakut cream mash.[7] We had to spend another half a day, till noon, exchanging the teams. From here there are two trails to the Amga River. One takes off to the left, which I took together with Gavrilo, my servant, and with Mr. Berckhan's servant, as well as Aleksei Danilov; the other goes to the right along a lake, which Mr. Berckhan, Ushakov, Gorlanov, and my convoy took so that we were separated and didn't see each other again until the following day on the Amga River. Mr. Berckhan's horse spilled its guts like the traitor Judas [see Acts 1:15–19]. We therefore had to send back for a new horse. Today we covered forty-five kilometers on a mountain trail with a forest of larch and Scots pine to our left and had to contribute a lot of blood to horseflies and mosquitoes. We spent the night in the forest. I found the lesser *Pyrola* [probably sidebells wintergreen, *Orthilia secunda* (L.) House; Jäger] with white flowers, a species of lousewort [*Pedicularis*], dogwood with white and red berries,[8] and the lesser lousewort with yellow flowers and a fernlike leaf.[9]

Wednesday, July 2. The weather was pleasant all day, clear and warm. Having covered fifteen kilometers past many lakes, we came to the Amga River. I discovered a lake that was totally overgrown with a species of bladderwort and beautiful to look at.[10] The low-lying areas were a lot grassier and the grass much taller than before. I again noticed Siberian horseradish in abundance, chives [*Allium schoenoprasum* L.; Jäger], meadow rue with a purple-turning flower [*Thalictrum simplex* L.; Jäger], a species of thoroughwax [*Bupleurum sibiricum* Vest ex Spreng.; Jäger], and a species of cow parsnip [*Heracleum dissectum* Ledeb.] called *puchki* by the Russians and the stems of which I munched on.[11] I also found a species of skullcaps ["Cassida," *Scutellaria*],[12] another species of dragonhead [possibly *Dracocephalum stellerianum* Hildebr.; Jäger], a species of lovage,[13] *Thysselinum* [may be similar to *Kitagawia baicalensis* (Redowsky ex Willd.) Pimenov; Jäger], a member of the parsley family [Umbelliferae, cannot be further identified; Jäger], water hemlock, the Russians' *omeg*, which the horses are supposed to be immune to.

At the ford on the Amga River is a yurt [presumably another way station]. The river is about 350 feet wide there and in spring badly floods the low-lying areas. There are many lakes along it. It flows from the south to the north into the Aldan, which is the Yakut word for copper. We ferried across in a boat with a load capacity of nine hundred pounds. We made the cattle and the horses swim across. The following fish are found in the Amga: Eurasian dace, European perch [in text, *okuni, Perca fluviatilis* L.; WH, Anm. 908; northern pike, common whitefish, and Arctic grayling; at the mouth are common sturgeon, sterlet, and also *nalim*, a burbot [*Lota lota*; Bond, pers. comm., May 14, 1991].

Notes

1. In text, *Papaver* of *Hortus Elthamensis*, identified as *Papaver jacuticum* Peschkova, one of the microspecies of *P. nudicaule* L. s. l. Jäger.
2. In text, *Corallorhiza*; *C. trifida* Chatel. is the only species of this orchid genus in Siberia. Jäger.
3. In Steller's *Fl. Och.* under 382 *"sub Jaceae nomine descripti"* mentioned as *Cirsium rhaponticoides*, possibly a species of *Saussurea* or sawwort; the horseradish is most probably the wild *Armoracia sisymbrioides* (DC.) Cajander, and the dyer's woad *Isatis jacutensis* (N. Busch) N. Busch. Jäger.
4. Knowing how Steller sometimes mentions later events before earlier ones, we wonder if this is the calf just butchered or a replacement for it.
5. *Onobrychis arenaria* (Kit.) DC, a member of the legume family and the only species of this genus in Siberia. Jäger. Literal translation of Onobrychis (Greek): devoured by donkeys.
6. *Artemisia tanacetifolia* L. refers to a mugwort with the leaves of *Tanacetum*. It is excluded because its leaves are neither silky nor woolly and thus could not be used as tobacco. Jäger.
7. Dwarf water lily, *Nymphaea tetragona* Georgi, or small yellow pond lily, *Nuphar pumila* (Timm) DC; rhizomes of these species of the water lily family are edible, containing a high percentage of starch. Jäger.
8. Siberian dogwood, *Cornus alba* L., is the only Siberian shrubby dogwood, but the berries are white, sometimes bluish white. In his *Fl. Och.*, Steller lists this species only under Nr. 529 as *Cornus foemina* C. B. P.—i.e., *C. sanguinea* L.—but *sanguinea* has black berries and is absent from Siberia. On July 1, Steller would not have found ripe berries. Jäger.
9. Perhaps *Fl. Och.* Nr. 92; not enough information to identify; *Flora of Siberia* lists fifty-three species of *Pedicularis*. Jäger.
10. Either flatleaf bladderwort, *Utricularia intermedia* Hayne, or lesser bladderwort, *U. minor* L., or greater common bladderwort, *U. vulgaris* L., all with showy yellow flowers. Jäger.
11. *Heracleum dissectum* Ledeb. is a somewhat smaller species than *H. lanatum* Michx. (syn. of *Heracleum maximum* W. Bartram) with triangular leaves that are longer than wide. Jäger. Cow parsnips are still called puchki in Alaska.
12. Either *Scutellaria ikonnikovii* Juz. (syn. of *S. regeliana* var. *ikonnikovii* (Juz.) C. Y. Wu & H. W. Li) or *S. galericulata* L. or possibly a species of dragonhead, *Dracocephalum*. Jäger.
13. Possibly alpine lovage, *Ligusticum mutellinoides* (Crantz) Vill, a syn. of *Neogaya simplex* (L.) Meisn., but it only grows in high mountains; Steller was in the valley of the Amga on July 2. Jäger.

14

FROM THE AMGA TO THE YUNA RIVER (7/3–7/21)

THURSDAY, JULY 3. THE WEATHER WAS LIKE YESTERDAY. We were still waiting for our convoy, which arrived in the evening as expected. Today I noticed a wild iris [*Iris setosa* Pall. ex Link; Jäger], northern Indian paintbrush with white and red flowers [*Castilleja pallida* (L.) Kunth], a cinquefoil with long runners [*Potentilla flagellaris* D.F.K.Schltdl.; Jäger], the wild blood-red Siberian lily [*Lilium pensylvanicum* Ker Gawl.], and a species of lousewort.[1]

The Amga River has its source across from Vitimsk Sloboda. Two hundred and fifty kilometers from the ford is Amginsk Sloboda, where both barley and rye tend to grow well, and that was especially the case in 1739. But the people have no taste for bread, just as they are forgetting their own language and are more Yakut than Russian. In July the Amga is so shallow that you can safely cross it on foot. On the left bank, upriver from the ford, there are mountains of grayish-white and yellowish-gray sandstone between which are veins of metal and layers of pitch and coal. At the foot of the mountains are found pieces of rough iron ore, also some pieces of petrified larch containing iron.

Friday, July 4. The weather was like yesterday until evening. For thirteen kilometers we traveled along at the foot of the mountains. The trail is absolutely wretched when it is raining. We were in luck, however, that the muddy ground was dry though very uneven. To the right of the trail and in the low-lying areas is nothing but boggy ground with hummocks and small shrubby birch, dwarf bog birch [*Betula fruticosa* Pall.; Jäger]. From there we rode across a bog and in the evening came to a halt at a mountain near a lake. Toward evening, it turned so cold that, unequipped for it in my peasant tunic, I was frozen through as I would be in Germany in November. We had the wind directly from the northeast. I noticed St. John's wort [*Hypericum*], yellow dot saxifrage [*Saxifraga stelleriana* Merklein ex Ser.], and a species of milkvetch [*Astragalus*] with white-brown flowers.[2]

Saturday, July 5. It was calm, clear, warm, and sunny in the morning when we left our night's camp. There are no dense forests along this trail because tall trees grow only in the mountains. Not a single real tree grows in the low-lying areas, just willows, small alders [*Alnaster fruticosus* (Rupr.) Ledeb.], and dwarf bog birches. The soil in these areas consists of peat riven by huge fissures. In the hilly or mountainous places the soil is loamy; in rocky ones, which occur along the trail on the Amga, it consists of white and yellowish gray sandstone. You also find bald mountains in the midst of forests, or at least the trees on these mountains are very sparse. Their valleys are all oriented toward the north, and up to this point you find few very steep or high places, if any at all. But there are many grouse.

Sunday, July 6. The weather was like yesterday. Today we arrived at the large Aldan River, having covered a distance of ninety kilometers from the Amga to the Aldan, crossing over a total of four mountain ranges, which, though not very high, are almost impassable in bad weather. In dry weather it was just doable. Between the mountains there are lakes all over, becoming larger the closer you get to the Aldan. On the Aldan I noticed a beautiful, large, completely violet Japanese iris with the fragrance of prunes [*Iris laevigata* Fisch..];[3] also the false spirea or false goat's beard, which had not yet opened up, however [*Sorbaria sorbifolia* (L.) A. Braun];[4] Dr. Gmelin's Jacob's ladder, "*Polemonium humile hirsutum*" [in reality, the small Siberian phlox, *Phlox sibirica* L., see June 20];[5] the unusual campanula—that is, the spotted bellflower—with flowers that are white with purple dots and leaves like nettles [*Campanula punctata* Lam.; Jäger]; a *Hesperis*—that is, dame's violet—with lanceolate-shaped leaves and white flowers [*Hesperis sibirica* L.; Jäger]; *Lychnis* covered in foam with azure flowers;[6] the alpine bells with the fragrance of honey, very broad leaves, and purple flowers [*Primula matthioli* (L.) V. A. Richt. subsp. *sibirica* (Andrz. ex Bess.) Kovt.; Jäger];[7] and the sardana of the Russians—that is, alpine sweetvetch—with red and white flowers [*Hedysarum alpinum* L.; cf. *Flora Ochotensis* 347; Jäger]. I have had drawings made of the last two. As much as I pursued a white hawk who had an ashy coloring only at the tips of the wings [*Accipiter gentilis*, northern goshawk, a best guess; Springer, pers. comm., August 24, 2016], I could not get a shot at him. At the ford the Aldan is half again as wide as the Neva is across from the pharmacy. At that spot a storage facility and two earthen huts have been erected.

Monday, July 7. The weather was like yesterday. Today we had our horses and cattle, 101 heads in all, brought over in two vessels, which make the crossing three times a day, every time landing far downriver and having to be pulled back to the ford with ropes. I botanized, and we butchered the cow that the mother of the girl I baptized had given me [see above, p. 123].

Tuesday, July 8. The weather was like yesterday. We crossed the Aldan with our gear. I botanized and delighted in the abundance of red currants, which, however, were not yet ripe. Toward evening the instrument maker [apprentice Stepan] Ovsianikov arrived, bringing with him my horse that had been lost on the trail two hundred kilometers back.

Wednesday, July 9. Around ten o'clock we left the Aldan and spent the night about fifteen kilometers from the ford. The weather was like yesterday. We traveled through forests, staying along the Aldan. Its banks on both sides are steep and precipitous. Part of the trail was altogether miserable and the brush so thick that we had to carefully guard our eyes.

Thursday, July 10. The weather was like yesterday. We left very early and for approximately ten kilometers had an awful trail with nothing but boggy ground and hummocks, so we had covered only twenty kilometers by twelve o'clock. Where we had our noon meal, I saw the first orchid with a long spur, the keyflower [*Dactylorhiza cruenta* (O. E. Müll.) Soó, syn. of *D. incarnata* subsp. *cruenta* (O. E. Müll.) P. D. Sell; Jäger]. Toward four o'clock we moved on. Covering about fourteen kilometers by eight o'clock, we came to the Belaya River, where we fed the horses and spent the night. There are excellent pastures on the Aldan that are not used, however, except by the convoys, because during the expedition the Yakuts all moved away. The ones living close by are very poor, having no cattle but living on fish from the lakes, Scots pine and larch [*Larix gmelinii* Kuzen.] bark, and game. If they catch some game animal, they stay put until it has all been eaten. . . . A Russian reported to me that these people, lacking bread and good nourishment, were so lightweight that it was impossible for a Russian to follow a Yakut on snowshoes. When the Yakuts' snowshoe tracks were barely visible in the snow, those of the Russians were half a foot deep. I have also observed our driver's lack of strength in loading the horses.[8] Around the fords the snow falls at the most . . . deep. The shortest day is approximately three hours long. There are no blizzards or storms all winter; . . . they start around the time of Lent.

. . . In the Aldan there are common sturgeon; sterlet, which have wider, fatter heads than in any other places; northern pike; Arctic and common grayling; European perch; Eurasian ruffe do not occur;[9] and very large burbot.... The Belaya River has a terribly fast current and varies in width, but ... in sunny weather ... you can swim across it with horses and gear. The river is full of rocks, among them cherry-red and green jasper and black agate or earth wax—that is, ozocerite [a naturally occurring odoriferous mineral wax or paraffin]—which can be used in place of flint. Like the Yuna River, when it rains the Belaya becomes so swollen in a few hours that travelers have to wait two to five days until the water recedes. This stems from four causes. First, the Belaya River originates in high mountains and continues to visibly flow downhill. Second, not only its source but the whole river flows at high elevation. Third, the many rocks make the impact of the current more violent, and fourth, the many bends make it so turbulent that it knocks the horses over if they get too close to a deep spot.... We should have watched more closely for the shallow places.... The current turns the swimming dogs around ... and ... pulls them far downriver. One of ours couldn't ... make it at all.

Friday, July 11. It was very hot in the morning, almost unbearably so. From two to six in the evening, there was constant thunder, and the storm moved all around the horizon. Toward seven o'clock it rained for half an hour. Afterward, it was very pleasant all night long. We stayed until seven in the evening on the Belaya because one of the surveyor Ushakov's horses had bit the dust, and the driver had escaped during the night with the remaining two horses. [Not clear if this was a troika and they had lost a whole team or if these were pack horses.] I therefore occupied myself with botanizing. While around Krasnoyarsk and Lake Baikal, rhubarb [*Rheum compactum* L.; Jäger] grows on the highest mountains, on the Belaya it frequently grows in low, boggy forests because, on the whole, the countryside itself is pretty high. In addition, I found a *Lychnis* with flowers turning azure [probably *Gastrolychnis violascens* Tolm. or *Silene uralensis* (Rupr.) Boquet, see July 6; Jäger], northern jasmine [*Androsace septentrionalis* L.; Jäger], the tiny purple mountain saxifrage [*Saxifraga oppositifolia* L.. subsp. *ajanica* (Sipliv.) Vorosch.; Jäger], a species of sweet coltsfoot [*Petasites sibiricus* (J. F. Gmel.) Dingwall, syn. of *Endocellion sibiricum* (J. F. Gmel.) Toman; Jäger], and perhaps broadleaf chives [*Allium senescens* L.; Jäger], which I had Mr. Berckhan make a drawing of. Toward seven o'clock we departed and for ten kilometers ... passed through nothing but boggy areas.

Saturday, July 12. It was very hot all day long. We traveled through absolutely beautiful forests, though boggy at times, upriver along the Belaya;

after having covered fifteen kilometers, we ate our noon meal on the river. In the afternoon we forded the river for the first time. Turning first east, then south for eight kilometers, we traveled through forests of Scots pine, spruce, larch, and willow. Then we passed a high mountain . . . , along a cliff across a bog, covered about fourteen kilometers, and spent the night on a lake. Today I found a star gentian [*Swertia obtusa* Ledeb.; Jäger]; a *Fumaria* with a longish, hollow root), fragrant purple flowers, and very wide leaves [*Corydalis paeoniifolia* (Stephan) Pers.; Jäger]; and an alpine bistort [*Bistorta vivipara* (L.) Delarbre; Jäger].

Sunday, July 13. It was incredibly clear and the heat almost unbearable if the winds . . . hadn't refreshed us. We had to stay here to wait for a lost horse and the gear to catch up. I went to the river and found a very tall, sticky cinquefoil with white flowers—that is, rock cinquefoil [*Potentilla inquinans* Turcz., which is up to twenty inches tall and frequently found throughout Yakutia; Jäger]—from which I also collected ripe seeds. Mr. Berckhan shot a bird, a young diver [in text, *gagara* or loon, species unknown]. We were surprised to hear the mother lament her young with the most pitiful cries. I dried my plants and journaled. Here, ninety kilometers from the Aldan, the steep, rocky mountains and cliffs begin, extending all the way to the mouth of the Belaya River.

Monday, July 14. We left our camp in the morning, crossed the Belaya River a second time, traveled through unending larch and Scots pine forests, and, after eight kilometers, passed a volcano called Windy Mountain about which lots of lies are told. Then we crossed the river for the third time. We traveled through boggy areas for six kilometers, then crossed a mountain on the right, turned east again over lots of boggy ground, and toward one in the afternoon once again reached the Belaya River, where we ate our lunch and gave the horses a rest. Mr. Berckhan shot a female tufted duck [*Aythya fuligula* L.; WH, Anm. 1031; Springer, email, November 9, 2016], which I described. I noticed how abruptly the land rises toward the east and south. Having traveled ten to twelve kilometers on our level trail, we saw on the horizon mountain peaks that were at least 2,400 feet high. That alone can easily explain the fast current of the Belaya and Yuna Rivers as well as their sudden flooding. At the same time, it is amazing that this high plateau is filled with so many lakes and bogs. Today I noticed a bog saxifrage with spotted yellow flowers [*Saxifraga hirculus* L.; Jäger]; a greater bog milkvetch with a three-cornered husk and blue flowers [perhaps alpine milkvetch, *Astragalus alpinus* L.; Jäger], which I had seen last year on Lake Baikal, and also a lesser one [unidentified] (the former grows on streams, the other in low forests); and the greater white or yellow-white *Astragalus* with a black flower banner [perhaps *A. frigidus* (L.) A. Gray; Jäger]. At four in the afternoon, we departed, traveling upriver on the Belaya, where now and then we could see ice. [Literally "on which there were points of ice"; these could be on the banks or in the river.] Having covered seven kilometers along the mountains on the right bank, we crossed the Belaya a fourth time where the right bank turned into cliffs. Here I found a pair of beaded boots of soft leather. Avoiding the bogs, we proceeded another eight kilometers in the woods, and around ten at night we came again to the Belaya River, where we camped for the night. Part of our convoy caught up with us around midnight, but the rest didn't arrive until morning.

I had the bad luck that one of my horses with all my gear fell into the river, and the river carried away thirty-six pounds of my brick tea, but I fished it back out and dried it the next day without any noticeable loss of strength. At the same time, my Yakut soldier was even worse off because the river carried away his winter clothes.[10]

The morning was cool and dreary, the afternoon clearer and warmer. It's amazing how many detours we had to take. Until we got to the Amga, we had to walk single-file around the lakes on twisting trails; from the Aldan to here, we had to detour around the mountains to avoid crossing them in order not to tire out the horses too much. Some mountains, particularly the volcanoes and certain crags, have trees only on their summits, their steep slopes being bare. The soil on them is grayish-yellow clay that is five to seven feet thick high up on the cliffs. Many mountains are also burned over in order to dry out the trail by exposing it to the air, and in the evenings we entertained ourselves by energetically participating in these air-inducing fireworks.[11] In the pastures trees sport boards where travelers, according to their mood, have recorded when they fed their horses here.

Tuesday, July 15. It was very hot all day. To give the horses a rest, we stayed put till three in the afternoon. I dried my wet tea and plants. Then we left, crossed over a mountain, and having covered six kilometers, we forded the Belaya River a fifth time because there were too many cliffs on the left. After another ten kilometers, we came to a channel of the Belaya where we spent the night. There I found an Arctic marsh marigold with finely edged leaves; a *Phalangium* with white flowers [*Tofieldia cernua* Sm., a species of false asphodel], which I had sketched; a beautiful rush; alpine bells with very broad leaves; a coltsfoot with longish leaves [*Endocellion sibiricum*

(J. F. Gmel.) Toman; Jäger] and yet another unknown pod-bearing plant.[12] In the Belaya I noticed the most beautiful pieces of black marble with white veins and very large pieces of green jasper.

Wednesday, July 16. My crew left camp around six in the morning. I stayed behind a few hours with Mr. Berckhan, who was making a drawing of the *Phalangium*. In the meantime I journaled while sipping my improved tea, finding it acceptable. Afterward I went botanizing in the woods and found a single delight wintergreen.[13] Then we went on a terrible trail up and over a mountain, descending its very steep side. At the foot I found a saxifrage with tripartite, rough-haired leaves and white flowers.[14] Then we went through interminable forests with mountains on both sides and forded the Chagdala stream three times, which flows into the Belaya and is at most a foot deep but incredibly clean and clear. After covering twelve kilometers, we had lunch at the river between two mountains, separated by about two kilometers at the base. I climbed one of them, which is quite high to the northeast and looked at the precipitous side to the south, but on it I found only a sawwort [*Jacea* or *Centaurea* is absent from Eastern Siberia, presumably Steller found a species of *Saussurea*; Jäger], a red lousewort (*Pedicularis*) with dark-red leaves, and a narrow-leafed anemone.[15]

These mountains extend lengthwise from east to west and fall away steeply on the south and north sides. They are as craggy as the ones around Lake Baikal and the Lena River, are quite dry, and are made of gray rock; some are brick-red, tainted by rust. If you throw rocks on the ground, they barely make a sound. Gray-black slate is lying on the summits of the crags; it is easily split into thin, very fragile flakes. There is no trace of ore or fossils to be seen. Only *slanets* or Siberian dwarf pine [*Pinus pumila* (Pall.) Regel] and alpine blueberry bushes [*Vaccinium uliginosum* L.] grow on top. On these mountains you don't find *byssos* [any algae of the genus *Trentepohlia*, H. Dörfelt; Jäger], just a lot of moss, and I have observed that the more broken up mountains are—that is, eroded without passages and veins—the fewer byssos there are. The totally shattered mountains have no byssos at all.

Then I went back to my convoy and ate, and soon thereafter we left. In the afternoon we passed through nothing but forests between the mountains, and, having covered twenty-five kilometers from morning till evening, we came to a mountain range that faces north but extends like the previous one—that is, it stretches from east to west. I climbed up it and found it to be like the previous one, although there were several other plants on it. It was overgrown with eight-petal mountain avens [*Dryas octopetala* L. var. *viscida* Hultén, syn. of *D. viscosa* Juz.] with sticky leaves and with the narrowness of the leaves increasing the farther up the mountain I got. Up there I also found a dame's violet [*Hesperis sibirica* L.] with white flowers, a jasmine with pointed rough-haired leaves, red lousewort, and Labrador tea with whitish, long-tubed flowers and leaves like *Lentiscus*, of which I had a drawing made. Down below, on the river, I collected a lovely arrow grass with white flowers, and a poppy, which always has orange-red flowers around here.[16] Then I went back. All day long it was very hot and clear, but up on the mountains it was constantly foggy.

Thursday, July 17. The weather was like yesterday. Six kilometers from where we had camped for the night, we climbed up and over a horribly high mountain with all our gear. On it I found a rhododendron with very broad, sulfur-yellow flowers; a butterwort; two rare heathers; a naked bishop's cap; a stem-bearing sphagnum with a silky, purple, yellow, and white capsule; and a beautiful lousewort of which I had Mr. Berckhan make a drawing.[17] After going another fourteen kilometers, we fed the horses. At three o'clock we took off again, made approximately eight kilometers, and camped again on the Belaya under a tall mountain. This area is littered with lots of horse bones left there courtesy of the Yakuts' knives and mouths, continuing as the hallmark of the "road to Okhotsk." When the trail is bad, the Yakuts habitually encourage and cheer on their horses by joyfully shouting *yuyul* or by barking like dogs, which often in the midst of mud and mire made me laugh.

Friday, July 18. The weather was like yesterday. In the morning we left Yunakan and made our way up and over a lot of dreadfully tall mountains and through deep valleys, crossing rivers and streams more than fifty times, all of which wore out our horses; some of them even broke their hooves on the rocks. Today I found three new species of saxifrage, a second species of bittercress [in text, *Cardamine*], and an unknown plant with roselike flowers.[18] About four kilometers from the night's camp at the foot of a mountain, I found huge boulders of green jasper, weighing 660 to 1,100 pounds, as well as liver-colored and black marble with white stripes in boulders of equal size.

We ate our lunch at a deserted hut, where I found a species of butterwort but lost my handkerchief. In the afternoon we climbed a high mountain and descended it again only to come to another high mountain, from

Fig. 14.1. In the high mountains (Arnold).

the summit of which we saw eighteen mountains encircling the whole horizon. They were a spectacular sight but for us travelers dreadful to behold, especially if you looked at the abysses and valleys. I wished the esteemed senators in St. Petersburg could have this view from their windows for half an hour to properly evaluate this project of the Kamchatka Expedition and the insight and conscience of its planners. We climbed up over this mountain and two more and spent the night at a stream between sheer cliffs, from which one of my own horses fell to its death and to their joy into the Yakuts' cook pots. Today we covered thirty-five kilometers.

Saturday, July 19. The weather was like yesterday. We stayed put until four in the afternoon. I botanized, dried and described several plants, collected seeds, and took a look at the schist rocks that stretch from here to the Yuna River. Although my feet and especially my inflamed big toe caused me much pain, we took our leave around four in the afternoon, crossing over many mountains and through valleys and bogs, and at 11:00 p.m., after twenty kilometers, we came to a halt on boggy ground by a small stream. Today on a rock of green talc, I found a beautiful *Artemisia*, the first since the Aldan; an *Arnica* with white flowers, of which I recently had

Mr. Berckhan make a drawing; and a gentian with leaves of *Hypericum* and sky-blue flowers with four or five points, respectively.[19]

Sunday, July 20. It was downright hot. We traveled along the valleys with mountains above us and made lunch at a little stream beneath a cliff, where I found a beautiful *Fumaria* [actually a *Corydalis sibirica* (L. f.) Pers.; Jäger], a bittercress, a *Salvia*,[20] and a new species of saxifrage [unidentified] with stiffer leaves. We spent the afternoon climbing up and down mountains. Having traveled eighteen kilometers during the day, we came to a small stream, where we stopped for the night. There I found—at the source of the little stream under the rocks—a small yellow violet, which on the Aldan I had found in seed, along with a beautiful fern,[21] but in my joy I left behind my brass tobacco pipe as a tip.

Everywhere you pass a tall mountain, a bog, or an otherwise nasty place, you find trees along the trail festooned with white horse hairs like a fringe, at once thanking God or the devil for overcoming the adversity. Occasionally the Yakuts also hang rags on the trees or put a stone on a stump.[22] In this beautiful religion the lid is generally made to fit the pitcher, in that the Yakuts only treat the devil to things they no longer have any use for. When the Yakuts have gobbled up a horse that has become too weak or died on them, in gratitude they give the devil the skull as well as some bones for dessert. Consequently, their sacrifice costs them nothing while the Lord Satan can't complain about wealth.

Monday, July 21. We left early in the morning. Two kilometers from our night camp in some woods, I found a Yakut mausoleum on four posts [obviously a burial platform]. Having traveled twelve kilometers, we reached the Yuna River and some lakes where we stopped for lunch. In the afternoon we traveled another two kilometers downriver, and while jumping across a channel the student Gorlanov and I fell into the mud with our horses. Under great danger we crossed the river, which was rather deep and fast, and camped two kilometers from it between two large lakes full of the nicest carp, lake minnows, and ducks.

A few Yakuts live there in two yurts. They do not pay yasak and on top of that had received twenty head of cattle and twenty horses for breeding. However, because of lack of feed, deep snow, and the powerful storms in fall and spring, all of the animals had already bit the dust. They told me they have just fish, plants, and hares for food. There are reindeer around here, but the Tungus, the Yakuts claim, keep coming here in spring and threaten to shoot them if they catch them hunting reindeer, so they're limited to hunting hares. Thus envy can be found in even the vast wilderness. The Yakuts do praise the Tungus' helpfulness; they reported that they would have croaked in the spring had they not received reindeer jerky from the Tungus. In return, the Yakuts had to give the Tungus *pal'mi*—that is, hunting spears, axes, clothing, buckles, and other belongings. I took a break on one *kurgan* [R., burial mound], and Mr. Berckhan on another. In the evening we once again enjoyed a meal of fresh fish for the first time in ten days. Up until then we had eaten only barley mush with ham, a diet that causes wretched gas, especially if you have nothing but water to drink with it.

Notes

1. Northern paintbrush has white and purple-red flowers and is common in meadows, steppes, and open forests in Yakutia.

Despite its scientific name, the Siberian lily is found from Siberia to northern China and Kamchatka but not in Pennsylvania. Jäger. The misleading Latin name is due to an error by the botanist John Bellenden Ker.

2. Any one of the species of *Hypericum*: *H. attenuatum* Fisch. ex Choisy or *H. ascyron* L. and its subsp. *gebleri* (Ledeb.) N. Robson. The species of saxifrage with undivided, grasslike leaves was named in honor of Steller.

With ninety-two species of *Astragalus* in Siberia, one can only hypothesize which species Steller meant; perhaps *Astragalus frigidus* (L.) A. Gray, which is a beautiful plant with yellowish white flowers. Jäger.

3. The basal leaves of the Japanese iris are 0.8–1.2 inches wide, and the diameter of the flowers is 3–4 inches; it is found around lakes and backwaters of the Aldan, Yuna, and Belaya Rivers. Jäger.

4. This species of *Sorbaria*, false spirea, is widespread in south, central, and east Yakutia. Jäger.

5. Literally translated, "rough-haired Polemonium of small stature," but Polemoniums are not rough-haired. Jäger.

6. No member of the Caryophyllaceae-Silenoideae subfamily has blue flowers, but perhaps the violet flowers of *Gastrolychnis violascens* Tolm. Syn. *Silene violascens* (Tolm.) V.V. Petrovsky & Elven) and *Silene uralensis* (Rupr.) Boquet become blue when dry; see also June 17 and below, July 11. Jäger.

7. There are several subspecies of now-named *Primula matthioli* (L.) V. A. Richt. in Eastern Asia and around Lake Baikal; here it is subsp. *sibirica* (Andrz. ex Bess. Kovt). Jäger.

8. In text, *beim Jutschen*, a seemingly German verb no longer used that makes no sense in the context. More likely, it is a germanized corruption of the Russian verb *v'iuchit'*, to load a horse; (Tchaikovsky, email, March, 14, 2017). Words or a complete sentence following seem to be missing, ending in . . . *weisen*, which could be short for *beweisen*, meaning to prove. Conceivably Steller meant to say that this lack of strength would confirm what his Russian informant had told him.

9. Our guess; in text, *werden nicht verführet*, are not enticed; could be a variant of *geführt*, carried.

10. In text, *Mein Jakut Caper*, literally my Yakut pirate, if translated from German. Since Steller occasionally confused the letters in the Roman and Cyrillic alphabets (Roman *c* equals Cyrillic *s*), we are certain that the Russian *sapër* is meant—i.e., a soldier from an engineering battalion (like the US Navy's Seabees), who built bridges and fortifications.

11. In text, *Lustfeuerwerken*, literally fun fireworks; but since in German script nonfinal *s* and *f* are very similar and since Steller mentions that these fires were set to get air into the forest to dry out the trails, we assume that he meant to write (or wrote—it could just be hard to decipher) *Luftfeuerwerken*, literally air fireworks.

12. Arctic marsh marigold, *Caltha palustris* subsp. *arctica* (R. Br.) Huth; Jäger. *Phalangium*, perhaps *Tofieldia cernua*; Jäger. Rush, in text, *Juncus*—"beautiful" is not enough to guess which species; Jäger. Alpine bells—see July 6 and footnote 7; Jäger. Coltsfoot, in text, *Tussilago*, which does not reach eastern Yakutia—perhaps the related genus *Petasites*, *P. sibiricus* (J. F. Gmel.) Dingwall, Syn. of Endocellion; Jäger.

13. Wintergreen, *Moneses uniflora* (L.) A. Gray, single-flowered relative of *Pyrola* that is distributed from Europe to the Far East and Alaska. Jäger.

14. *Saxifraga lactea* Turcz. In text, *Geum*, now known as the genus *Saxifraga*. This species was found again and described by Turczaninov exactly one hundred years later in the same place where Steller found it and recognized it as a new species of saxifrage. Jäger.

15. Species with narrow digitate leaves are *Anemone narcissiflora* subsp. *calva* (Juz.) Hultén; syn. of *Anemonastrum calvum* (Juz.) Holub and *Anemone tamarae* Kharkev. Jäger.

16. Eight-petal mountain avens, *Dryas punctata* Juz. or the closely related *D. viscosa* Juz.; syn. of *D. octopetala* L.? A jasmine, probably *Androsace incana* Lam. "Like *Lentiscus*": *Pistacia lentiscus* is a Mediterranean evergreen shrub with lanceolate leaflets. Arrow grass, in text, *Juncago*, now named *Triglochin*; two species grow in Yakutia, but they have inconspicuous, not white flowers. Perhaps Steller meant *Rhynchospora alba* (L.) Vahl, a similar plant with white flowers. The poppy, *Papaver jacuticum* Peschkova, has orange flowers and belongs to *P. nudicaule* s. l.; common name is Iceland poppy, which has white, yellow, or orange flowers. Jäger.

17. A rhododendron, *Rhododendron aureum* Georgi, a small evergreen shrub with flowers 1.2–2.0 inches wide. A butterwort, a species of *Pinguicula*. Three occur in Yakutia: *P. spathulata* Ledeb., *P. vulgaris* L., and *P. villosa* L.; impossible to determine without a description of the flowers. Two rare heathers, *Cassiope tetragona* (L.) D. Don, common name, arctic bell heather, or *C. ericoides* (Pall.) D. Don; the second may be *Phyllodoce coerulea* (L.) Bab., common name, mountain heather. A naked bishop's cap, *Mitella nuda* L.; "*Doronicum* or *Arnica* with leaves like *Plantago*": *Arnica intermedia* Turcz. A sphagnum; with over three hundred species of *Sphagnum*, peat moss, these characteristics are not enough to identify which species. Jäger.

18. Unknown plant with roselike flowers, now known as spring beauty, *Claytonia soczaviana* Jurtzev; syn. of *Claytonia angustifolia* Pall. ex Willd. A genus described as new by Steller with the name *Belia* after Belaya River, *Fl. Och.* 296. Jäger.

19. "... a beautiful *Absinthium*": *Artemisia*, not enough information to determine the species; perhaps *Artemisia sericea* Weber et Stechm., a beautiful silvery plant of the Far East. "... a *Doronicum* with white flower," but *Fl. Och.* 419: "*Aster montanus omnium minimus . . . primo intuitu pro Doronici species habui*": *Arctogeron gramineum* (L.) DC. (or *Aster alpinus* L.?, cf. the

drawing by Berckhan). *"Gentiana florum laciniis quaternis"*: *Gentianopsis barbata* (Froel.) Ma has blue flowers and four crown segments. Common name, fringed gentian. Jäger.

20. Bittercress—the description in *Opred. Rast.* 7 (1995) corresponds to that in *Fl. Och.* 160; perhaps *Macropodium nivale* (Pall.) R. Br. Jäger. "... a *Salvia*," cf. *Fl. Och.* 117: "*Salvia minor hederae terrestris folio*": It is not *Salvia* but may be a member of *Scutellaria alpina*-group or *Glechoma hederacea* L.?; see below, July 24. Jäger.

21. *Viola uniflora*, which has a single, rather large, golden-yellow flower. Jäger. "... a beautiful filicula," *Fl. Och.* 474: This fern is now called Steller's rockbrake, *Cryptogramma stelleri* (S. G. Gmel.) Prantl. Jäger.

22. To put a stone on a stump or a hill of stones was common practice with the Yakuts and Mongolians. It both marks the way and is a sacred rite to satisfy the spirits at the site. Jäger.

15

FROM THE YUNA RIVER TO YUDOMA CROSS (7/22–8/8)

Tuesday, July 22. We stayed put here and allowed our horses to rest up, fill up, and pick up their health.[1] We washed the felt saddle blankets, which were covered in blood and pus. I dried my plants and collected some seeds. Afterward we treated ourselves, again for the first time [since July 6], with beef from an ox we butchered. The weather was pleasant and sunny in the morning though still a bit cool. At one in the afternoon it turned windy, and I had to gather up my plant stuff and rather speedily at that. Toward evening the wind increased more and more, the mountains all around became shrouded in fog, the air turned dark and thick, and we saw rain in the offing. From the Belaya to here there are no more birches, but along the Yuna River are mongolian poplar [*Populus suaveolens* Fisch. ex Poiteau & A.Vilm., a tree of the river plains; Jäger] reappear with increasing frequency. Nor did we see any birds except for ravens until the Yuna, where we once again saw the yellow wagtails [*Motacilla flava*; Springer, email, September 5, 2016] and gulls. The jay can be seen and heard now and then in the mountains.[2]

Wednesday, July 23. The strong wind had continued all night long and during the entire day, which was also bright and sunny though already rather cool. But to our joy the anticipated rain did not materialize. Mr. Anton Emmanuilovich Devier [new commander of Okhotsk] arrived with Basso[3] and an interpreter. It was actually Mr. Devier who woke me up because I recognized his voice immediately. So I hurriedly got up. Over a nice cup of tea, we debated the improvement of this region and its occupation by the Yakuts. I mentioned the many difficulties this area and its peoples had, and we asked the Yakuts what they thought. Mr. Devier thought, with good reason, that growing grain on Kamchatka would not be profitable at all for Her Majesty because the game living in these parts would be frightened and driven away forever by the burning of trees and roots. Then we dined on [crucian] carp and a piece of beef and parted. I went to the Yakuts' yurt and discovered that in order to convince strangers of their poverty and move them to pity, they moan and groan, pretending to be sick and weak, just like the Yakuts are wont to do. I returned home with wet feet and packed for our departure the next day. I cooked myself soup from the marrow of a whole ox [sic], topped it off with a good cup of tea with milk, and, having given orders for an early departure, went to bed.

Thursday, July 24. The wind kept blowing all night, but toward morning it calmed down; the day turned cool and dreary, and a few rain drops fell. Nevertheless, mosquitoes swarmed around me like bees, so I myself immediately started a fire to chase them away. We loaded the horses and left the place even before sunrise. We passed a mountain and around noon came to a boggy valley. On the right a very fast river with a rocky bottom flows from east to west. It drains many forest streams, and forty kilometers above where we crossed, it forks into many branches. After that we passed a very high mountain, the third on this trip that deserves to be noticed, and after putting twelve kilometers behind us, we came to a grassy place along the Ancha River where we stopped for lunch. There I found seeds from a *Salvia* and a sticky five-leaved plant with yellow blossoms.[4] We left after two hours and for the first four kilometers had a very good trail; then we passed a cliff on the left along streams with all the rocks poking up, making it hard for the horses to walk. Then came bogs for several kilometers until, having covered fifteen kilometers, we made camp for the night by a mountain. My horse had the misfortune of badly wounding its genitals on a stick in the bog, so that once again my soup at supper turned out too salty. All day it had been drizzling.

Friday, July 25. We had pleasant weather all day: It was calm, and the sun was shining. We traveled over steep and rocky terrain and through stands of Mongolian poplar to the Ancha River, and having covered twelve kilometers we camped on the river where we would have to ford it. Here I found the first currants [*Ribes spicatum* E. Robson; Jäger] since the Aldan River [see p. 128], which I turned into a delicious dish for our noonday meal by boiling a beef tongue, peas,[5] and kidneys with them. Two hours later we left. Fording the river, I and my gear once again had the misfortune of getting into deep water and thus all wet. We passed through continuous steep terrain and saw a lot of snow still lying on the crags. After covering fifteen kilometers, we reached a meadow along the river, where we all enjoyed blueberries and camped for the night. I collected a few seeds from a small gentian and from a *myosotide*.[6]

Saturday, July 26. We left in the morning, traveled through continuous rocky terrain along the mountain range, and came to two places where the ice never melts but stays year-round.[7]

After traveling another fourteen kilometers, I found in a meadow by a creek a type of buttercup I had never seen before and from which I collected ripe seeds.[8] In the morning the weather was mixed—now sunny, now cloudy. But in the afternoon a severe thunderstorm broke over us, and a heavy rain fell, which caused the mountains and crags to smoke like baking ovens. Even though we had gotten thoroughly drenched, we decided to continue on our way and made such good time that by evening we had covered twelve kilometers. Not far from our camp that night, I saw a curious phenomenon in the woods. A stream flowed between two mountains separated from each other by half a kilometer. On both sides the cut banks were made of ice up to two feet thick [permafrost]. On top of the ice were soil and muskeg and very tall larch trees. I gathered that this ice has never thawed and has been lying here since times immemorial and represents solid ground. Around here we heard wolves howling and were on our guard lest they scatter our horses and cattle.

Sunday, July 27. We had cool, cloudy weather all day. But it gradually became clearer from noon on. We left our camp early in the morning; traveled along valleys between mountains; crossed many forest streams, some several times; and, after covering thirteen kilometers, arrived at a meadow on a stream where we took a two-hour midday break. After that we traveled just in the valleys between mountains for eleven kilometers, coming to an ice patch. Here I noted the following curiosities: (1) Toward the east, among and right at the base of the mountains, was a sheet of ice almost one and a quarter kilometers wide and from south to north four kilometers long. An icy stream flows around this ice, originating partly from up the valleys and partly from the thawing of the ice. It flows very fast on all sides and is very rocky, clear, and icy cold. (2) The ice in the middle is raised up and then slopes down toward the edges. What thaws in the middle gathers in rivulets and channels on the ice and flows constantly confused around and around like in a labyrinth. Toward the south is a lake on the ice about a hundred feet long and forty-two to forty-eight feet wide, whose water and the edges of the ice are incomparably beautiful to behold, like Cyprian copper sulfate. The rivulets in the ice look more greenish. (3) The whole sheet of ice is situated right on rocks torn from the surrounding cliffs and polished by meltwater. The site is just like in the previous three places. [Presumably the other icy phenomena mentioned above.] Toward the east rise many very high cone-shaped mountains like sugar cones, not separated by valleys but contiguous at their base. In front are also low forested foothills of approximately ninety feet,[9] and thus they do not let sunlight through.

In comparison to those, the mountains toward the north are lower. Their slopes are less steep and flatten out further until in three to four kilometers they form a valley across from this sheet of ice, giving the north winds freer access. Toward the south a series of high, very broad mountains rises, so you have both very cold weather in the summer and a steady wind from various directions, as it is repelled whenever it hits the mountains and valleys. Toward the west, however, are dense larch forests about four kilometers behind this icy mountain range; consequently, warm winds are blocked from this direction as well. The ice itself is located in a bowl-like valley. When you have crossed the low mountains of 108 or so feet high, there is an ice-free lake one kilometer to the east, which contains lake minnows and [crucian] carp. But this lake is located 48 to 54 feet higher, and because there are no mountains close to its shore for 300 to 360 feet, it is more exposed to the sun. By the way, there is nothing mysterious about this sheet of ice or about the wind rock on the Belaya River as the fantasizing Yakut inhabitants believe, who have no insight into physical phenomena. Then we passed a moss-covered mountain and landed in a bog. From there we crossed another moss-covered mountain and entered a beautiful forest on the river, where we spent the night, having covered fifteen to sixteen kilometers. This sheet of ice is assumed to be halfway between Yuna and Yudoma Cross. The evening was rather pleasant, and we anticipated a good morning.

Monday, July 28. Our hopes for good weather were dashed. In the morning it started to rain so hard that I—having taken pity on my servant and given orders not to bother with putting up the tent and thus sleeping out in the open—got so wet, my bed included, that there was not a dry spot on me. On top of that, all my traveling clothes, including stockings and shoes, suffered the same embarrassment. While it was still raining, I had to stand by the fire, barefoot and wearing only a shirt. When I was dry in front, I'd gotten wet in the back again, until finally the rain slowed down and my clothes quickly dried. But I had barely put them on when I suffered acute abdominal pains, which subsided after a quick case of diarrhea and a cup of spirits with Mynsicht's Elixir.[10] Toward evening the sun started to shine a bit, if only momentarily and mockingly. We made ready for the next morning's departure, dried out our gear, rigged a tarpaulin, set up tents, and thus ended this day full of grief and work. But as he did in the past, may God grant me a good stomach to digest everything well in the future. Up to now I've been hardworking and high-spirited.

Tuesday, July 29. The rain continued all day, and we had to stay put. I found the first mushrooms—red-capped scaber stalk [*Leccinum aurantiacum* (Bull. ex St Am.) S. F. Gray s.l.; Jäger]—and lettuce [*Lactuca sativa* L.; Jäger] from seed lost en route, but I despaired of finding vinegar and oil. A roast, which is to say a dead horse, lay nearby. Other than that, I examined my plants.

Wednesday, July 30. It was pleasant all day, but rather cool. Toward evening, however, it started to rain and continued off and on all night. In the morning we went for approximately eight kilometers through a lot of bogs and forest streams. And with great effort, via an amazingly bad trail at the base of a rough sandstone cliff covered with Siberian dwarf pine trees, we came to a rain-swollen river that the Yakuts call Lying Crosswise because you have to cross it diagonally to the trail, and there most of my gear fell into the water. Much of the gunpowder in particular was spoiled, as well as Chinese paper and my books; and, worst of all, *Willoughbey's Ichthyology* was totally ruined. I had to take it apart leaf by leaf and dry it out as well as all my observations, among which my journal fell into the other extreme and caught fire.[11]

Across the river the terrain between the mountains was broader, clearer, and flat, and covered by a sparse forest of larch trees, through which we covered seven kilometers and then made camp at a small river, stayed the day, and dried out our gear, assessing the damage to mine at a hundred rubles, which, tired of moisture as I was, I had to view with dry eyes. I was especially chagrined by the loss of two and a half buckets of double brandy that alone, counting the local value with freight, amounted to thirty rubles. I discovered that it had leaked out en route. The remainder turned out to be just about a bottle, which I emptied together with my companions in order to bid the broken bottle [*sic*; presumably Steller meant the bucket] farewell. I then had it hung in a tree like a magic drum. We butchered a cow here, too, which had lost its ability to ruminate, so that we might replace its cud-chewing with our eager teeth. Around midnight we dined without light in our tent, reminding ourselves that the banquets in the realm of the dead would be set up in the same way, and after that we betook ourselves, wet as we were, into our wet beds to rest.

Thursday, July 31. The weather was nice all day; we saw the sun again in its splendor, in which we continued to dry out our gear. Toward evening a Scottish merchant and [helmsman] Khitrov's convoy passed us. The former had made it here from Yakutsk in four weeks.

Friday, August 1. We started out very early. We had barely covered two kilometers when one of my driver's horses impaled itself, dying on the spot, and right before my eyes was butchered and quartered into a Yakut banquet. After covering six kilometers, we came to another sheet of ice, the makeup of the place similar to the previous one. Today ice formed for the first time on the water. After three kilometers we came to the Akachan River, which flowed very fast and high. I found a shallow place and crossed it with twenty horses without a problem. The rest of my convoy coming after me could not find the place and got so scattered that my servant went with Aleksei [Danilov] across the mountains, and I didn't see him again until the next day toward evening. The two other soldiers with ten horses took yet another route.

Toward noon we had covered fifteen kilometers but had had nothing to eat or drink. Here again we found a very large sheet of ice, which had the same characteristics as the previous one, though it was much larger than the one we came across five days ago. I found here another beautiful saxifrage, which I had sketched the other day. And smoking my pipe because I had no food, I continued on my way across a mossy and very boggy mountain with a large lake on the summit. From there we descended, and I went ahead with the student Gorlanov to reconnoiter the Akachan River, which we had to cross again way behind the sheet of ice, both of us getting in so deep that we were swimming up to our belts with the horses in the river. Here we caught sight of my servant with Aleksei, but they couldn't join us. Ivan Almasov, however, was ahead with the surveyor, Ushakov, and the [apprentice] instrument maker, Ovsianikov. Because I met Mr. Berckhan here, I downed a bowl of elixir with him in celebration. I then left the student Gorlanov behind to show their convoy the ford, that is, the shallow place in the river, while I went with Mr. Berckhan into the forest at the foot of the mountains.

At a burned-over place, we came to terrible boglands. After covering seven kilometers, we happened upon Khitrov's party, who was spending the night in a bog. In answer to our question, they replied that our people were ahead, camping not far from us. So even though it was already quite dark, we continued on our way over mountains and through valleys, grassy tundra, and bogs. Seeing only lakes on the right, we traversed one mountain after another; finding neither our advance party nor a place to camp, I and Mr. Berckhan just about decided to light a fire and spend the night together in the woods but kept on going. That's when I noticed that my horse, named Daurken, was a very good botanist and more knowledgeable about nature than I, because it wanted to make its way consistently on the white cushion moss [*Leucobryum glaucum* (Hedw.) Angstr.; Jäger], not on the green sphagnum, aware that rocks lie right under the former, which gives you a sure step, but pitfalls and big bogs underlie the latter.

Then we came into a valley and once again went up a mountain covered with moss. Proceeding diagonally down a mountain to another lake, Mr. Berckhan informed me that he couldn't see or distinguish anything with his eyes anymore but would follow me blindly, taking his chances with my pair of spectacles. Luckily I found the way across the marsh around the lake, and we came to another rocky, burned-over mountain. We climbed up it and saw the moon rise, as well as a phenomenon that lit half the horizon like the brightest bolt of lightning starting at the moon. The colors of the rainbow were clearly recognizable in it.[12] After we had crossed the scene of the fire down the slope, we came to nonstop rocks on the left bank of the Akachan River. With our horses we clattered across those, without a trail, guided only by my imagination, and finally heard Mr. Berckhan's dog bark. Thinking that our advance party couldn't be far now gave us new courage. Our horses noticed that and began to pace, having previously been walking like exhausted altos.[13] We got across the rocks to a trail leading into the woods, where I, too, lost my ability to see and transferred the office of trail-finder to my Daurken. Shortly thereafter we saw campfires and joined our crew who had gone on ahead of us. As upset as we were with them for having preceded us by forty-five kilometers seemingly without realizing it, we were, nonetheless, immediately mollified when they explained that they had not found fodder for the horses anywhere, and at the same time we noticed the teakettle and the meat pot on the tripod, the contents of which, famished as we were, we attacked with great gusto. After we had eaten and drunk, we intended to sing the *Te Deum Laudamus*. But I didn't want to start because Mr. Berckhan had greater reason for it than I; he had his servant, his tent, and his bed, while I was deprived of all those. So I lit another pipe, lay down in front of the fire, put my head on my saddle, and congratulated myself on having this illumination lit for me alone all night. But since I was lying barefoot and in my shirt on the bare ground, I became very cold during the night when the fire went out, and not wanting to bother the servants, I took my hunting knife into the woods and dragged out as much wood as roasting my carcass would require.

Sunday, August 2. We departed at noon, advanced five kilometers, and again had to stay put because of the rain. By evening all my people were with me again. But then once again I received two pieces of happy news: (1) that my own horse with a local value of fifteen rubles had gotten lost and (2) that a draft horse was busy giving up its ghost with all fours in the air. This reminded me of the little rhyme I had often written in my exercise book at school: "If you love to write, a boring time you can fight." So I wrote in my journal as I was thinking about the history of the Yakuts. I especially like the way the Yakuts name their children, examples of which follow.

I had a driver called Uthghysaeh, which is Yakut for daughter of a dog. Because he was also a shaman, he sometimes—falsely—pretended to have fanciful revelations all night long, like a *studiosus daemonologiae* of old. If a horse got lost, he shamanned, just for practice, where it was and when it would be found. He told a driver named Slepushka, meaning the blind one, that his eyes must be hurting. Another driver had paronychia [L, an inflammation of the nails]; thus with his prophecies this shaman served his people as a traveling pastor.[14]

So I asked the reason for his name, especially since, even if his father and mother had been dogs, he was not a daughter but a son of a dog, and he told me the following story. His mother had been barren in her marriage for a long time, and so her husband came to hate her and was ready to trade her in. But because she had a bitch in her yurt who had whelped a sizable number of pups twice every year, his mother had gotten the idea of secretly transferring the dog's fertility to herself. To that end she had offered the dog a piece of fat horsemeat as if to feed it to her. When the dog had half swallowed it while she had the other half still in her hands, she pulled the dog around with it until the dog angrily had to let it slide out of its throat, slathered in saliva. Immediately the woman had greedily swallowed the piece of meat and had become pregnant shortly thereafter, had given birth to him, and in commemoration of this event had given him the name Dog's Daughter. When I asked him how he thought this could have happened, he answered—it sounds ridiculous—that both the human and the dogs' gods hang on one horsehair, by which he meant to say that the gods work together. And what you could not receive from your guardian spirit, you could just as well ask and receive of another idol, and that would not create jealousy between them.

My second driver was called Myrsilla, and he gave the following etymological reason for his name: "When I was born, I was quite puny, skinny, and full of wrinkles like a piece of leather shrunk from too much heat. When, in spite of that, I continued to grow and even thrived, my mother named me in memory of my miserable birth, Myrsilla, Shriveled One."

My third driver's name was Erkaehwill. He was named after a Tungus with the same name who was the first to come into the yurt after my driver's birth. In Tungus this name means a mother's boy, a spoiled one, and the meaning of his name truly applied to him, because he was not only the smallest and weakest but also the messiest, laziest, and least likable among all the drivers. He caused more damage to my gear than the bastard was worth in body and soul.

Ushakov's driver was named Sobong, and he told me that his father had been a wealthy man. At the time of his birth, his father had caught a huge mess of carp, and because two happy events had occurred in his family at the same time, his father had named him in commemoration Sobong Karasnik, Carp Child—*sobo* being the Yakut word for carp, and *karasnik* the Russian for aficionado of carp [WH, Anm. 1301, 1302].

Gorlanov's driver was called Polloss, which in Yakut means sausage mouth, in Latin *labeo*, having thick lips, in Russian *guban*, fat mouth. He told the following story. His father had been a well-to-do man who'd had many horses, including mares, and consequently also had a lot of kumis, a great abundance of which stood all around the yurt in *simirren*, leather hoses. Polloss had not yet been given a name, but because he could already walk, he had always had ready access to the kumis. So it happened that, while tippling, he had once fallen and badly cut his mouth on a hose. His lips had swollen, and so his father had named him Sausage Mouth.

As a joke the Russians had named our cattle driver at birth Sachot, meaning a two-year-old reindeer, a name many are said to have. A few days later, the commissar had come and written down the families' names, but he had not wanted to record this name in the book again and so named him Üth, meaning Dog. On this occasion I also heard that the Yakuts do not like to be called by their full name because they are afraid the devil could learn the name or, hearing it, could remember it and then eat or ruin them. The biggest cuss word among them is *kaeraech*, meaning old baldy or old fogey [literally, used-up one, burned-out one; WH, Anm. 1312, 1313], and they get very embittered when they are called that.

Sunday, August 3. It was dreary all day, and the night before it had rained heavily again and continued until noon. We took off after noon and had gone two kilometers when we came to a stream that ran so high from the rain we had to go to the trouble of building a bridge across it. But the swift, rising water kept sweeping the bridge away, so that we had to keep repairing it again and again until midnight and still could not prevent some horses with the gear falling in. To my utter chagrin, this misfortune had the severest consequence for my packet of dried plants, so that I spent the following day drying them out again, some by the fire and some in the air. My crew didn't arrive until the next day, but I went ahead with Mr. Berckhan.

Covering four kilometers across just moss and bogs, we again came to an even larger, swifter, swollen forest stream. Several times I tried to determine its depth but had to turn back drenched and freezing, the only hope being that the water would go down overnight. On top of that, I had to spend the whole night by a fire without a tent or bed, being invigorated by a steady drenching rain.

Monday, August 4. We noticed that in spite of the rain the water had gone down quite a bit. As soon as my convoy arrived, I had them build another bridge across the stream. While they worked, I dried my newly baptized plants. Toward evening we moved our gear across our ingenious larch bridge and made another five kilometers until the night and bogs forced us to stop by a stream. Thank God, it was pleasant, sunny weather all day.

Tuesday, August 5. The weather was pleasant and sunny during the day and the night without rain, though it froze so hard that in the morning all the streams were covered with an icy skin. Here the plain between the mountains gradually widens. In the morning we had covered approximately four kilometers when once again one of my mares got stuck in the morass, and we actually had to leave her behind. We again came to a forest stream over which we had to build a bridge. From here we had a good trail for about eight kilometers, but then till Yudoma Cross we had to get through big marshy areas. After we had covered fifteen kilometers, we took a one-hour lunch break on a lake, into which I sank my pilgrim's beard after I'd had it shaved off. From there we traveled through nothing but more marshland for eight kilometers and came to the Yudoma River, across which we saw Mr. Gregorei Gregor'evich [Skornyakov-] Pisarev's [then still commander of

Okhotsk, being replaced by Devier] ambars and house and two kilometers upriver the other storage sheds and houses.

I, Gorlanov, and Ovsianikov [apprentice instrument maker] had ridden ahead and lost our way, crossing awful bogs and streams and finally coming to a branch of the Yudoma in which Ovsianikov, along with his horse, almost drowned while trying to reconnoiter. Even though we didn't drown, we ended up plenty wet. Luckily we encountered carpenters and soldiers who ferried us across the swift and terribly swollen Yudoma. There we found our crew, who reported how our convoy was standing at the same branch of the river but couldn't cross because of the high water and had to wait for it to go down. They thus ruined my hope of getting hold of my bed, food, and brandy. So I stuck to my pipe and tobacco. I found that Professor la Croyère's wife, Mar'ia Dmitreevna, was here [in Yudoma Cross], but in my shabby clothes I did not want to pay her my respects. However, she immediately sent me tea and had a piece of salted meat prepared for me. I was staying right across from her in a black room by the fireplace.[15] And I was overjoyed to once again have soft bread to eat because I was pretty tired of chewing hardtack. And because I received a nice feather bed from the professor's wife, I slept in sweetest comfort all night long.

Wednesday, August 6. The weather was pleasant and sunny all day. To my delight the water in the Yudoma and its branches receded so much that by 10:00 a.m. I saw my entire crew by the fire. I immediately had a wagon sent across the river for transporting our gear to us, and by evening we had brought over all of it. Together with my entourage I paid Madame de la Croyère a visit, and we dined with her; afterward I stayed in my quarters in order to further dry my plants. The others, however, retired a kilometer upriver to stay with the gear.

Thursday, August 7. The weather was like yesterday, but the night was freezing cold. I went back for my gear, and we finished transporting it and also had the horses and cattle swim across. I took a beef quarter, green and black tea, and sugar to the professor's wife, took a bath, and prepared myself for the next day's travel.

Yudoma Cross was built on the Yudoma River, which flows into the Maya River, and they together flow into the Aldan River and so on into the Lena River. The Yudoma has Siberian taimen, common whitefish, sharp-snouted lenok, burbot, and Arctic grayling but not in large numbers. On both sides of its banks, horrendous mountains alternate with cliffs, and the riverbed itself is so rocky that no oven clay or clay deposits have yet

Fig. 15.1. Transporting gear by wagon to Yudoma Cross (Arnold).

been discovered in the whole area. Nevertheless, even with all the rocks, everything in this area is boggy and full of puddles, and thus many yellow cloudberries [*Rubus chamaemorus* L.; Jäger], lingonberries [*Vaccinium vitis-idaea* L.], and currants grow here. And I noticed that from the Belaya River to here all the berries are longish, more oval than round. The grass is very short, thin, and hard, and only poor *Carex* grass [Jäger] grows from the Belaya River to here, but there is a great abundance of lichen for the reindeer. The reason for this lack of fertility is undoubtedly all the flooding icy streams and rivers that freeze the roots.[16] Half a kilometer above Yudoma Cross, a river flows into the Yudoma from the right.

Friday, August 8. The weather was the same as yesterday. But toward evening after sunset, it began to rain. We spent almost the whole day rounding up our horses, who had scattered far and wide to find forage. I had to leave my roan acquired in Ust'Ilginsk behind because it was impossible to find him. We traveled through nonstop mountainous and hilly terrain that was covered with moss and provided our horses constant admittance to two, three, or four feet of boggy muck. Finally, around nine at night, we came to a beautiful grassy place and a well-built foliage hut, where we spent the night.

Notes

1. In text, *ausruhen, ausfressen und ausheilen*, an unconventional play on words we have tried to emulate.
2. The Eurasian jay, *Garrulus glandarius*, or oak jay, with many subspecies. Springer, pers. comm., August 24, 2016; in text, *Ronsche*.

3. Presumably Emel'ian Basov, an Okhotsk sergeant. WH, Anm. 1170.

4. Salvia is commonly known as sage. Possibly not *Salvia*, which has only two species in the Far East, neither of which fits Steller's description in *Fl. Och.* No. 117; perhaps a member of the *Scutellaria alpina* L.-group, but it grows on moist sites. Unidentified; see above, July 20. The sticky five-leaved plant is possibly *Potentilla longifolia* Willd. ex D.F.K.Schltdl. syn: *P. viscosa* Donn. Jäger.

5. Peas a best guess for filling the hole in the manuscript, . . . *sen*, presumably *Erbsen*.

6. Abundant species in Yakutia are *Gentiana aquatic* L.; *G. prostrata* Haenke , common name, pygmy gentian; and *G. pseudoaquatica* Kusn. syn. of *G. aquatica* var. *pseudoaquatica* (Kusn.) S. Agrawal. Not a *Myosotis*, forget-me-not, in the actual sense, but a relative of *Stellaria aquatica* (L.) Scop., water chickweed, Caryophyllaceae, *Fl. Och.* No. 186. Jäger.

7. Probably an ice patch. It "exists in a delicate balance between winter snow accumulation and summer melting. The snow is gradually compressed into ice." *Frozen Past. Yukon Ice Patches*, Gov. of Yukon, 2011. "The largest, longest-lived ice patches in Alaska and the Yukon seem to be found on the northern sides of rounded or flat-topped mountains with large snow accumulation areas. The tops of these mountains are generally below the altitude where glaciers form. Snow blows across the mountaintop in the winter and accumulates in the snow patch, which, if it doesn't melt away the next summer, can develop an ice core. If ice patches get big enough, they might creep but don't actually flow like a glacier." Richard VanderHoek, Alaska Office of History and Archaeology, email, January 27, 2017. "Ice patches are not rare in Eastern Siberia and Central Asia and can be preserved for centuries." Jäger, email, January 20, 2017.

8. In text, literally, "a type of buttercup I had never seen before"; not mentioned in *Fl. Och.*, both *Ranunculus monophyllos* Ovcz. and a species of *Halerpestes* Greene are possibilities. Jäger.

9. In text, fifteen fathoms, which seems rather low.

10. A tincture developed by Adrian von Mynsicht (1603–38), a German physician and alchemist. WH, Anm. 1232.

11. Possibly the missing part from March 30 to April 20 from Kirenskoi Ostrog. WH, Anm. 1241; see above, p. 97.

12. Unclear if these were northern lights or some other celestial phenomenon.

13. Likely a reference to Steller's participation in his school's choir. WH, Anm. 1278. As a former member of the *Alumneum*, the boarding school, Steller may recall here the fatiguing weekly serenades the singers were required to present at well-to-do citizens' houses.

14. In text, *paronychiane*. Quoting Pierer, author of a nineteenth-century encyclopedia, Hintzsche suggests Steller is making a pun between paronychia, considered an early symptom of syphilis, and a church congregation—that is, parishioners (WH, Anm. 1292). That would explain Steller's follow-up reference to the traveling pastor. Steller clearly considers the shaman to be a charlatan.

15. A black room has a stove but no stovepipe. WH, Anm. 1327.

16. Perhaps the temperature also has an influence on fertility, but the main factor would be the low content of nutrients in the bedrock. Jäger.

16

FROM YUDOMA CROSS TO OKHOTSK (8/9–8/13)

Saturn-Jupiter Saturday, August 9.[1] It rained the entire morning, but in the afternoon it was bright and clear though the night was rather nippy and cold. We had ridden about two kilometers through fearsome bogs when I suddenly heard yelling and my name called out several times in quick succession. My curiosity drove me willy-nilly through the muck, and there I saw Captain Spangberg, whom I no more expected to see than Death himself and therefore didn't recognize; that is to say, I couldn't believe my eyes because in Yakutsk we had accompanied him up the Lena River and wished him well on his trip to St. Petersburg. We fell into each other's arms. Right away he explained how the Cabinet in St. Petersburg had ordered him, via courier, to go to Okhotsk, and so he had returned from Ust'Kutsk. We joked about this and that until we came to a stream, which [Skornyakov-]Pisarev had wanted to link to the Urak River by a canal even though one of them flows north and the other toward the south, and thirty kilometers of impregnable rock would've had to have been dug through. Here we stopped to eat lunch under a *balagan*,[2] recorded our meeting on a tree, and, while lunch was being prepared, held a target-shooting match with the prize being a cup of spiced brandy, the competition continuing until not a single drop was left in the bottle.

After the meal my convoy arrived and reported that once again a horse had fallen and died. I decided to join the captain in riding ahead as couriers. The captain gave me a spare horse so that I could give up my Daurken to the convoy to replace the fallen one. We had ridden ahead for barely two kilometers when I had the luck to sink, along with my horse, into the morass for the first and last time on this trail. In jumping off I landed under the horse and was hospitably received by the muck, becoming, so to speak, the meat

Fig. 16.1. Eating lunch under a balagan (Arnold).

in the mud soup. I crawled out with my peasant smock newly dyed brown, washed myself off, and continued the journey, wet as I was; therefore, the sun felt especially good to me. We were riding along, a bunch of disintegrating limestone mountains covered with Siberian dwarf pine to our left and only bogland and hummocks to our right. Here, too, the mountains from the headwaters of the Urak came into our view, lining the whole horizon in front of us. After making thirty kilometers, we came to a lake between the mountains separated here by only two kilometers. On this lake, which is said to be full of fish, there is a hut [presumably another way-station].

We passed between the mountains through endless bogland, and at the headwaters of the Urak we came to a very rocky, forested trail. The dark night robbed us of our vision—we couldn't see a thing—but we continued through the valleys for fifteen kilometers until around midnight. Having braved and overcome breakneck perils, we came out of a valley at a tall cross, where the captain, who had ridden ahead, welcomed me with tea and congratulated me with brandy on my initiation as a courier. We ate a quick meal of butter and hardtack; then, lying down on my saddle, I went to sleep by the fire and dried my clothes until morning when, having drunk our tea, we imbibed a cup of brandy, grabbed some hardtack, and continued our ride between the mountains.

Sunday, August 10. After five to six kilometers, we came to another cross on a dry plain along the Urak; crossing it, we saw Basov's convoy still asleep to our right. We rode along the right bank of the Urak through beautiful forests. Approximately seventy kilometers from Yudoma Cross, a rocky stream flows into the Urak on the left from the north, widening the Urak's channel and turning it into a river. We crossed the Urak several times, and at about 1:00 p.m. we arrived at Uratsky Wharf, built to the right of the Urak on a hill. It includes a magazine, a dormitory for workers along with a room for the officer as well as several peasant houses, and a stockaded powder magazine, which was built by Lieutenant Walton on Captain Spangberg's orders. In winter, provisions from Yudoma Cross are brought here with incredible exertion on sleds, sometimes pulled by dogs, sometimes by people. Beside provisions for people and dogs, only 180 pounds can be transported in one load. In spring, flat-bottomed boats that can carry 108,000 pounds are built here. Because lumber is abundant, five people can accomplish this in three days, and then the boats are floated to Okhotsk in the spring at high water. Without landing along the way, they get to the mouth of the river and into the sea in thirteen hours, which is what Lt. Waxell did. Usually, however, it takes thirty-six hours. The boats are then towed from the mouth fifteen kilometers along the coast to Okhotsk, where they are unloaded and reused for building houses. The Urak is very shallow and spreads out wide in summer. But that there is no other river with such a swift current can be seen from the fact that it takes the boat only thirteen hours to go the 250 kilometers [at most 200; Jäger] from the wharf to Okhotsk.

Besides the fish that migrate from the ocean in July and August, the Urak has grayling that, even though they do not differ overall from the

Siberian ones [Arctic grayling], nevertheless look quite different. First, they are much blacker; second, the dorsal fin is so incredibly long that the outermost spine of the composite fin reaches the adipose fin; and, third, the gill fins are longer too. Thus, one can see that the length of each fin is not commensurate with the proportions of the fish.

Transporting provisions from Yakutsk to Yudoma Cross costs a ruble per thirty-six pounds whereas purchasing these same provisions in Yakutsk costs twenty to fifty kopecks. Transportation to the Uratsky Wharf costs thirty-five kopecks per thirty-six pounds and to Okhotsk forty kopecks so that in Okhotsk thirty-six pounds of flour come to between one ruble seventy-five kopecks and two rubles. No prince in Europe lives so extravagantly when it comes to eating bread. While Captain Spangberg had the meal prepared, I climbed up a tall mountain and noticed two species of saxifrage and a *Symphytum* with leaves like *Vincetoxicum* [*Mertensia rivularis* (Turcz.) DC.; Jäger] and collected their seeds. On the summit of the mountain, I found very large pieces of green jasper and at its foot a green but not very dense siliceous soil in which perhaps the Isaac Hollands' green is halfway turning into the redness of universal soil.[3] But what most surprises me is that I found good ferruginous soil and rock very close to the wharf, which no one has observed so far even though there is a great need for it and, especially now with the expedition, this metal is almost as precious as silver. The lazy and unreliable assay master, Gardebol, being paid a sinful salary of 3,200 rubles for nothing, has not been able to find in eight years what struck me just in passing on my courier ride, and even if the metal were poor, there must clearly be richer finds in the vicinity. After we had spent approximately two hours there, we continued on our way, sometimes through forests, sometimes across mountains, but mostly through plains, and at nine in the evening we camped in a place that had excellent pasture for our cattle. All day long we had fine, sunny weather.

Monday, August 11. The weather was the same as yesterday. We left our camp before daybreak, crossed the first or smaller channel approximately twenty-five kilometers from our camp, and met Poluekhtov, a syn boyarskoi from Okhotsk, who was on his way to Yudoma Cross to transport provisions. He reported that the captain commander was planning to sail in three days and that the wives of both the commander and Captain Chirikov were on the way back, being carried in sedan chairs. After having traveled thirty-five kilometers, we took an hour's break, ate, and then went through exceptionally beautiful meadows and forests at the foot of the mountains and across a river, in the evening camping on the Bludnaya River, which flows into the Urak. The Bludnaya—that is, Lost River—gets its name from the fact that soldiers en route from Okhotsk to the Urak lost their way and mistook it for the Urak, crossing it upriver. The area is extraordinarily pleasant; it produces very tall, excellent grass that grows along the Urak to Okhotsk. Therefore, Pisarev ordered Yakuts to be settled here to herd Her Majesty's cattle.

Tuesday, August 12. The weather was like yesterday—that is, sunny. We left early in the morning and toward noon arrived at the second large river channel, which, because it was so deep and fast, we forded under great peril, swimming across with our horses. We continued ten kilometers upriver, not far from the dangerous falls. In this area the banks of the Urak are rocky, not too high, but very steep; and we soon went up a rocky hill where we found a lot of yellow cloudberries [see above, August 7]. I collected the seeds from a species of saxifrage with sticky leaves [unidentified; Jäger]. When we were on top of the hill, Captain Spangberg—to my delight—called to my attention that we could see the area of Okhotsk. Then we went slowly down the mossy hill, and because I was picking cloudberries I became separated from my companion and at the same time lost my horse. But I found it again after having run after it for a few kilometers. Then we—my horse and I—passed through the loveliest of meadows and forests, where I found a bushy clubmoss and purple mountain saxifrage.[4] So I continued on my way until around ten in the evening, when I found the captain already camped on the river. At that point we were still ten kilometers from Okhotsk.

Wednesday, August 13. The weather was sunny like yesterday. In the morning we proceeded through the most beautiful meadows, where we came upon some Yakut stations. I noticed a *Senecio* with triangular leaves and smaller, snowy white blossoms with purple tips, but I couldn't dismount to gather it for my collection.[5]

After covering thirty kilometers, we came to a river, forded it, and continued along its high, rocky, clay-colored bank until we again came to a flat area. In another ten kilometers, we came to the *Medvezh'ya Golova*, the Bear's Head [WH, Anm. 1428], a mountain that got its name from a bear who had killed several people in this area. Captain Spangberg had first wounded it with a shot and had ultimately done it in with a hunting knife. In commemoration the captain had its head hung in a tree, which promptly gave the place its name. Four kilometers further, we came to some Russian fisher yurts.

Fig. 16.2. Steller and Spangberg riding toward Okhotsk (Arnold).

We rode until two in the afternoon, at which time we reached the swift-flowing Okhota River, which is incredibly wide and dotted with a lot of islands. On its left bank are very tall, big mountains. From there we came to the place where the old ostrog had previously stood four kilometers from the present Okhotsk and then to a channel of the Okhota, which we were ferried across, and there, for the first time, we laid eyes on the ocean, the Sea of Okhotsk. This channel and its mouth did not exist until four years ago, 1736, and are three kilometers away from the other main mouth and the harbor. Unfortunately, its division into two channels has so weakened the current in the main mouth that it isn't strong enough to wash away the sand that the ocean frequently deposits there. Over time the mouth has become so clogged that you can only sail out to the right in the calmest weather or with a very light north or northwest wind. And if you sail between the sandbar and up the coastline until you are parallel with the church, you can then run northward freely into the ocean. While there is still a channel in the middle of the Okhota, it is dangerous even when the tide is in, as Mr. Sofron Fedorovich Khitrov discovered, to his dismay, in the double sloop that ran aground on a sandbar and barely escaped from suffering considerable damage.

From the first mouth we rode toward the Okhotsk sandbar [that appears at low tide] across continuous gravel or small washed-up stones, which clattered as if we were riding on hazelnuts, and at four in the afternoon arrived in town. All heads went up at our arrival; all of Okhotsk came alive, everybody bursting with curiosity to know what in the world it meant seeing Captain Spangberg arrive with me, having assumed him to be back in St. Petersburg or not far from it.

We dismounted at Captain Commander Bering's house, whose dear wife was just then lounging in the window, looking down at the sedan chairs all ready for the next day's departure. After we had greeted her, and Bering's son had mistaken me in my peasant smock and raincoat for Captain Spangberg's servant, this young commander gave me the first order—namely, that I was to escort my dog out the door, my faithful Lastochka [a gift from Devier?; see above, p. 110] being overly excited to see all these high-class people. I obeyed his order to the merriment of the others, who had just been advised by the captain that I was the new adjunct, and told them that I sincerely wished this might be the first and last dog I had to escort. Amid the laughter the captain commander himself appeared and embraced us, and shortly thereafter Captain Chirikov and Lieutenant Chikhachev also showed up.

We asked leave, and I went home with Captain Spangberg, where we were greeted by Lieutenants Waxell, Walton, and Plautin; midshipman Scheltinga, who had recently returned from his Japanese trip; Mr. Dement'ev [helmsman]; and Khitrov. Here I received two packets of letters and plants from Dr. Gmelin. After having dined there, I went with Mr. Chemodurov to see Professor la Croyère, and from there we secured our quarters, where I enjoyed a long conversation with midshipman Krasil'nikov until almost midnight and after midnight went to bed at my host Paramonov's [yasak collector] place.

Notes

1. Saturn-Jupiter Day: when Saturn and Jupiter are both visible twenty degrees from each other above the horizon. WH, Anm. 1347; Jäger. "These meetings of Jupiter and Saturn, called 'Great Conjunctions,' usually happen in years divisible by 20—and always in the constellation of Taurus, Virgo, or Capricornus, although sometimes on the boundary of some adjacent constellation, which is why the Virgo conjunctions are sometimes listed as Libra.... The Great Conjunctions in Taurus, every 60 years find the planets very high up, and thus particularly noteworthy. We last saw that in 2000. The next are in 2016 and 2120." "Jupiter and Saturn and the Great Conjunction Curse," hudsonvalleyone.com.

2. For the Yakuts a balagan is a mud-covered winter dwelling built of wood, consisting of living quarters and stable; in Kamchatka, storage sheds on stilts. WH, Anm. 1355. Possibly here, too, a shed on stilts.

3. The Isaac Hollands were Dutch father and son alchemists who lived at the beginning of the fifteenth century. WH, Anm. 1395. Presumably Steller meant the transition from iron disulfide, *Eisenkies*, by way of the mineral iron vitriol—green vitriol—through weathering to the resulting iron trisulfate and thus reddish, red-brown iron trioxide. WH, Anm. 1397.

4. A bushy clubmoss is probably either *Lycopodium complanatum* L. or *L. alpinum* L.; both are bushy and occur on the Urak. Jäger. In text, "a creeping saxifrage with leaves like thyme."

5. This *Senecio* is *Parasenecio hastatus* (L.) H. Koyama (syn.: *Cacalia hastata* L.), a frequent member of the Senecioneae in the Eurasiatic taiga zone. Jäger.

17

IN OKHOTSK (8/14–8/26)

Thursday, August 14. The weather was sunny like yesterday. I visited Mr. la Croyère, dined at his place, then went botanizing on the beach, and from there went together with the professor to Mr. Spangberg's.

Friday, August 15. The weather was again like yesterday. At the professor's place, I found four boxes of plants and artifacts sent from Kamchatka by the student Krasheninnikov that were to be shipped to St. Petersburg. I examined the boxes and found them much too big for transport; I therefore decided to have them repacked into smaller ones. I put into leather sacks whatever could be transported in them. The fish and birds as well as the animals and clothes had begun to acquire a patina; I had those cleaned.

Saturday, August 16. Mr. Devier sent word that a whale had been stranded forty kilometers from Okhotsk. I received visits from Corporal Plenisner [later commander of Okhotsk]; an aristocrat from Courland, an especially skilled and well-mannered man; Mr. Furman, a Livonian nobleman; surgeon Feige; the two assistant surgeons Lau and Bethge; Mr. Vasilei Alekseevich Rtishchev, helmsman of the packet boat *St. Peter*; commissar Lagunov; midshipman Choglokov, the shipbuilder—ha' ha'[1]—and Mr. Anton Emmanuilovich Devier. After they left, I took the boat to the other side of the Okhota River, accompanied by three soldiers and Mr. Lau. From there we took horses to the Marikan River. En route we encountered a stranded porpoise or pig of the sea [possibly a Dall's porpoise—*Phocoenoides dalli*—abundant in the Sea of Okhotsk; Slaght, email, July 20, 2018], which I dissected. It breathes via lungs and eats fish, stones, and various shellfish. But because it stank badly and lots of those are to be had on Kamchatka, I left it behind. I found the following plants: a gentian with sky-blue flowers and leaves like pimpernel; a low-lying succulent with short, thick leaves and purple-red blossoms; a succulent with pale yellow flowers, leaves generally

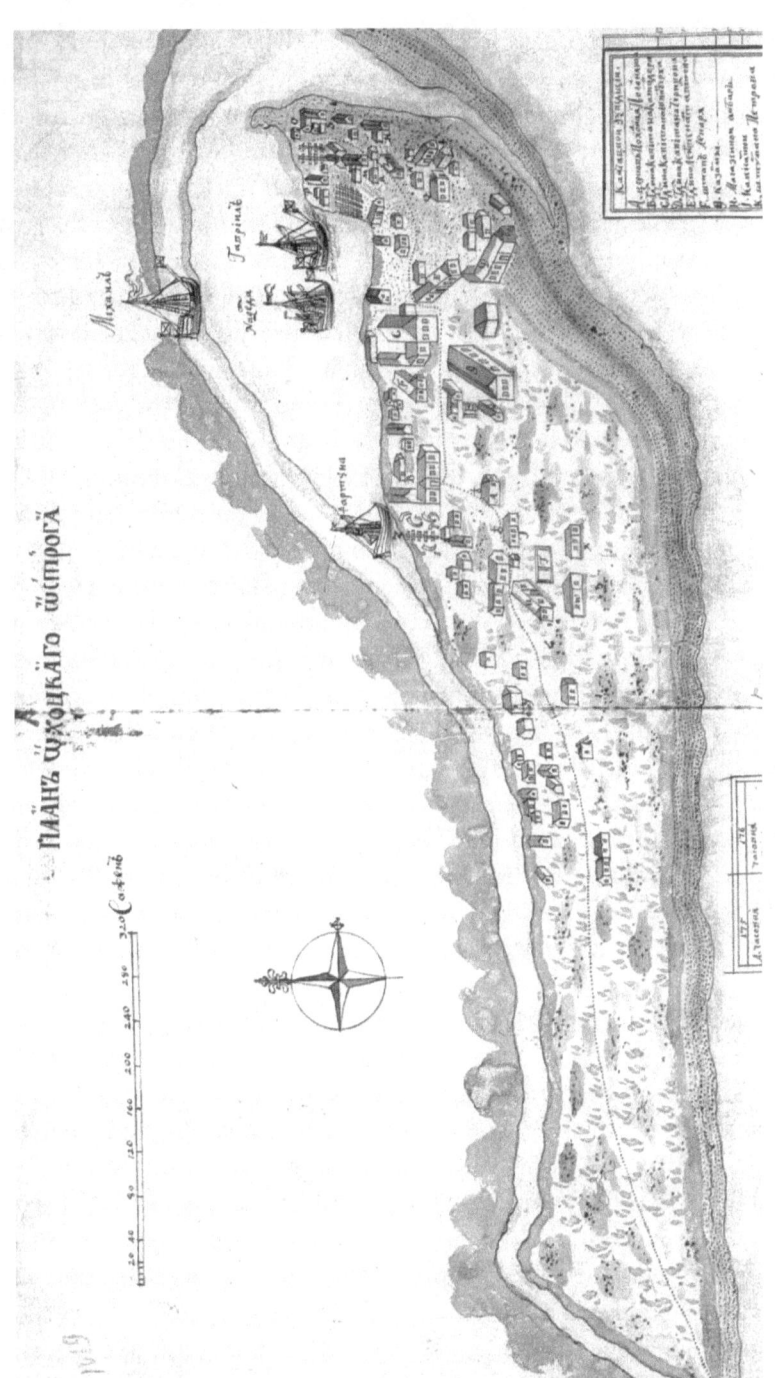

Map 17.1. Okhotskoi Ostrog, 1737 (State Marine Archive St. Petersburg; Wikimedia Commons).

deeply serrated; a rhododendron with showy rose-red blossoms and round, green leaves flecked with dark brown; dwarf Swedish dogwood; a sarana lily with small, back-bending flowers; mountain ash with egg-like, very scarred berries; a burnet with rather long, white and red spikes; and beach aster [beach fleabane] shaped like *Helenium* with thick, grass-green, long leaves that are generally notched or scalloped. I was further told that cow parsnips are said to grow at the mouth of the Urak. I also found an oyster leaf, which is used in Okhotsk in place of lettuce; scurvy grass; and a kind of wild celery, which looks and tastes just like celery. I've cooked it several times with fish, and it aroused in me such a strong appetite for sex that I would not have declined having some.[2] Around nine in the evening, we came to the Marikan River, where we staked our horses and slept out in the open. This river is thirty kilometers from Okhotsk. It was pleasant all day, but the north wind was so strong, especially during the night, that I caught such a bad cold I had a runny nose and cough for several days.

Sunday, August 17. It was very cold and windy in the morning with old snow still on the mountains. We went another nine to ten kilometers and then came upon the whale washed up on the beach. But the head with the tongue, which the local people consider to be the greatest delicacy, was already gone, and the bears had already taken their share too. Because the whale was chewed up a lot and half buried in sand, I contented myself with having seen my first whale, having measured its length at fifty-four feet as well as having tasted a piece of boiled blubber. So I departed again around 11:00 a.m.

After we had been ferried across the Marikan River by the Tungus, I asked them about the so-called *zemlianaia smetana* or sour cream earth [the soft bolus soil that tastes like sour cream; WH, Anm. 1512]. Captain Spangberg had told me that during famines in earlier times working people had traveled to where it was found and eaten whole pots full. They had also administered it as dependable medicine for diarrhea caused by eating fish. Right away one of the Tungus assured us he was willing to lead us to the place, telling us at the same time that the Russians had learned the use of this mineral from the Tungus, who boil it in reindeer milk and eat it like mush made from flour, which, it is said, causes it to lose its astringency. During this conversation we came to a clay mountain, extending west to east, where I collected seeds of mountain heather with a square stem and white flower and of sorrel.[3]

At the foot of the mountain is a pond, and in it are three to four pits or springs in which this mineral is abundant, and no matter how much of it is taken, it constantly wells back up. It is white as snow, has the consistency of gelatin, tastes sweet, and if mixed with flour is like clabber milk. What lies lower than two feet is coarser and less pure, but I found rocky ground at six feet by pushing a stick down. You feel no astringent effect whatsoever in your mouth but a little in your throat. I didn't have time to test this at great length. I therefore took along a teakettle full and sent some of it in a beef bladder to Dr. Gmelin. I am thinking that it is a fine white clay corroded by underground salt, with the pond water diluting and rinsing and cleaning out the salt. By the way, this stuff could be used to manufacture fine porcelain.

On the trip home I found two special crabs, which are different from the Dutch ones, concerning which cf. *Catal. Insectorum*,[4] and a smaller purple sea urchin. The larger ones, frequently found on the Kurile Islands, are eaten and are called *morskaia repa*, sea turnip, by the Russians [red sea urchin, *Mesocentrotus franciscanus*]. I also found a sea raspberry [probably *Alcyonium* L. Gmelin], various marine plants, and other things. Toward evening I came home and relaxed.

Monday, August 18. It was very cloudy and windy. I began to write letters to Dr. Gmelin, voevod Pavlutskoi in Yakutsk, Kychkin, Ivan Volodimerov [Yakutsk sluzhiv], and Ivan Shestakov [Yakutsk syn boyarskoi]; cf. Letter Journal.

Tuesday, August 19. I made clean copies of my letters to be mailed. The weather was like yesterday. Mr. Berckhan and the rest of my crew arrived today.

Wednesday, August 20. I got the student Krasheninnikov's collection ready for shipment. Today my baggage arrived and was loaded on board.

Thursday, August 21. I wrote instructions for my soldier Aleksei Danilov and sent a memorandum about the soldiers' provisions to the office. Today another whale was stranded at the mouth of the Urak.

Friday, August 22. I cataloged my plants as well as the seeds I sent, albeit in a cursory manner on account of the time constraints; I have a copy.

Saturday, August 23. I packed up at home and took all my belongings to the galleon *Okhotsk* for departure.

Sunday, August 24. I collected a few more plants around Okhotsk and spent the evening with Professor la Croyère, Mr. Devier, Chikhachev, Khitrov, and Plautin at Lieutenants Waxell and Walton's.

Monday, August 25. I went to the beach and collected various things that had been washed ashore by the previous day's storm, such as two sea stars;

two specimens of crossed sea raspberries, which glow in the dark; a type of soft coral; a sponge; a fat *Madrepora*, stony coral, yellow inside; a worm; a snail shell resembling a top; a few dark-blue mussels containing impure pearls; and various types of seaweed and corals that are described in my *Verzeichnis der Pflanzen* [List of Plants; manuscript not found; WH, Anm. 1567].

Tuesday, August 26. I received from Mr. Devier bismuth and marcasite from the headwaters of the Okhota and four kinds of immature pearls from Tauiskoi Ostrog; I sent samples to the Academy. Today we went aboard the galleon and slept our first night there.

Notes

1. We are not sure if Steller is laughing at the fact that the midshipman served at some point as shipbuilder or if he meant to say that he had another visitor whose nickname was Ha' Ha'. The fact that *ha' ha'* is not capitalized favors the former interpretation since even Steller usually capitalizes names.
2. Scientific names for the following thirteen plants, all identified by Jäger:

    A gentian, *Gentianella auriculata* (Pall.) J.M. Gillet.

    Perhaps western roseroot, *Rhodiola integrifolia* Raf., syn. of *Sedum integrifolium* (Raf.) A. Nelson,

    A succulent, perhaps Aizoon's stonecrop, *Sedum aizoon* L, syn. of *Phedimus aizoon* (L.) t'Hart

    Rhododendron camtschaticum Pall.

    Dwarf Swedish dogwood, *Cornus suecica* L.

    Sarana lily, *Fritillaria camtschatcensis* (L.) Ker Gawl.

    Mountain ash, *Sorbus sambucifolia* (Cham. et Schltdl.) M. Roem.

    A burnet, *Sanguisorba tenuifolia* Fisch. ex Link, Beach fleabane, *Senecio pseudoarnica* Less., syn. of *Jacobaea p.* (Less.) Zuev,

    Cow parsnips, *Heracleum lanatum* Michx., syn. of *H. maximum* W. Bartram; see July 2.

    An oyster leaf, *Mertensia maritima* (L.) Gray, distributed along the boreal Arctic coast; in the Pacific region subsp. *arctica* Takeda.

    Scurvy grass, *Cochlearia officinalis* L. subsp. arctica (Schltdl. ex DC.) Hultén, syn. of *C. groenlandica* L.; a widespread coastal plant with three subspecies.

    A kind of wild celery, perhaps *Sium suave* Walter, syn. of *Apium lineare* (Michx.) Alph. Wood; Jäger. In folk medicine wild celery was indeed considered an aphrodisiac.
3. Mountain heather, *Cassiope ericoides* (Pall.) D. Don; Steller was the first to collect this heather around Okhotsk, and his collection is the standard of the species, conserved in the herbarium in St. Petersburg.

    Sorrel, *Rumex acetosa* L. subsp. *acetosa*; Jäger.
4. Only one short *Catalogus insectorum marinor* could be located; WH, Anm. 1526.

18

SALMON FISHING AND PRESERVING (8/27)

WEDNESDAY, AUGUST 27. WE STAYED PUT IN THE harbor because of adverse wind. Here I contemplated the fishery at Okhotsk. First of all it must be noted that, according to the unanimous testimony of the inhabitants of Okhotsk, the fishery here has been as rich since the founding of Okhotsk as it is now in the year 1740. The implements are nets made exactly like our lark nets. The front part, equipped with a loop, is fastened to a pole and from shore is pushed into the water, where it hangs diagonally underwater. The fish, swimming upriver in the Okhota in large numbers, enter the looped opening and immediately make their capture known by moving the net. The fisherman, likely standing alone on the shore, pulls out the net, beats the fish on the head with a wooden club, takes them out, throws them on a pile in the sand, and immediately pushes the pole with the net back into the water. Pushing it in and pulling it out commonly takes about two minutes, and he gets one or more, up to six fish. But those who want to do a better job enlist the help of another person, who stays on shore [presumably holding the net]. The fisherman himself stands in a boat next to the net and drifts along the net like on a ship's rope. And he can club just one fish and toss it in the boat when right away two or three other fish are in the net.[1]

The nerpi or seals, of whom from thirty to a hundred are seen close by wanting to partake in the fishing, are so tame that they approach the net. To keep them from tearing the nets—since people do not care much for these animals—the fisherman standing on shore drives the seals away by throwing rocks at them. This much is certain that if people in Russia and other places were to fish with nets like these used here in the rivers of Siberia, they would come up short and not have enough fish for themselves to eat.

But locally, you could fill such a huge sack net so full that you would not be able to pull it ashore without tearing it. Or, if you did manage, four to five individuals would—in one fell swoop—have three-fifths of their entire food supply, bread and vegetables constituting the remainder.[2]

Toward the end of August, when the fishery at the mouth and on the beach close to the mouth is finished, it moves upriver from twenty to a hundred kilometers where the fish are then more suitable for salting since they've lost almost all their fat swimming upriver. When the rivers flood their banks and where, because of sandy soil, some standing water remains in low places once the river has receded, these remaining low places on the Okhota and Urak Rivers teem with so many fish that you can just scoop them up with your hands or with sacks or, as often happens, even with linen pants tied to poles. When the water finally seeps completely into the sand, the fish remain on the dry ground, where they die and become gratuitous dinner for gulls and crows. What's remarkable is that these fish—as I know from my own experience—have no teeth or very small teeth when they swim out of the ocean, but the farther they swim upriver, the bigger the teeth become so that a dog salmon [*Oncorhynchus keta*] that had traveled up the Amur and been caught in the Shilka, and which I got ahold of in Irkutsk, had such big teeth that the old inhabitants of Okhotsk, who were under arrest there because of Mr. [Skornyakov-]Pisarev[3] and were asked to see me, agreed, unanimously, to have never seen such one-inch-long teeth in a dog salmon.

These fish are utilized in eight different ways. They're eaten fresh, and because there's such a huge supply, you can get some just by asking without having to pay for them. However, people who are more concerned about satiation than taste (in the opinion of gourmets) throw away the best parts—that is, the heads and milt, which indeed are the best in all fish, especially those from saltwater. To dry the fish heads for dog food, people hang them in large numbers in the sun—you could mistake each house for the Roman Capitol.[4] The milt and offal are lying all over in front of the houses and create such a stench that, on his arrival, Mr. Devier, who likes things neat and orderly, right away decreed, in no uncertain terms, that it all be buried.

The second way is to salt the fish. You have to pay attention to the fact, though, that if you use fresh fish when they first leave the ocean, they will spoil in just a few days because the fat softened by the salt will lie on top of the brine as an orange-colored oily layer and the remaining fat prevents the salt from further penetrating the flesh. That is not the case with the skinnier fish, having migrated far upriver. If you want to preserve the fat fresh fish, however, you have to proceed as follows: you gut the fish and cut them from the belly to the back into two parts [filleting them], rub them well with salt, pile them one on top of the other in the grass, and leave them there for twenty-four hours until the orange-colored liquid fat has drained off and only the white, so-to-speak bacon-like solid fat remains. You then rinse them again in seawater, which extracts the salt and all the fat it has attracted. Then you salt them anew in barrels to preserve them well and store them in a cool place to keep them tasty all year long.

The third process is drying the salted fish fillets in the sun and wind, and the fourth is drying them in smoke, which is the best way because it does not turn the fish bitter or pungent. The fifth process turns the fish, without first salting them, into *iukola* [unsalted dried fish], which the rich Tungus and Kamchadals eat dry like bread with other fish or cook in water with groats or roots.

The sixth process converts the filleted unsalted fish (that is, the iukola) into so-called *porsa* (that is, fish meal) which is made in two different ways. The best, destined for your own use, is roasted on the grill, then pulverized, and dried in the sun. The other, destined for sale or to be saved for emergencies, is boiled in kettles, the fat taken off, and then dried, but it tastes like straw. The people who do not have kettles put the fish in barrels, pour water over them, and put in glowing stones until the water boils. The porsa results when these unsalted roasted or boiled fish fillets are scraped off the skins and crumbled into meal; that is to say, porsa is the remnants of iukola.[5] In Zhigani they have a special way of preparation called *caacha*, which is said to be very tasty.

Both ways of iukola and porsa preparation have two flaws. First, the fillets, lacking salt, get moldy or rot when the weather turns wet and prevents drying. The moist ocean air also contributes to this problem even on dry days, especially since even on the hottest days, toward evening or at night, rain-like drops of moisture fall, which the Russians call *busa* or drizzling rain, and which wets down everything anew, as I myself have experienced, to my amazement, during my trip to the Marikan River and much more often than Kolb relates in his travel report to the Cape of Good Hope.[6] That is why the dried fish in spite of the glut of fish in 1739 in Kamchatka was sold at five to eight kopeks per thirty-six pounds. Second, because of the fat content and constant moisture, the fish meal turns bitter, which the Russians call *progor'knut*, turning rancid. But the iukola and porsa from Zhigani are not subjected to either of these adversities because the ocean is far away and the winds are strong, and so the fish can be dried properly and are therefore exported as far as Yudoma Cross. The Russians cook this porsa with cabbage or other greens and roots, but what is left over or spoils is fed to the sled dogs on the winter trips to Yudoma Cross or Tauiskoi Ostrog.

The seventh way consists of digging pits, putting the gutted fish in them, covering them with boards, and then piling dirt on top; there the fish stay all year, rotting or, as the Russians say, souring, which is why they call it *kislaia ryba* or sour fish [in Alaska referred to as fermented fish]. Although this is usually the sled dogs' food at home, some Russians, especially on Kamchatka, have become as fond of this sour fish as the natives are, so that they consider it the best food and eat it daily, despite the fact that it stinks so badly when cooked in kettles or troughs—which the Russians call *koryto*—that you can smell it from twelve hundred feet away and be knocked senseless by it in the yurts. The Russians on the Lena call this dish *argyhs* in Yakut. On Kamchatka.... [omission in text][7] The Kamchadals cook this sour fish for both themselves and their dogs in one and the same koryto, from which they eat it together peaceably, like brothers.

The eighth way consists in drying the fish roe, which cannot be eaten raw because it causes diarrhea. The roe is dried partly in the wind, partly in smoke, and after some time it's eaten by itself or with crowberries[8] or with larch bark, at times even willow bark. This is usually what the Kamchadals eat while traveling.

It should be noted that the saltwater fish, either salted or unsalted, glow in the night like phosphorus while they are being wind-dried. If you rub these fish with your hands, the fingers glow too as if they had been coated with sulfur. Thus, in the month of August, Okhotsk is lit up even in the dark of night because the drying racks are to be found in front of every house, as if they were theatrical lights.

The time of fishing here is from the beginning of July to the end of August. From then on, it begins in the upper reaches of the rivers. The fish maintain the following order in migrating up the rivers, which determines the various time periods for fishing. Toward the end of June and the beginning of July, the red salmon [*Oncorhynchus nerka*] is the first to enter the Okhota, Kukhtui, and Urak Rivers. This is the best fish, but it isn't caught too frequently because the other species following it cause the inhabitants at the mouth too much work. It is not caught at all upriver even though it is said to migrate up as far as the headwaters. [Red salmon usually spawn in lakes—that is, the headwaters.] For more information, see my *Historia piscium* and description of Kamchatka.[9]

The second fish is the dog or chum salmon [*O. keta*], which enters the river toward the middle of July and almost exclusively is kept by the inhabitants for winter provisions because it is the most numerous; but it is also much worse than the red salmon, especially those fish that are caught upriver toward the end of July until the end of August.

The third fish is the Dolly Varden trout [*Salvinus malma*], which migrates up with the two previous ones but alone at the beginning of June as soon as the beach is free of ice. In size and shape it resembles the Arctic grayling with vermilion spots, has reddish flesh, and is especially tasty.

The fourth is called *lomok* [identical to the red salmon; WH, Anm. 1633], which is different from the dog salmon only in that it has red flesh and a blunter and shorter upper jaw. This one migrates up the rivers from the beginning of August until the twenty-fourth.

The fifth is the *kundsha*, the Arctic char [*Salvelinus alpinus*], which swims up at the beginning of July and is eaten fresh but not preserved for the winter. The sixth is *kambala* or flatfish, which is caught at various times with the others but not much appreciated, rather most often thrown away.

Besides these, in spring there come the so-called *seldi* or herring, mistakenly called that because they are not herring at all but, as their other dorsal fin clearly indicates, belong to the genus *truttaceae* [*sic*, eighteenth-century classification; unidentified]. They have another fish in Okhotsk that they call *koriukha* or smelt [perhaps *Osmerus mordax*]; I cannot decide whether it is identical with the one in Petersburg because up to now I have not seen it. At any rate, it is said to smell exactly like it, but without experience I do not judge odor, which Eunus in Catullus must be better able to do.[10] *Uiky* or capelin[11] are similar to Eurasian dace and also found around Okhotsk. The sculpin is said to be similar to *uranoscopo* or ugly *pizda*.[12] I have not seen it either in the rivers Urak, Okhota, or Kukhtui, the latter joining the Okhota at the mouth and together with it forming the harbor. Besides the anadromous fish of the genus truttaceae, there are the Arctic grayling and the round whitefish in those rivers as well as in the Marikan River thirty kilometers from Okhotsk, the Ul'ya forty kilometers from the Marikan, and the Inya ninety kilometers from Okhotsk, all three flowing into the sea. In addition to the saltwater fish, I myself caught a Ray's *aphyam aculeatam*, probably sea stickleback [*Spinachia spinachi*], from the beach.

As for the other marine animals: whales are beached almost every year, from which the baleen goes into the government coffers, the blubber and meat, however, to the inhabitants and the Tungus, who use the fresh blubber instead of butter in their cooking; they fry fish and pancakes in it as we do in butter. The second marine animal is the beluga, which up to now I haven't seen either and which is not hunted here but is hunted frequently in Udskoi and Anadyrskoi Ostrogs. The third are *phocaenae* [small dolphins], or marine pigs, which the Tungus shoot with arrows, whereupon they wash up dead on the beach after several days. The Tungus eat their blubber as well as the meat. The fourth are seals, large numbers of which swim up the Okhota for several kilometers without any timidity and are to be seen all over on the beach. The Tungus kill those with arrows and with a *nosok* or harpoon. Their blubber is well accepted without the least aversion as a butter substitute by the Russians as well as the natives here, on Kamchatka, and on the Kuriles. The fifth are small, round marine creatures, called marine sponges, which are twenty-eight inches long and move in the ocean in the form of a ball, but they are very rarely caught or thrown up on the beach.

Notes

1. In Alaska dip-netting salmon is a popular subsistence fishery on certain rivers to this day. We have dip-netted from shore on Alaska's Copper River and wading in the Kenai River and have seen others dip-net from boats, but we find it impossible to visualize or understand the method Steller describes. He likely had not observed it but described it from hearsay, losing something in the retelling. He could be describing a type of setnet.

2. Literally translated, "the fish would constitute three parts, with regard to bread and vegetables"; alternate reading: "three-fourths" rather than "three-fifths of the supply."

3. Grigorei Grigor'evich Skornyakov-Pisarev, commander of Okhotsk until 1739, was infamous for his vicious temper and unjust treatment of people. We have been unable to find out why he had these inhabitants of Okhotsk arrested.

4. In ancient Rome the heads of decapitated enemies were displayed at the Forum. Jäger, pers. comm., October 4, 2016.

5. Steller's wording is more convoluted; literally it reads, "But the porsa is scraped off after the iukola has been taken off the skin; thus, the fish flour is what's left of the dried fish."

6. Peter Kolb (1675–1726) went to Kapstadt in 1705 and stayed there until 1712; Steller apparently had read Kolb's *Caput bonae spei hodiernum, das ist vollständige Beschreibung des Afrikanischen Vorgebürges der Guten Hoffnung*, published in Nuremberg in 1719. Stejneger, 17.

7. Perhaps Steller intended to provide additional information after his return from Kamchatka. On p. 118 of our translation of his *History of Kamchatka*, Steller mentions that on the Bol'shaya River sour fish is called *chuigul*.

8. In text, R, *shiksha*, *Empetrum nigrum* L., a black berry similar to the blueberry.

9. No manuscript called *Historia piscium* has been found. WH, Anm. 1632. Instruction number 37 (pp. 19–20) above specifies that Steller was to write a detailed description of Kamchatka.

10. Gaius Valerius Catullus (Roman poet, 87–54 BC) epigrams 82 and 87, against his rival Eunus; Jäger, email, January 17, 2017.

11. Uiky, *Mallotus villosus*, cited as identified by Bond in Steller's *History of Kamchatka*, note 27, 124; also known as candlefish or grunion. In his *History of Kamchatka* Steller writes about these fish: "Such an incredible number of little fish, capelin five to six inches long, are washed ashore every year in June and July by the easterly wind around Avacha and the mouth of the Kamchatka River that they lie along the beach two to three feet deep, with usually the male and female attached to each other. They are called *uiky* in both Itelmen languages and are gathered in large numbers and air-dried on the sand or on straw mats out in the open" (107).

12. The sculpin—in text, R, *byki*, oxen—with the most prominent set of horns is *Enophyrus diceraus*, antlered sculpin. Bond, in Steller's *History of Kamchatka*, note 36, 124. Uranoscopus, the stargazer. WH, Anm. 1653. Uranoscopidae is a family of fish with eyes on top of their heads.

19

FROM OKHOTSK TO BOL'SHERETSK (8/28–9/16)

Thursday, August 28. We are still in the harbor.

Friday, August 29. Still the same because of adverse wind.

Saturday, August 30. Today I bid farewell to all our good patrons and friends in Okhotsk and had the honor of hosting some of them that evening on the galleon.

Sunday, August 31. In the morning we saw Mr. Khitrov's double sloop sitting on a shoal in the mouth of the river, which scared our seamen so much that we stayed in the harbor for another seven days until the eighth of September.

In the morning of September eighth, around ten o'clock, the captain commander sailed from the harbor into the Sea of Okhotsk. We followed him, and behind us came the sloop commanded by Captain Chirikov, who had to wait till the next day because he took too long and the tide went out. During the day we sailed out into the sea for about thirty kilometers and were welcomed by two whales, who had their fun showering us with water for about three hours about a kilometer from our galleon. During the night under a light wind, we covered another twenty kilometers, making it fifty altogether from Okhotsk, and toward morning we anchored opposite the mountains at the mouth of the Inya River, where a bend constitutes the last point of land you see this side of Kamchatka.

Tuesday, September 9. There was no wind, so we enjoyed rocking in the swells. Like the previous day, this one was very pleasant and bright.

Wednesday, September 10. The weather was the same, so we fared the same. At night I saw that the sea raspberries glow like phosphorus in the dark and that the sea is full of them. But I haven't been able to figure out whether this phosphorescence is a marine or animal excretion. I remember this much, that in 1734 I saw almost the same phenomenon at the Danzig [Gdansk] anchorage in the Baltic Sea. I also saw a *pulmonem marinam* [sea lung? WH, Anm. 1688] as described by John Johnstone [1603–1675; European physician and scholar].

Thursday, September 11. The weather was moderate like yesterday. At night a good wind came up, and we made good progress. Cf. *Journal itineris maritimi* [probably refers to the logbook of the galleon *Okhotsk*; WH, Anm. 1691].

Friday, September 12. We had good weather and progressed accordingly.

Saturday, September 13. The weather and our progress were like yesterday.

Sunday, September 14. It was very cold in the morning but clear. We saw Captain Chirikov's ship, the *St. Paul*, above us in the sea, but a headwind came up. [Implication unclear.]

Monday, September 15. The wind changed considerably, but we had good weather. Toward morning we saw the mountains of Kamchatka located about seventy kilometers inland from the coast. I want to have Mr. Berckhan paint a picture of this view.

Tuesday, September 16. We had excellent, beautiful, and pleasant weather. But because we had a headwind till about eleven o'clock and were still about sixty kilometers from the coast and the mouth of the Bol'shaya River, we could enjoy the view of this camel-backed paradise only from afar. Toward eleven o'clock we got a good wind and got so far that toward morning of the next day we were at the mouth of the Bol'shaya River. I observed two kinds of gulls that live on the sea: one was black-and-white spotted on the back [a juvenile gull? Springer, pers. comm., August 24, 2015]; the other was all black, longish, and gaunt with long, narrow wings [a storm petrel or black tern? Springer, ibid.]. I will make every effort to get ahold of these.

AFTERWORD

So what did we learn about Georg Wilhelm Steller that we want others to know, too? Along with letters and documents we consulted in volumes 1 and 3 of *Quellen*, the translated texts greatly increased our understanding and appreciation of the complexity of Steller's character and achievement, not to mention the scope of his assignments and the challenges he faced in carrying them out. In contrast to the man in frequent conflict with the people on board the *St. Peter*, the Steller we have come to know got along well with most people. The urge to give unsolicited advice, which caused him so much grief on the sea voyage, is also evident—albeit apologetically—in letters to the president of the Academy and others. But in the journal of his trip from Irkutsk to Kamchatka, Steller rarely has anything bad to say about the people he worked with; people who were lazy and did not do their jobs well, such as one of his drivers, the assay master Gardebol, and the helmsman Khitrov, his bête noire on the sea voyage, were the exceptions. On the difficult overland trek, Steller seems to have lost his temper only once in utter frustration over the lack of help in loading the unruly horses. That good help was sometimes hard to come by is illustrated by the answer Steller received to a request made on May 24, 1740, to the administration in Yakutsk for a huntsman, a sluzhiv who is "a good shot as well as an upright and sober person" (*Quellen* 1:194). The voevod responded on June 4 that the Cossack chief had advised that "among the Yakutsk sluzhivs none is both an experienced shot and an upright and sober person" (ibid., 210).

Steller's camaraderie with Captain Spangberg, the glee with which he reports how happy the new commander of Okhotsk, Devier, arriving in Yakutsk, was to see him, and the somewhat smug declaration that Bibikov, the vice-governor of Irkutsk (to whom Steller dedicated his *Flora Irkutiensis*), loved him so much that he wanted to keep him there all winter (letter to Müller, *Quellen* 3:261) attest to Steller's good relationships with his equals and those of higher rank. That he flew off the handle when learning of Gmelin's interference with his travel plans to Kamchatka and immediately resolved not to accede to the professor's wishes is certainly understandable, just as is Gmelin's unhappiness with Steller's ignoring some of Gmelin's prior discoveries. Apart from Steller's having set his heart on getting to Kamchatka, he had already spent considerable energy and not inconsiderable sums of his own money preparing for the trip, as he wrote to Baron von Korff on December 23, 1739 (*Quellen* 3:387). But it is clear that the need to be his own man—illustrated by his emphasis on being under not the professors' but the Academy's command—lay at the root of his anger. When Gmelin later wrote a conciliatory letter, Steller responded in kind, apologizing profusely for causing the rift. A few memoranda and letters prove that he also helped mitigate the conflicts of others.

Several of his letters contain candid revelations of what motivated him, how he saw himself, and how he wanted to be seen. He discloses his own self-interest when he tells Müller he supported Gmelin's request to be allowed to return to St. Petersburg (ibid., 213) or emphasizes to von Korff that he, Steller, travels at less cost to the Crown than the professors do (ibid., 269–70). He also openly admits his ambition for further travel, not only to China as mentioned in the "Description of Irkutsk" but also to Japan, asking von Korff (letter of April 20, 1740, *Quellen* 1:152) to be allowed to go there after finishing his work on Kamchatka. Steller always craftily emphasizes that his eagerness is not for his own gain but for the good of the country, for Her Majesty's gain, or to "further the sciences and increase the reputation of the Academy" (ibid.). He could be cheeky, as when he tells Schumacher, librarian and office manager of the Academy of Sciences, to tell Professor Amman, botanist at the Academy, that if he does not write to him, Steller will send him fewer plants because he has the upper hand (letter of December 24, 1739, *Quellen* 3:413). And to Gmelin (letter of November 17, 1739, *Quellen* 3:340) he admits in St. Petersburg having affected ignorance in things political, lack of initiative, and negligence in promoting his affairs, so any possible problems he might cause himself in Siberia would be attributed to his being a country bumpkin and therefore excused. In other words, he found dissembling a useful method of getting along in the world. He also points out that he is less demanding than the professors though that does not always get him what he needs. As a mere adjunct, he cannot afford to shoot off his mouth. On the other hand, he brags about his God-given gift of gab to persuade people to do his bidding (letter to Müller of December 23, 1739, *Quellen* 3:392).

In the letter to Schumacher (see Appendix C), having once more offered unsolicited advice on how the government could encourage gainful discoveries in Siberia, Steller again protests his disinterest in selfish gain and his modest ambition to gain merely a *rabotnik*'s (worker's) fame while emphasizing his "high spirits while working very hard." He obviously had a sunny disposition, enduring hardships cheerfully, and while he enjoyed an occasional cup of brandy, he did not need it to keep his spirits up. For from the documents we consulted, we also learned—and hope future commentators take note—that much of the brandy Steller requested (for example, in document 107, *Quellen* 3:304) was not for his own consumption but for preserving specimens. Admittedly, some readers may question the reliability of this positive assessment of Steller because it relies exclusively on what he tells us. But the negative image that has dominated the literature so far was also self-generated. The newly published texts at least establish a more balanced picture.

While the man Steller may not have been much admired up to now, the scientist's achievement has all along been recognized by scholars, early on and most notably by Stejneger, and praised by popularizers such as Ford, Littlepage, and the Suttons; Bell called him the only true explorer on board the *St. Peter*. Yet as one of the group of the academicians in the eighteenth century who established the baseline of knowledge in the natural and certain social sciences, Steller deserves greater recognition than he has received. But until all his scientific writings in Latin have been translated, his contribution to that foundation cannot be properly assessed.

As Germanists without the Russian language skills to have read any Russian sources of the period, we could not attempt to assess how the two texts we translated enlarge the understanding of the immense enterprise that was the Second Kamchatka Expedition or of life in eighteenth-century Siberia. What we do get are revealing details of daily life on the expedition and of social and business life in Irkutsk in 1739–40. Because of the large scope of Steller's observations—not only demanded by his instructions but seemingly innate to his nature—they provide much valuable information not just in history but in many different fields. Historians, however, especially those who concern themselves with the common folk, may find the minutiae of daily life particularly intriguing. We were, for example, reminded of the high value of seemingly insignificant items we take for granted, such as a handkerchief, the loss of which Steller records, or a brass pipe, left, regretfully, as a "tip" for finding a beautiful flower.[1] Pipes were a comfort to Steller; he used them on several occasions to take his mind off the lack of food or bed. We were also intrigued by what he says about women's employment and child labor, by his comparison of the hardworking peasants along the Lena River with the lazy women of Irkutsk, and by his sharp criticism of the exploitation of the peasants by usurers.

But Steller not only observed; he was a problem solver and had his own ideas for correcting unfair practices and reorganizing bloated institutions. He argues against government monopolies of trade goods and for a type of free enterprise. He presents a case for taking an accurate inventory of who lives where and how rich or poor they are so that everyone may be taxed fairly. He proposes solutions to prostitution and the resulting high rates of sexually transmitted diseases. We do not think of Steller as a social scientist, yet he offers intriguing descriptions of social life and insight into his own sense of what a good society would entail.

In Germany, scholarship has focused primarily on Steller's contribution to ethnography in the *Beschreibung vom Lande Kamtschatka* (*History of Kamchatka*). Steller is given credit for his pioneering role by Erich Kasten (preface to the 2013 edition of the *Beschreibung* and *Lachsfang und Bärentanz*), Marcus Köhler (*Völker-Beschreibung: Die ethnographische Methodik Georg Wilhelm Stellers (1709–1746) im Kontext der Herausbildung der "russischen" etnografija*, 2013), and Han Vermeulen (2013, 2015). What Steller has to say about the Yakuts, the Gilyaks, and others in our texts should be of considerable interest to ethnographers, too. According to Hintzsche, among the remaining manuscripts may be further ethnographic material, but written in Latin it remains untranslated (email, January 17, 2018).

As recognized already, Steller's greatest contribution was in the field of botany. Steller's sea cow and Steller's jay are familiar names; less familiar are *Saxifraga stelleriana* (a species of saxifrage), *Artemisia stelleriana* Besser (beach wormwood or hoary mugwort), and *Arabis stelleri* (a species of rockcress). Along with four genera honoring Steller, some plant species were dedicated to him, most of them during the century after his death.

In addition to Steller's distinct enthusiasm for plants, he had a practiced eye for distinguishing their most important characteristics. And he must have had an extraordinary memory, because he could remember if he had already seen a plant species and thus recognize those species that were new to the scientific community. His observations about the distribution and the local growing conditions were unusually good for the period. For example, he describes how birch trees are diminishing along the Belaya River, then are not found at all as far as the Yuna, and from Yudoma to Okhotsk are once again common. Or how in the boggy valleys found in mountain ranges, no trees grow but only dwarf birch. And he notices that the elevation at which mountain plants grow becomes lower the further north you go (Jäger).

During the very short time of two and a half months in 1739, Steller had recorded over 1,050 plant species, resulting in his *Flora Irkutiensis*, which, edited by Heike Heklau, is soon to be published for the first time, using contemporary plant names. Steller summarized all his botanical observations from this travel journal in his still unpublished *Flora Ochotensis*, comprising fifty-five pages with 543 numbered listings, 50 of which Steller recognized as new.[2]

Today Steller's works are considered of particular interest from the standpoint of human-caused changes to the flora because they provide a baseline against which the present distribution and frequency of plants can be measured, as well as the first appearance of invasive species (Jäger).

Scholars in the fields of fishery biology, health science, nutrition, environmental studies, and ecology, as well as those who have an interest in folk medicine (see "Treatise of Folk Medicine," translated by Lukina), are bound to discover aspects they had not known before. Scholars with a reading knowledge of Russian may find additional material in the Russian editions of the *Quellen zur Geschichte Sibiriens und Alaskas aus russischen Archiven* (see bibliography).

There is more to be discovered about Georg Wilhelm Steller in the volumes of *Quellen* published so far, the anticipated publication of his *Flora Irkutiensis*, his journal of his trip from Moscow to Yeniseysk, and possibly other manuscripts. There is much left to translate into English. But with the two texts here presented, the man and his work should be much better understood.

Notes

1 Littlepage and Bown took similar note in the journal of the sea voyage, Littlepage by observing that on board the *St. Peter* seventy-eight people were crowded into a smaller space than in our country is "routinely" occupied by two people in the average house (58), Bown by commenting on the fact that the chocolate Steller was served on his return to the ship from Kayak Island, having presumably originated in South America, had traveled farther than the mariners; it had practically circumnavigated the globe (136).

2 Hintzsche graciously made available the manuscript according to AAWRI, op. 104, d. 25 (no. 18) to Jäger for identifying the plants in this translation.

APPENDIX A:
GEORG WILHELM STELLER'S LIFE

(Excerpted and translated from *Die Große Nordische Expedition*)

1709

March 10, Georg Wilhelm Stöller is born in Windsheim, Franconia, Germany, the fourth child of Johannes Jacob Stöller, organist and choirmaster at St. Kilian's Church and music teacher at the local *Gymnasium* [Latin school], and his wife Loysa Susanna, née Baumann; the child is named after his godfather, the town's mayor, Georg Wilhelm von Keget.

1713

At age five, Georg Wilhelm is admitted to the gymnasium; at age fourteen, he advances to the upper class and, at his father's request, is admitted to the *Alumneum*, the boarding school for deserving children of parents of limited means. Sparse meals; unheated, poorly insulated sleeping quarters; and tiring weekly obligatory vocal performances the alums have to give at well-to-do citizens' houses are characteristics of this beneficent establishment [Uhlmann, passim], memories of which are evoked in his journal.

1729

Georg Wilhelm graduates first in his class and delivers the valedictory address, in Latin, on the topic of "Thunder as Expression and Proof of God's Working." The city of Windsheim grants him a scholarship to study theology at the university in Wittenberg. As a serious student and candidate in theology, he is soon allowed to deliver sermons in Wittenberg and churches of neighboring communities. He attends lectures in ethics, politics, and law, as well as the lectures and demonstrations of Abraham Vater, a well-known professor of anatomy.

1731

Steller leaves Wittenberg to register in the college of theology at the university in Halle, switching soon to the medical college to further his interest in the natural sciences, especially botany. He attends lectures by noted professors of medicine and expands his knowledge of botany with field trips into the Harz Mountains, where he also visits the mining centers of Stolberg and Eisleben. Having lost his scholarship upon switching from theology and leaving Wittenberg, he earns his living as a tutor in August Hermann Francke's orphanage and boarding school and as a lecturer in botany. In an entry in the 1731 lecturers' record of Francke's orphanage evaluation, he is found to be lacking in religious devotion, showing mediocre student enrollment, and being a poor lecturer and occasionally too severe. Possibly aching eyes and his maintaining satisfactory order are listed as somewhat mitigating circumstances [cited by Vermeulen 2013].

1734

On the recommendation of his mentor, Friedrich Hoffmann, a famous professor of medicine, Steller travels to Berlin in August in the hope of securing a position at a German university by undergoing an examination at the *collegium medicum*. But in spite of an excellent test result, no position becomes available. Steller therefore decides to seek his fortune in Russia, as many young German scholars have before him. In Danzig [now Gdansk] he joins a Russian troop transport to care for wounded soldiers and in November arrives in St. Petersburg. He is befriended by Archbishop Feofan Prokopovich and soon makes the acquaintance of many of the European scientists at the new Academy of Sciences, all of them communicating in Latin. Discovering that there is no *ö* in Russian, he changes his last name to Steller. When he learns that additional academics are sought for the Second Kamchatka Expedition, he applies to join it.

1737

On February 7, Steller is offered a contract as adjunct of natural sciences by the Academy of Sciences at a salary of 660 rubles per year for the duration of the expedition. He prepares himself by studying all available information, including the papers of the botanist Daniel Gottlieb Messerschmidt, who died in 1735 after having traveled in Siberia for seven years. Steller marries Messerschmidt's widow Brigitta Helena, and on December 24 the couple leaves St. Petersburg for Moscow.

1738

With his wife opting to stay behind, Steller leaves Moscow in March for Tobolsk, then travels downriver on the Irtysh and upriver on the Ob and arrives in Tomsk in September, where he falls ill. After his recovery he travels on, arriving in Yeniseysk on December 7. Steller is warmly received by the professors Johann Georg Gmelin and Gerhard Friedrich Müller, who, tired after six years' travel in Siberia, had asked for an assistant.

1739

The two professors issue Steller detailed instructions for his journey to Kamchatka and the research he is to conduct. In early March Steller leaves Yeniseysk for Irkutsk with the painter Johann Christian Berckhan and the student Aleksei Gorlanov. Lack of transport and provisions makes it impossible for him to continue traveling east. So from the end of July to the beginning of September, Steller travels to Barguzinskoi Ostrog to investigate the flora, fauna, and minerals on the eastern shore of Lake Baikal. His major botanical work, the *Flora Irkutiensis*, with 1,150 plant descriptions, which results from this trip, is finished in December.

1740

From mid-January to mid-February, Steller travels to Kyakhta on the Chinese border to purchase Chinese paper needed for the preservation of collected plants. On March 5, he is finally able to leave Irkutsk, arriving in Yakutsk May 24 and in Okhotsk August 14, where he meets Vitus Bering, the commander of the expedition, for the first time. After arriving on Kamchatka on September 16, Steller begins his research in Bol'sheretsk and also takes his first trip to Avacha Bay on the east coast.

1741

In February, on his return from a trip to Cape Lopatka and Lake Kurile in the south, Steller receives Bering's letter inviting him to join the voyage to America. The *St. Peter* sets sail on June 4; Steller faithfully records the voyage in his journal, high points being his one-day exploration of Alaska's Kayak Island and meeting the first Alaskans in the Shumagin Islands. On November 6, the *St. Peter* is shipwrecked on an uninhabited island, today's Bering Island, where Bering dies on December 8. Steller tends to his shipmates, many of them sick with scurvy, and explores the island. He writes the first description of the sea cow together with those of the sea otter, fur seal, and sea lion in *De Bestiis Marinis*, completed on the island but not published until years after his death.

1742

Having constructed a smaller vessel from the shipwrecked *St. Peter*, the survivors leave the island at the beginning of August and on the twenty-sixth arrive in Avacha Bay. Steller returns to Bol'sheretsk, where he spends the winter and works on the manuscripts of the "Journal of the Sea Voyage" and the "Description of Kamchatka."

1743

In May and June, Steller travels to southern Kamchatka and to the Kuriles. In July he travels north as far as Karaga Island, returning to Bol'sheretsk only in June of the following year.

1744

Steller receives the news in January that the expedition has been officially terminated as of the previous September, but he does not leave for Okhotsk until August 3. From there he continues on to Yakutsk, where he stays until the following July.

1745

In September Steller arrives in Irkutsk, where he is confronted with the accusation of having incited Kamchadals to rebellion but exonerated after a hearing before Vice-Governor Lange.

1746

In January Steller is free to continue his journey to Moscow, reaching Tomsk at the end of the month and Tobolsk on March 4. In April he travels to Krasnoye Selo near Solikamsk for a visit with the well-known Demidov family. In May he sends his luggage with Berckhan and Gorlanov ahead to Moscow, while he investigates the flora of the Perm region. The news of his exoneration not having reached St. Petersburg, a ukase is issued to escort Steller under guard back to Irkutsk. In October he has reached Tara east of the Ural Mountains when another order sets him free and allows him to turn west again. When he arrives in Tobolsk, he is already very sick but continues his journey to Tyumen, where Dr. Lau, who has also been a member of the expedition and whom Steller has met in Okhotsk, tries in vain to save his life. Georg Wilhelm Steller dies here on November 12.

APPENDIX B:
SCHNURBUCH ACCOUNT LEDGER

Fedot Klimovskoi's Expense Account for Georg Wilhelm Steller from Barguzinskoi Ostrog, August 1739 (translated from *Quellen* 3:317–21)

In the handwriting of Fedot Klimovskoi (translated from the Russian)

Extraordinary expenses: what was needed for which things is itemized below.

		Rubles	Kopeks
purchased 7 oz. gall apples, paid			15
purchased 7 oz. ferrous sulfate, paid			5
paid for 9.7 yd. black gauze			60
paid for a box for storing curiosities			33
paid for a box for storing insects			15
	total	1	28
paid for wrapping the instruments with gauze			5
paid for 3.6 lb. of alum			40
paid for 54 yd. of linen			96
paid for a skein of sewing thread			7
paid for 50 flints			6
paid for cutting the linen to size			90
paid for 14.5 oz. of mica			24
	total	2	68
Your personal expenses, sir			
paid the shoemaker		3	88
paid for a couple of pieces of fine china			80
paid for a big tin to store tea in			80
When it pleased you, sir, to travel to Dement'ev's Zaimka, the servant, was given for foodstuffs			32
for the sewing of towels			3
	total	5	83
to the rope maker for loops to close the tent with			15
paid for red leather to cover a box			45
paid the blacksmiths at the smithy for covering a box			40
for blueberries			1
the prospector was paid			5
paid for a box for the fine china			30
for making a tent			10
paid for a bridle			35
paid for 5.4 lb. of soap			30
	total	2	11

184 | Appendix B

paid for 2 brandy glasses			10
paid for a tuia [round birch basket with lid]		2	
you, sir, deigned to take		2	
paid the shoemaker for 3 pairs of shoes and 1 pair of slippers		2	35
paid for 153 lb. of wheat flour			61
paid for 108 lb. of salt			66
36 lb. of sugar			15
for a lamp			10
for 72 lb. of meat			60
you, sir, deigned to take		2	
paid for a watering can			10
	total	9	35
	[should correctly read 8.69 rubles]		
paid for candles			20
378 lb. of rye provisions [flour]			94
paid for spinning work			12
Matfei was given			50
paid for rendered blubber			3
you, sir, deigned to take		4	
	total	5	79
the sum total of the above-listed expenses		27	4
	[should correctly read 26.38 rubles]		
remaining after expenses		12	46
	[should correctly read	13	2]

APPENDIX C: LETTER TO JOHANN DANIEL SCHUMACHER

(Translated from *Quellen* 3:412–17)
December 24, 1739, from Irkutsk

Honorable Sir,
Highly Esteemed Councillor,
Gracious Patron,

    I have once again taken the liberty, Honorable Sir, with these lines, to attest to my most devoted respect even though I am not certain they will be graciously received by you. While I shall happily and contentedly continue my work in Siberia, I will nonetheless not deny that I shall consider these regions as if cursed until I receive a few lines from you assuring me of your grace and goodwill. I, for my part, am directing all my thoughts and desires toward making myself more worthy to the exalted head of the Academy and to you, Honored Sir.

    Last year, it is true. I discovered very little that was worthwhile, but that is not my fault because I myself did not create the miserable areas on the Ob River; if I had, I would certainly have adorned them as Paradise and eaten so much from the tree of good [Steller's humorous derivation from the Tree of the Knowledge of Good and Evil; Gen. 2:9, 3] that I would not have become sick in Tomsk. But this year I hope to have done everything well. So I am sending my observations and collections to the Academy as an example of the way I will investigate Kamchatka even though I am sending hardly half now of what remains to be sent. As I have said before, I shall not ask for anything but what is absolutely necessary for me to do my work; thus, I am most humbly requesting of your Honor

    (1) To replenish the depleted supply of gray paper [used for pressing and drying plants] as quickly as possible with ten reams. With what paper I have left, I cannot even press a single plant. Dr. Gmelin cannot help me because he has none either. I will use all the newspapers, notes, and whatever can be found in the professors' Yakutsk stockrooms for this purpose, especially since the local inhabitants are fonder of handwritten promissory notes than of printed notations.

    (2) My second request concerns revealing the [composition of] *Ruysch's Liquor balsamicum*,[1] so that I can send, unspoiled, my Siberian fish, particularly the marine fish from the Sea of Okhotsk and Kamchatka, along with many other marine creatures, to St. Petersburg. I promise not to reveal how this solution is made, and after my trip is over I will happily forget it again myself.

(3) I most humbly request that someone write to me annually to let me know if my [scientific] reports and collections have actually been received, considering that I still do not know if the first box sent from Kazan has been delivered.

(4) I request [a copy of] Agricola's Latin works, so at least I have a single book about mineralogy on hand to help out my memory.²

(5) The local coarse gunpowder that has deteriorated in the cellars deprived me of many birds and other noteworthy creatures. Although I have found someone to rework it, there is so much sand in it that I doubt I will be able to use it.

(6) The local lead from Argunskoi Ostrog, containing silver and being brittle, not only cannot be used to mold shot but ruins the best gun. It has happened to me and my servant that a musket cracked in my hand, and almost daily I fear the same thing happening with the barrel. So far I have kept buying guns, but they all use bullets that tear up small birds into two hundred pieces, which is why I am not able to [collect and] send on small birds. Even though I was able to examine and describe three hundred birds this year, I could barely stuff one in twenty. Thus, I beg you to send me 72 to 108 pounds of birdshot.

By the way, Honorable Sir, please pardon my sloppy handwriting because I have little free time. I am particularly occupied with getting my collection of seeds and plants ready, so that they may arrive in St. Petersburg in a timely manner and fulfill their purpose, which will especially please Professor Amman. But if Professor Amman does not write to me, in the future I will send only half [of what I have] because in this respect I have the upper hand. In April, I hope to send my remaining observations with the billing and a devotional memorandum to the High Senate. In this country one does not need a tongue because everything is dealt with in writing. I trust that, in the future, I could earn my daily bread as a clerk if I had to.

I would particularly like to know, Honorable Sir, if I stand in your good graces and if the Academy would favorably consider it if I were to discover—as I am obligated to—a thing or two that would benefit the public and enhance the Academy's reputation. According to the Academy's newly printed mining regulations, a lot of useful things could be discovered around here if the residents were not hesitant to travel to Petersburg for these special permits, thereby ending up in poverty. This is what holds the greatest enthusiasts back and makes them hide what they are able to do and what they know. If the Academy of Sciences would help one or another of those who discover something in Siberia for us to gain these privileges, I could in one way or another disclose quite a few things, since I have access to a lot of people. But please do not assume that I want to become a promoter of projects; that is something I am as afraid of as I am of original sin. I am only trying to do everything possible to fulfill my instructions and to contribute to the favorable reputation of the Academy of Sciences. For me, however, the good reputation of a simple *rabotnik* [worker] will be enough. And if I am allowed to fish as I want to, I will certainly achieve something in the field of natural history and thus come somewhat close to the work of Dr. Gmelin, who has become awfully infatuated with rocks and birds. By the way, I very much enjoy my hard work and am pleased that I now have such a fine fox pelt and beautiful sable hat, which I could never have had in St. Petersburg. May God grant that I keep my cheerful mind longer than the professors did. If I find a new plant or get a beautiful bird, fish, rock, or historical narrative, I will whistle like the pied piper of Hamelin[3] or jump [for joy] like Robinson Crusoe's man Friday when his father was released from the cannibals.[4] Irkutsk is unusually happy about the arrival of the governor, Councillor Lange,[5] about which everyone should rejoice. Finally, Honorable Sir, I have the honor to wish you, from the bottom of my heart, an enjoyable New Year and, with it, all imaginable well-being as much as you, Honorable Sir, and your family can handle. I, however, commend myself to your benevolence and grace,

Honorable Sir, Highly Respected Councillor, and Gracious Patron,
Irkutsk, December 24, 1739
Your Most Humble Servant,
Georg Wilhelm Steller, Adjunct

Notes

1. Frederick Ruysch, 1638–1731, was a Dutch anatomist and botanist who developed an embalming fluid, which he sold in 1717, together with his collection of embalmed specimens including human parts, to Peter the Great. Before it was made public in 1743, only a few persons, including Schumacher, had the formula. WH, Anm. 9; *Quellen* 3:416.

2. Georgius Agricola, 1494–1555, a German mineralogist and metallurgist, is considered the father of mineralogy.

3. Traditional German folktale recorded by the Grimm Brothers in which a piper wearing a many-colored (pied) garment agrees to rid the town of rats by playing his pipe or flute, but when the townspeople refuse to pay him, he lures all the children out of town the same way.

4. In chapter 16 of Daniel Defoe's novel *Robinson Crusoe*, published in 1719.

5. Lorenz Lange (ca. 1690–1752), vice-governor of Irkutsk, 1740–52.

APPENDIX D:
PLANTS NAMED AFTER STELLER[1]

Genera Named after Steller

Dendrostellera (C. A. Mey.) Tiegh. and *Stelleropsis* Pobed. (Fl. SSSR 15 [1949]: 503), both with about ten species of annual and perennial herbaceous plants with reddish, white, or green flowers lacking petals and found in central and southwest Asia, had been included by Kit Tan (*Notes from the Royal Botanic Garden, Edinburgh* 40 [1982]: 219) in *Diarthron* Turcz. as subgenus *Stelleropsis* (Pobed.) Kit Tan, but both should be reinstated according to Galicia-Herbada (Plant Systematics and Evolution 257 [2006]: 159–87) based on an investigation of DNA sequences in Thymelaeaceae.

Stellera L. is a genus with one species *Stellera chamaejasme* L. (*Chamaejasme stelleriana* Kuntz). It is a perennial plant with heads of white, pink, or yellow flowers, grown as an ornamental plant in rock gardens; found in mountainous regions of central and south Asia.

Species Named after Steller

Allium stellerianum Willd., also known as Steller's leek/onion, is a small (6–20 cm) plant with pale yellow flowers in dense clusters; found in western Russia and temperate Asia.

Arabis stelleri DC. is a densely pilose biennial or perennial rockcress with clustered white flowers, growing on sandy beaches, along streams, and on disturbed ground; found in Siberia, the Russian Far East, Korea, Japan, and Taiwan.

Artemisia stelleriana Besser, also known as hoary mugwort, is a species of plant in the sunflower family, widely cultivated as an ornamental because of its silvery leaves; found in China, Japan, Korea, the Russian Far East, and on the Aleutian Islands.

Cryptogramma stelleri (S. G. Gmel.) Prantl, also known as fragile rockbrake, Steller's rockbrake, and slender rockbrake, is a small (3–20 cm high) fern found in the United States, with circumboreal distribution in Asia, Russia, the United States, Canada, and northwestern Mexico.

Dracocephalum stellerianum Hildebr., also known as Steller's dragonhead, is a tuft-forming perennial, 5–20 cm high with blue flowers 45 mm long in dense racemes; found on rocky alpine slopes in Siberia, Yakutia, and the Russian Far East.

Harrimanella stelleriana (Pall.) Coville (*Cassiope stelleriana* Pall. ex DC.), also known as Alaskan mountain/bell heather, is a small, mat-forming subshrub of the heather family with single white flowers at the ends of the twigs; found in Central Japan, the Russian Far East, the Yukon, Alaska, and Washington.

Limnas stelleri Trin. is a species of grass growing in woodlands of pine and larch trees; found in northeast Asia.

Linum stelleroides Planch., also known as Steller's wild flax, is found in Japan, Korea, Kyrgyzstan, the Russian Far East, Tajikistan, Turkmenistan, and Uzbekistan.

Saxifraga stelleriana Merklein ex Ser. is a species of saxifrage found in Yakutia and the Russian Far East.

Veronica stelleri Pall. ex Link, also known as Steller's speedwell, is a perennial creeping herb, 15 cm high, with dense racemes of white flowers; found in northern China, Japan, Korea, and the Russian Far East.

There are about fifteen other plants named after Steller, but these either have been transferred into other genera, have not been validly published, or have been antedated by an older name of the same plant, or the name has not yet been resolved. Three such examples are the species *Lomatogonium stellerianum* Kostel., *Scrophularia stelleriana* Steud., and *Pedicularis stelleriana* Pall. ex Steven.

Note

1. Eckehart J. Jäger compiled this list and wrote the last paragraph.

GLOSSARY OF FOREIGN WORDS

(All are Russian except those marked G, for German)

balagan for the Yakuts, a mud-covered winter dwelling built of wood, consisting of living quarters and stable; in Kamchatka, a storage shed on stilts (Hintzsche)

bobyl'skie the lower class of peasants usually without arable land, some without any property, some having only small households; day laborers or field hands (Hintzsche; Pushkarev).

cassa/kazna government coffers; office receiving and paying out money.

chokania from R. *chokan'e,* clinking of glasses while toasting; Yakut summer celebration and banquet (WH, Anm. 861).

Cossacks term applied to a great variety of men—adventurers, outcasts, restless misfits, homeless men—all of whom served either on horse or on foot to supplement the streltsy, sharpshooters (Pushkarev).

derevnya a village without a church (Hintzsche).

doshchenik (doshchanik) a flat-bottomed, single-decked, one-masted cargo vessel, rowed with up to ten long oars.

dvoryane a part of the active military forces. They held landed estates and were under obligation to perform military service until the end of their lives or up until their permanent disability. They also occupied various posts in civil administration (Pushkarev).

Geleitukas G/R, escort pass.

gostinii dvor prerevolutionary arcade; the market square with merchants' rows; a large hall with stores inside (Hintzsche; Pushkarev).

head tax/poll tax/**Kopfgeld** G. mainly to finance the army, Peter the Great introduced this tax in 1725, which applied to all males subject to being taxed, e.g., peasants, posadskie, merchants. Initially it was set at eighty kopeks a year (Hintzsche; Pushkarev).

inozemtsy literally, foreigners; at the time, usually foreigners in Russian service, but *iasachnye inozemtsy* meant yasak-paying Siberian tribes (WH, Glossar); Gmelin and Müller use the term to refer to the indigenous peoples.

iukola unsalted dried fish.

kastak distillery.

kislaia ryba sour (fermented) fish.

krest cross.

Kunstkammer G, established by Peter the Great in St. Petersburg and completed in 1727; dedicated to preserving natural and human curiosities and rarities.

Marienglas G, a selenite or satin spar, varieties of gypsum, used in place of glass.

nerpi in the text referring to both Baikal and common or harbor seals; in today's usage, ringed seals.

ostrog originally a small fort in Russia and Siberia, encircled by twelve- to fifteen-foot-high palisades made from sharpened tree trunks, with a garrison. Later many of these forts developed into towns and cities.

pashennie krest'iane in Siberia, peasants who had received government land allotments, livestock, and agricultural implements and in return were obliged to till fixed plots of the czar's arable lands to supply local service men with foodstuffs (Pushkarev).

pisani kameni literally, painted rocks (petroglyphs).

podval special station for brandy distribution and taxation.

podvodi government-sponsored wagons and sleds for hire.

porogi rapids.

porsa fish meal.

posad settlement outside the town center or fort where chiefly traders and craftsmen lived but also other social groups, including some peasants. They were required to pay certain taxes and perform required services for the government (Hintzsche; Pushkarev).

posadskie residents of the posad.

prikaz ministry, office, department, e.g., Siberian Office (*Sibirskoi prikaz*).

prikazchik chief administrator of a village or of a district.

progon toll collected per verst (kilometer) traveled.

promyshlenniks strictly speaking, men who worked for themselves and exploited the natural resources of the land; contract workers drawn largely from the serf and townsman class who fished and hunted for furs in Siberia and later in Russian America (Pushkarev).

prorva isthmus.

protok channel.

puchki cow parsnips.

raznochintsi commoners belonging to no clear legally defined group but liable to taxation, e.g., craftsmen who did not belong to a guild; often people who had left class or estate of their parents but had not formally entered another legal class (Hintzsche; Pushkarev).

Schnurbuch G, government ledger for travelers on official business to record their accounting.

shiveri rapids, rocky places.

sliuda mica.

sloboda large communal village settled by voluntary colonists with government assistance.

sluzhiv, *actually* **sluzhivoi, sluzhivie liudi,** *from the verb* **sluzhit',** *to serve* a general term applied to state employees in both civil and military service, mostly peasants and posadskie, but also including Cossacks and streltsy, who were sent to Siberia to protect Russia's vital interests (Hintzsche; Dmytryshyn in Wood, 22).

sosna flour made of or mixed with Scots pine bark.

streltsy literally shooters; units of guardsmen who carried firearms.

suslo a mush made with malt.

syn boyarskoi literally a boyar's son; originally the impoverished or younger sons of military men who had not achieved the rank of a boyar (a member of the higher nobility). These were the lowest-ranking nobles in the country but nevertheless ranked higher than ordinary Cossacks though Cossacks were sometimes promoted to the rank of boyars' sons (Hintzsche; Pushkarev; Hartley, 42–43).

ukase an edict of the Russian government.

utesi steep cliffs.

voevod chief administrator of a district with far-reaching legal, economic, administrative, and police powers; old Slavic, originally meaning military commander, leader of warriors.

yasak head tax paid in furs or money (see p. 8, note 4).

zaimka in Siberia, a small settlement with only a few houses, without an owner, arbitrarily acquired or occupied.

zakazchik a village's chosen representative, subordinate to the prikazschik; often responsible for collecting the yasak.

zapor ice jam.

zimov'e hut or way station used by hunters and travelers primarily in winter.

Obsolete Russian Measurements We Have Converted

arshin = 28 inches, standardized by Peter the Great in the eighteenth century

bakcha = funt = 0.903 pounds

desiatina meaning a tenth or ten; 1 = 117,600 square feet

funt = 14.5 ounces

fut = foot = 1 English foot

pud, pood = 40 Russian funt = 36. 11 pounds = 16.38 kilograms

sazhen' = Faden (G) = fathom = approximately 6 feet

tsentner = Zentner (G) = 110 pounds

vedro = bucket = 3.47 gallons

verst = 1.067 kilometers; converted to 1 kilometer

GLOSSARY OF PEOPLE

Johann Christian Berckhan (1709–1751), German, painter; traveling with Gmelin, Müller, and De l'Isle de la Croyère and then with Steller from Irkutsk to Kamchatka.

Vitus Jonassen Bering (1681–1741), Danish, captain commander of the Second Kamchatka Expedition; captain of the First Expedition; died and was buried on what is now Bering Island in the Commander Islands.

Aleksei Yur'evich Bibikov, vice-governor of Irkutsk from 1737 to 1740, died after 1741; Steller dedicated his *Flora Irkutiensis* to him.

Aleksei Il'ich Chirikov (1703–1748), Russian naval captain; participated in both the First and Second Kamchatka Expeditions, commanding the *St. Paul* on the voyage to America.

Aleksei Fedorovich Danilov, corporal sluzhiv from Okhotsk; accompanied Steller from Yakutsk to Okhotsk; later became a Yakutsk syn boyarskoi.

Ivan Andreevich (?) Daurkin, secretary to the Yakutsk voevod office; Steller refers to his horse as Daurken, likely named after secretary Daurkin; consistent spelling was not Steller's strong suit.

Louis de l'Isle de la Croyère (1688–1741), French, professor of astronomy, member of the Academic Group; died of scurvy in 1741 upon arrival on Kamchatka from the voyage with Chirikov on the *St. Paul*.

Anton Emmanuilovich Devier (1682–1745), new commander of Okhotsk when Steller arrived there in 1740; replaced Skornyakov-Pisarev after endless complaints about him had reached St. Petersburg.

Simon Gardebol (actually Hardebol; died 1750), Dutch, assay master; in 1732 was assigned to the Academic Group. Steller describes him as lazy and unreliable.

Dmitrei Giliashev, huntsman (to assist with collecting scientific specimens).

Johann Georg Gmelin (1709–1755), German, naturalist, chemist, physician; one of the three professors in the Academic Group. His observations and collections are contained in his *Flora Sibirica*. He described his journey as part of the Second Kamchatka Expedition in *Reise durch Sibirien von dem Jahr 1733–1743*.

Aleksei Gorlanov (died 1759), student, Steller's assistant and translator. Among other assignments he kept track of the toll paid out per kilometer of travel between Irkutsk and Kirenskoi Ostrog (*Quellen* 2:263–67). Together with A. Ivanov, I. Yakhontov, and S. Krasheninnikov, he described the Lena River from Verkholensk to Yakutsk in 1736, giving the direction of flow and every one-quarter kilometer describing islands, streams flowing into the Lena, and any settlements on the banks (*Quellen* 2:271–370).

Carl Hencke, caravan physician in Kyakhta (?) (Hintzsche).

Fedot Klimovskoi, Yakutsk sluzhiv and interpreter; assigned to Steller's crew.

Johann Albrecht von Korff (1697–1766), president of the Academy of Sciences (1734–1740); Steller sent the results of his research to him.

Stepan Krasheninnikov (1712–1755), student sent ahead to Kamchatka to prepare for the professors' arrival there. Based on their detailed instructions, he did his own research beginning in 1737, studying mostly the southern part of the peninsula. He spent ten years as a member of the expedition, eventually became a professor of the Academy of Sciences, and was commissioned to write up the results of both his and Steller's research about Kamchatka, which appeared in 1755, the year of Krasheninnikov's death, with the title *Opisanie Zemli Kamchatki* or *Description of Kamchatka*.

Andrei Dmitrievich Krasil'nikov (1705–1773), surveyor and astronomer.

Dmitrei Kychkin, Moscow dvoryanin.

Gerhard Friedrich Müller (1705–1783), German, historian and ethnographer; one of the professors of the Academic Group. He is considered the father of Siberian history and ethnography.

Dmitrei Ivanovich Pavlutskoi (died 1747), voevod in Yakutsk from June 1740 to June 1742.

Grigorei Samoilov, prospector assigned to Steller's crew.

Grigorei Skornyakov-Pisarev (1686–1747), commander of Okhotsk 1731–1740. According to Lauridsen, quoted by Stejneger (207), "Made vicious by a long and unjust banishment, he became Bering's evil spirit. . . . He was violent, restless and firey as a youngster in both speech and action, dissolute, bribable and slanderous, a lying and malicious gossip."

Grigorii Soltner, Swedish merchant.

Martin Spangberg (1695–1761), Danish naval captain; took part in both Kamchatka expeditions, commanding the first Russian naval squadron to visit the Japanese island of Honshu in 1738. He also made voyages in 1739 and 1742 to survey the coasts of Sakhalin, Japan, and the Kuril Islands.

Moisei Ushakov (died 1742), surveyor.

Sava Lukich Vladislavich-Raguzinsky (1679–1738), Serbian count and diplomat; in the service of Peter the Great negotiated the Treaty of Kyakhta, signed in 1728, which regulated the trade between Russia and China.

Yakov, Steller's hired hand.

BIBLIOGRAPHY

Primary Sources

Steller, Georg Wilhelm. "Beschreibung der Stadt Irkutsk und der umliegenden Gegenden." In *Reisetagebücher 1735 bis 1743*, 1–75. Vol. 2 of *Quellen zur Geschichte Sibiriens und Alaskas aus russischen Archiven*. Edited by Wieland Hintzsche with Thomas Nickol, Ol'ga V. Novochatko, and Dietmar Schulze. Halle: Verlag der Franckeschen Stiftungen, 2000.
———. "Reisejournal von Irkutsk nach Ochotsk und Kamtschatka 4. März bis 16. September 1740." *Quellen* 2:77–216.
"Instruktion und Verzeichnis mitgegebener Sachen für Georg Wilhelm Steller von Johann Georg Gmelin und Gerhard Friedrich Müller vom 28. Februar 1739 aus Enisejsk." In *Briefe und Dokumente, 1739*, 71–93. Vol. 3 of *Quellen*. Edited by Wieland Hintzsche, assisted by Thomas Nickol, Ol'ga V. Novochatko, and Dietmar Schulze. Halle: Verlag der Franckeschen Stiftungen, 2001.

Other Steller Works Consulted

Briefe und Dokumente, 1739. Vol. 3 of *Quellen*.
Briefe und Dokumente, 1740. Vol. 1 of *Quellen*. Edited by Wieland Hintzsche, Thomas Nickol, and Ol'ga Vladimirovna Novochatko. Halle: Verlag der Franckeschen Stiftungen, 2000.
Dokumente zur 2. Kamtschatkaexpedition 1730-1733, Akademiegruppe. Vol. 4.2 of *Quellen*. Edited by Wieland Hintzsche in cooperation with Natasha Ochotina Lind and Peter Ulf Möller. Halle: Verlag der Franckeschen Stiftungen, 2004.
Dokumente zur 2. Kamtschatkaexpedition Januar–Juni 1734, Akademiegruppe. Vol. 5 of *Quellen*. Edited by Wieland Hintzsche et al. Halle: Verlag der Franckeschen Stiftungen, 2006.
History of Kamchatka. Edited by Marvin W. Falk. Translated by Margritt Engel and Karen Willmore. Fairbanks: University of Alaska Press, 2003.
Journal of a Voyage with Bering, 1741–1742. Edited by O. W. Frost. Translated by Margritt A. Engel and O. W. Frost. Stanford: Stanford University Press, 1988.
"Reisejournal von Enisejsk nach Irkutsk 6. März 1739 bis 2. Mai 1739." In *Reisetagebücher 1738–1745*, 1–158. Vol. 7 of *Quellen*. Edited by Wieland Hintzsche with Heike Heklau. Halle: Verlag der Franckeschen Stiftungen, 2009.

Steller's Scientific Works

Few of Steller's purely scientific works, almost all written in Latin, have been translated and published either in German or English. More or less available exceptions are *The Beasts of the Sea* (long out of print; see annotated bibliography below), excerpts translated into German in the *Briefe und Dokumente*, *1739* and *1740*, and the following ones primarily describing plants:

Jäger, Eckehart. "Die ersten Listen und Aufsammlungen von Pflanzen aus Alaska—Georg Wilhelm Stellers botanische Arbeiten in Amerika." Feddes Repertorium 111 (2000): 321–62. (On-line in *Steller-Studien 2010*, 321–68. http://www.steller-gesellschaft.de/steller-studien/.)

Thilenius, J. F. "Alaska Plant Specimens Collected by Georg Steller in the Linnean Society Herbarium." Grantee reports, American Philosophical Society, London, 1985, 12–14.

———. "Appendix: Analysis of the Plant Taxonomy of the *Catalogus plantarum intra sex horas*." In *Bering and Chirikov: The American Voyages and Their Impact*, edited by O. W. Frost, 413–43. Anchorage: Alaska Historical Society, 1992. [See Jäger (2000) above for the more accurate assessment of Steller's collection.]

"Treatise on Folk Medicine." Translated from the Latin by Tatiana A. Lukina, *Science First Hand*, April 30, 2010. *World in the Eye of Science* 25, no. 1.

While Steller's manuscript *Flora Irkutiensis* is now in press, his *Flora Ochotensis* (*Fl. Och.*) has not been worked on (Hintzsche, e-mail January 17, 2018).

Secondary Sources

"AgroAtlas: Interactive Agricultural Ecological Atlas of Russia and Neighboring Countries." www.agroatlas.ru/en/index.html.

Bond, Carl E. Professor Emeritus of Fisheries, Department of Fisheries and Wildlife. Oregon State University, Corvallis, Oregon. Personal communications, 1991.

Bown, Stephen R. *Island of the Blue Foxes: Disaster and Triumph on the World's Greatest Scientific Expedition*. New York: Da Capo, 2017.

Dauenhauer, Nora, Richard Dauenhauer, and Lydia Black, eds. *Russians in Tlingit America: The Battles of Sitka 1802 and 1804*. Seattle: University of Washington Press, 2008.

Die Große Nordische Expedition—Georg Wilhelm Steller (1709–1746): Ein Lutheraner erforscht Sibirien und Alaska. Edited by Wieland Hintzsche and Thomas Nickol. Gotha: Justus Perthes, 1996. Catalog to the exhibition held to commemorate the 250th anniversary of Steller's death, at the Franckesche Stiftungen in Halle, Germany.

Dmytryshyn, Basil, E. A. P. Crownhart-Vaughan, and Thomas Vaughan, eds. and trans. *Three Centuries of Russian Eastward Expansion. A Documentary Record*. Vol. 1, *Russia's Conquest of Siberia: To Siberia and Russian America, 1558–1700*. Western Imprints. Portland: Oregon Historical Society, 1985.

———. Vol. 2, *Russian Penetration of the North Pacific Ocean, 1700–1797*. Loc. cit., 1988.

"Fish of Siberia." http://www.sibrybalka.ru/ryby.

Fjodorova, Tatjana, Birgit Leick Lampe, Sigurd Rambusch, and Tage Sørensen. *Martin Spangsberg: A Danish Explorer in Russian Service*. Esbjerg: Fiskeri-og Søfartsmuseet, n.d. [2003].

German Names of U.S. Fish and Shellfish. Pamphlet. Anchorage, AK: Fisheries Development Foundation [no date].

Gibson, James R. *Feeding the Russian Fur Trade: Provisionment of the Okhotsk Seaboard and the Kamchatka Peninsula, 1639–1856*. Madison: University of Wisconsin Press, 1969.

Girdle, Ash, Ian Welby, and Robin Welcomme. *Fisheries Management: A Manual for Still-Water Coarse Fisheries*. Oxford: Wiley Blackwell, 2010.

Golder, F. A. *Bering's Voyages: An Account of the Efforts of the Russians to Determine the Relations of Asia and America*. 2 vols. New York: Octagon Books, 1968.

———. *Russian Expansion on the Pacific, 1641–1850*. Cleveland, OH: Arthur H. Clark, 1914.

Grimm, Jacob, and Wilhelm Grimm. *Deutsches Wörterbuch*. 33 vols. Munich: Deutscher Taschenbuch-Verlag, 1984.

Hartley, Janet. *Siberia: A History of the People*. New Haven: Yale University Press, 2014.

Kasten, Erich, in cooperation with Michael Dürr, Elena Dultschenko, Sergej Longinov, and Tjan Zaotschnaja. *Lachsfang und Bärentanz: Die Itelmenen 250 Jahre nach ihrer Beschreibung durch Georg Wilhelm Steller* [Salmon fishing and the bear dance: The Itelmen 250 years after their description by Steller]. Bonn: Holos, 1996.

Krasheninnikov, Stepan P. *Explorations of Kamchatka, 1735–1741*. Translated by E. A. P. Crownhart-Vaughan. Portland: Oregon Historical Society, 1972.

Kushnarev, Evgenii G. *Bering's Search for the Strait: The First Kamchatka Expedition, 1725 1730*. Edited and translated by E. A. P. Crownhart-Vaughan. Portland: Oregon Historical Society, 1990.

Kuschtewskaja, Tatjana. *Sibirienreise—die Lena: Vom Baikal bis zum Eismeer—Geschichte und Geschichten entlang dem großen historischen Fluss*. Translated by Ilse Tschörtner. Berlin: Wostok, 2007.

Massie, Robert K. *Peter the Great, His Life and World*. New York: Alfred A. Knopf, 1980.

"The Plant List: A Working List of All Plant Species." www.theplantlist.org.

Pushkarev, Sergei G. *Dictionary of Russian Historical Terms from the Eleventh Century to 1917*. Edited by George Vernadsky and Ralph T. Fischer, Jr. New Haven: Yale University Press, 1970.

Ricketts, Edward F., and Jack Calvin. *Between Pacific Tides*. 4th ed. Revised by Joel W. Hedgpeth. Stanford: Stanford University Press, 1968.

Romanenko, Olga, Dale L. Taylor, Vera Kanishero, Ora Gologergen, and Polly Schaeffer. *Biota of Central Beringia with English, Russian, and Native Names*. Anchorage, AK: National Park Service, 1997.

Stejneger, Leonhard. *Georg Wilhelm Steller: The Pioneer of Alaskan Natural History*. Cambridge, MA: Harvard University Press, 1936.

Sutton, Ann, and Myron Sutton. *Steller of the North*. Chicago: Rand McNally, 1961.

Uhlmann, Bernd. "Zu Georg Wilhelm Stöller in Windsheim." *Steller-Studien* 2010. http://www.steller-gesellschaft.de/steller-studien/.

———. *Zur Ehre Gottes und zum Wohl der Stadt: Idee, Geschichte und Ende der Armenschule in der Freien Reichsstadt Windsheim*. Electronic edition, privately provided.

Vermeulen, Han. "Halle und die Anfänge der Ethnologie im 18. Jahrhundert." *Steller-Studien* 2013. http://www.steller-gesellschaft.de/steller-studien/.

———. *Before Boas: The Genesis of Ethnography and Ethnology in the German Enlightenment*. Lincoln, NE and London: University of Nebraska Press, 2015 (Critical Studies in the History of Anthropology).

Wood, Alan, ed. *The History of Siberia*. New York: Routledge, Chapman, and Hall, 1991.

"WWW Irkutsk: Animals and Fishes of Lake Baikal." www.irkutsk.org/baikal/animals.html. www.uniport.org/taxonomy/3711.

Sources Consulted by Eckehart J. Jäger, Institut für Biologie, Bereich Geobotanik und Botanischer Garten der Martin-Luther-Universität, Halle, Germany

(Personal communication, 2014–20)
Drawings by Johann Christian Berckhan.
Drawings in Gmelin's *Flora Sibirica Siv Historia Plantarum Sibirae*.
Charkevic, S. S., ed. *Sosudistye Rastenija Sovetskogo Dal'nego Vostoka* [Flora of the Far East]. Vols. 1–8. St. Petersburg: Nauka, 1985–96.
Hultén, E., and M. Fries. *Atlas of the North European Vascular Plants North of the Tropic of Cancer*. Vols. 1–3. Königstein: Koeltz, 1986.
Jäger, Eckehart J. "Die ersten Listen und Aufsammlungen von Pflanzen aus Alaska—Georg Wilhelm Stellers botanische Arbeiten in Amerika." Op. cit.
Malyshev, L. I., I. M. Krasnoborov, G. A. Peshkova, and A. V. Polozhii, eds. *Flora Sibiri*. Vols. 1–14. Novosibirsk: Nauka, 1987–97.
Marzell, H., Wilhelm Wissman, and Wolfgang Pfeifer. *Wörterbuch der deutschen Pflanzennamen*. Vols. 1–5. 1943–79. Leipzig, Stuttgart, and Wiesbaden. New printing, Cologne, 2000.
Richter, Hermann. *Codex Botanicus Linnaeanus*. Rugel: A. R. G. Gantern Verlag K. G., 2003.
Steller, G. W. *Flora Irkutiensis*. Manuscript. 1740. After the handwriting by Aleksej Gorlanov. Source: AAW R. I., Op. 104, D. 4, Bl Ir-188r. Supplied by W. Hintzsche. Translated by H. Heklau with interpretation of plant names used by Steller. Manuscript prepared for submission.

Selective Annotated Bibliography of Published and Unpublished Works of Georg Wilhelm Steller in German and English and a Brief Survey of Books about Him

De Bestiis Marinis or *the Beasts of the Sea*. Original Latin published in 1751. Translated into English by Walter Miller and Jennie E. Miller, published in David S. Jordan, *The Fur Seals and the Fur-Seal Islands of the North Pacific Ocean*, 179–218. Washington, DC: US Government Printing Office, 1899. All are marine mammals that inhabit (or formerly inhabited) the arc of the North Pacific from Japan to California: sea otter (*Enhydra lutris*), Steller's sea lion (*Eumetopias jubatus*), northern fur seal (*Callorhinus ursinus*), and Steller's sea cow (*Hydrodamalis gigas*). None of these animals had been known to European scientists until Steller's description of them.

Description of Unpublished Steller Papers in Smithsonian Archives and the Library of Congress, O. W. Frost and Karen Willmore, Alaska Historical Commission, 1983. Described *Steller's Journal: The Manuscript Text* (see below); several letters and memoranda; *Catalogus plantarum intra sex horas*, which lists some of the plants Steller found on Kayak Island in 1741 and Bering Island in 1742; a list of Steller papers received by Krasheninnikov and a list of materials sent to St. Petersburg, together containing, for example, descriptions of plants and seeds, minerals, fish, birds and nests, sea and land animals, insects, medicine used by natives and Russians in Siberia, and vocabulary of different native languages; and "A Trip to Kayak Island, Alaska," by Leonhard Stejneger.

Steller's Journal: The Manuscript Text. Part 1, facsimile edition, and part 2, transliteration. Edited by O. W. Frost. Transliteration by Margritt Engel. Anchorage: Alaska Historical Commission, 1984. A facsimile assumed to be a direct copy of Steller's manuscript *Journal of a Voyage with Bering*, written with a quill pen by two or more copyists. Transliteration is more faithful to the original than the one done by Stejneger.

Georg Wilhelm Steller: Journal of a Voyage with Bering, 1741–1742. Edited by O. W. Frost. Translated by Margritt A. Engel and O. W. Frost. Stanford: Stanford University Press, 1988. This is a retranslation by Engel based on her transliteration described above. Steller departed Avacha Bay on Kamchatka on the *St. Peter* on June 4, 1741; landed on Kayak Island off the coast of Alaska on July 20; witnessed the first meeting between Europeans and Alaska Natives in the Shumagin Islands on September 5; ran aground on Bering Island November 16, where Bering and several more of his crew died, totaling thirty-one; and arrived back in Avacha Bay on August 27, 1742, one of forty-six survivors. What Steller revealed of himself here is what established his reputation as, in the words of Cory Ford, "one of the . . . most fascinating characters ever to appear on the western scene. He was brilliant; he was arrogant; he was gifted as are few men" (*Where the Sea Breaks Its Back*, introduction). In the earlier-written but much-later-published manuscripts and documents, Steller presents himself as a much more nuanced, complex person—empathetic, congenial, turning near disaster into humor, capable of playing the bureaucratic game but always standing up for what he thought was right.

Steller's History of Kamchatka: Collected Information Concerning the History of Kamchatka, Its Peoples, Their Manners, Names, Lifestyle, and Various Customary Practices. Edited by Marvin Falk. Translated by Margritt Engel and Karen Willmore. Fairbanks: University of Alaska Press, 2003. This translation was based on J. B. Scherer's printed German edition of 1774. In 2013 Erich Kasten and Michael Dürr published a new German edition based on Steller's original manuscript, *Georg Wilhelm Steller, Beschreibung von dem Lande Kamtschatka*, in which they corrected many of the misprints, errors, and inconsistencies found in Scherer's edition, who himself had written that Steller's manuscript was terribly difficult to decipher. This edition is also available electronically: www.siberian-studies.org/publications/steller.html. The student Stepan Krasheninnikov arrived on Kamchatka in 1737 with a detailed set of instructions for his research under the auspices of the Academy of Sciences. He left Kamchatka in 1743; Steller arrived in September 1740, leaving in May 1741 and returning from his sea voyage in August 1742 to remain for almost a year. In 1750 Krasheninnikov became a professor of natural history and botany in St. Petersburg and was asked to prepare a volume about Kamchatka using both his and Steller's research, though the part that Steller did was not made entirely clear. This work was translated into a number of languages, the Oregon Historical Society edition of 1972 by E. A. P. Crownhart-Vaughan being the most recent English-language version. With his description of Kamchatka, Steller has a much greater claim to fame than with his diary of the sea voyage. Scientific knowledge of Kamchatka's flora, birds, land and marine mammals, fisheries, and sea creatures began with his and Krasheninnikov's research. Steller's descriptions of the way of life of the Itelmen have been of particular value for being the only ethnography of these indigenous people before their culture was overpowered by European Russians; they are now using these descriptions to recoup their traditional knowledge and to protect their environment attested to by Erich

Kasten's *Lachsfang und Bärentanz: Die Itelmenen 250 Jahre nach ihrer Beschreibung durch Georg Wilhelm Steller* (Salmon fishing and the bear dance; see above). Much more like a native than a European scientist, Steller traveled light, ate native foods, and praised the use of dogsleds in winter, including the ability to stay warm curled up with the dogs. He even became a godfather to an Itelmen son. In the *Vorwort* (preface) to their new edition of the *Beschreibung*, Erich Kasten describes Steller as a "participating observer," as someone who respected strange cultures, perhaps heralding the beginning of cultural relativism, though he was very open about aspects of Kamchadal behavior he did not agree with.

Georg Wilhelm Steller: Briefe und Dokumente, 1739. Vol. 3 of *Quellen*, 2001. Although the Russian government was funding the Second Kamchatka Expedition, no one government office was responsible for all the supplies, crew, food, and salaries that Steller needed for his trip from Irkutsk to Kamchatka or for research he did around Irkutsk. Many of these documents show how frustrating and complicated it was to shake loose the funding and necessities he was lawfully due even though it was the local officials who actually held the purse strings, each theoretically supplying a portion of his requirements. Published in this volume are 157 documents, most of which are memoranda, letters, catalogs, instructions, reports, and trebovania (written requests to a person or institution of lower rank; WH, Glossar), dealing primarily with the Academic Group's concerns as part of the Second Kamchatka Expedition. All are in German though some have been translated from Russian or Latin. Of these Steller wrote twenty-seven memoranda, all to the Irkutsk Provincial Government, detailing all the supplies and support crew and their salaries that by law he was to be given for his trip from Irkutsk. Of the thirteen of Steller's letters in this volume, three are to Johann Albrecht von Korff, the president of the Academy of Sciences, reporting on his trip from Moscow to Yeniseysk, his arrival in Irkutsk, and all his observations and specimens he was sending to von Korff; seven letters are to his fellow scientists, Müller and Gmelin, about his research; one letter is in Latin to the botanist Johann Amman, about plants Steller has found and how happy he is to be going to Kamchatka; and one letter discharges his workers in Barguzinskoi Ostrog. One letter to the librarian Johann Daniel Schumacher of the Academy of Sciences we have translated and included above as Appendix C. Of the four trebovania Steller wrote, three were to the Barguzinskoi Ostrog's prikazchik, demanding that enough double brandy be provided to safely preserve his omul and sigi (fish) specimens, that transportation be provided for his sluzhiv Danilov, and that the miner, Samoilov, be paid for four months work. The fourth trebovanie was to the brandy inspector in Barguzinskoi Ostrog. Two documents accompanied Steller's scientific catalogs of minerals and of birds and animals and one of Johann Christian Berckhan's drawings of Steller's specimens; all were sent from Irkutsk. Included in this volume are two of Steller's instructions: one to Fedot Klimovskoi, requesting that he turn over his *Schnurbuch* to Aleksei Gorlanov; the other to Aleksei Danilov, detailing how he should go about fulfilling his assignment to investigate, among other things, the blue color of the steep bank on the Tsipa River and the hot springs in the vicinity of Lake Baunt.

Georg Wilhelm Steller: Briefe und Dokumente, 1740. Vol. 1 of *Quellen*, 2000. Published in this volume are 172 documents, most of which are also memoranda, letters, instructions, and catalogs of research results. All are in German, some having been translated from

Russian or Latin. Of these documents Steller wrote eight letters, of which the three most consequential—to Müller, von Korff, and Gmelin—present his case and apology over the controversy with Gmelin. The others concern administrative matters: thirty-six memoranda, half of which were to the Irkutsk government (Kanzlei) and the others to the Yakutsk voevod and the office of Okhotskoi Port (official name of the ostrog after its 1736 relocation to the mouth of the Okhota; WH, Anm. 1, p. 275), requesting pay for crew members and the promised necessities for his travels; thirteen trebovania of which ten were to the Bol'sheretsk prikazchik, asking the support Krasheninnikov was owed on Kamchatka; five documents of instructions to four different individuals; four documents of catalogs, two listing research results and two listing expenses that needed to be reimbursed; and three reports, two of which went to the Senate in St. Petersburg and one to the Academy of Sciences.

Georg Wilhelm Steller. "Beschreibung von Flüssen und darin lebender Fische auf dem Weg von Enisejsk bis zur Stadt Irkuck aus dem Jahr 1739." In *Reisetagebücher 1738–1745*, 159-80. Vol. 7 of *Quellen*, 2009.

The manuscript of Steller's travel journal from St. Petersburg to Yeniseysk, written between December 1737 and February 1739—long thought to be lost—was found by Wieland Hintzsche in St. Petersburg in 2001, its publication being delayed by the need to find Latin translators who would volunteer their services. Other manuscripts concerning folk medicine, ethnography, travels, fish, birds, plants, and so on also await someone who can translate from Latin and is willing to work for free (Hintzsche, email, January 17, 2018).

From the outset, the publication of the *Quellen zur Geschichte Sibiriens und Alaskas aus russischen Archiven* was a cooperative effort of the Franckesche Stiftungen and the Archive of the Academy of Sciences in St. Petersburg. The stated intent (*Quellen* 1:vi) was to make unpublished documents from the Second Kamchatka Expedition available to scholars and the public in both German and Russian. A list of those in print is found on the website of the Internationale Georg-Wilhelm-Steller Gesellschaft (steller-gesellschaft.de) under "Literatur." In addition to the ones we have cited, the following have been published in German (our translations):

Vol. 8, *Gerhard Friedrich Müller, Ethnographic Writings I*
Vol. 11, *Gerhard Friedrich Müller, Ethnographic Writings II*

The following volumes have been published in Russian (our translations):

Vol. 1, *Georg Wilhelm Steller, Letters and Documents, 1740*
Vol. 4, 1, *Second Kamchatka Expedition: Documents, 1730–1733—Marine Detachment* (Documents concerning the Academic Group in preparation)
Vol. 6, *Second Kamchatka Expedition: Documents, 1734–1736—Marine Detachment*
Vol. 8, *Gerhard Friedrich Müller, Description of Siberian Peoples*
Vol. 9, *Second Kamchatka Expedition: Documents, 1737–1738—Marine Detachment*

There are possibly more books about Steller in English than in German, but only two are scholarly works. The second volume of F. A. Golder's two-volume *Bering's Voyages: An Account of the Efforts of the Russians to Determine the Relation of Asia and America* contains Steller's *Journal of the Sea Voyage from Kamchatka to America and*

Return on the Second Kamchatka Expedition, 1741–1742, as translated by Leonhard Stejneger, along with a brief preface and biographical note, and Stejneger's biography of Steller. (Volume 1 of Golder holds translations of the *St. Peter*'s log books and the official reports of the First and Second Kamchatka Expeditions.) Since its publication in 1925—the first time the journal had been translated in its entirety—it has been primarily responsible for what others have thought of and written about Steller.

The later commentators have also drawn heavily on Leonhard Stejneger's biography, *Georg Wilhelm Steller: The Pioneer of Alaskan Natural History*, published in 1936, a most thoroughly researched, documented, and well-written biography. Though it has long been out of print and is therefore no longer readily available, many knowledgeable Germans consider it so good that they see no need for a German update. Yet while Stejneger was a formidable researcher who made use of many different sources in Russia, Germany, Denmark, and the United States, he himself laments the apparent loss of many Steller manuscripts. He thus presents a wealth of information on the historical context, the circumstances that Steller encountered, and the people he came in contact with. But of necessity Stejneger often had to rely on assumptions for Steller's actions, reactions, and interactions, especially those concerning his private life (e.g., his marriage), which led to misrepresentations by later commentators who mistook Stejneger's assumptions as facts.

Not surprisingly, some of the authors of popular books about Steller were attracted to him because, like him, they felt at home in the natural world: Ford was an outdoors writer, Littlepage a wilderness guide, the Suttons a park ranger and a geologist, respectively. These English books focus on the naturalist while the Germans are more focused on the ethnographer. All of these popular books essentially retell the events in the sea journal, and though they make for good reading, they often repeat misperceptions and misrepresentations. Some of the more sensational or surprising—definitely fictional—details (for example, about Steller's marriage or his love of liquor) occur in several works. For example, both Stejneger and Bown cite Lagunov's issuing liquor to Steller on board ship as proof that Steller was prone to drink too much. Knowing of memoranda requesting brandy for the preservation of specimens, we are certain that was its intended use on board as well. It is to be hoped that our translation will dispel some of these myths.

The Suttons' *Steller of the North* and Ann Arnold's *Sea Cows, Shamans, and Scurvy* are appealing books for young adults, Arnold's especially so because of her illustrations. Although they, too, rely heavily on the sea journal and on Stejneger, they are not preoccupied with Steller's marriage and do not speculate on Mrs. Steller's broken promise of accompanying him, while W. G. Sebald's poetic triptych, *After Nature*, in which the second part is devoted to Steller, and T Edward Bak's *Island of Memory*, first part of a planned Steller graphic narrative trilogy, place undue focus on them. The latest publication of interest in this context, Stephen R. Bown's *Island of the Blue Foxes*, while not merely about Steller but about the Second Kamchatka Expedition, already indicates by its subtitle, *Disaster and Triumph on the World's Greatest Scientific Expedition*, that to a large extent it also presents a retelling of Steller's sea journal.

An intriguing misunderstanding attests to how mistakes are perpetuated in the literature. In a letter to Gmelin (of November 17, 1739; *Quellen* 3:347), Steller rejects Gmelin's suggestion that he be more conciliatory toward Mrs. Steller and mentions that in her place—presumably for affection—he now has two young *Baben*, the Germanized plural of Russian *babi*, pelicans [*Baba ptitsa* in Latin]. We do not know who first misread *Baben* for *Raben*, ravens in German, but the ravens appear at least in Ford, Sebald, and Bak in this context.

After we had submitted our manuscript, we were alerted to two very recently published novels, Thomas McGuire's *Steller's Orchid* (Boreal Books, Red Hen Press, 2019) and Stephen Spotte's *The Singing Bones* (Open Books, 2019). With the help of the plant Steller did not find in the Shumagin Islands, McGuire, an Alaskan outdoorsman, tells an intriguing "old-fashioned adventure, mystery, and coming-of-age story" (Heather Lende, reviewer). Spotte, himself a well-known marine biologist, who subtitled his book "A Novel of the Life and Times of Naturalist Georg Wilhelm Steller" and who calls Steller "a superb marine biologist . . . in addition to his other achievements" (p. 247), obviously feels a deep kinship with Alaska's first western naturalist. He portrays Steller sympathetically and narrates the events in such an appealing way that it is hard to put the book down even if one already knows the story.

The following two books were our primary sources for the historical background:

Hartley, Janet. *Siberia: A History of the People*. New Haven: Yale University Press, 2014. A readable overview, but with errors concerning Steller and the Second Kamchatka Expedition. Gerhard Müller and Johann Gmelin—and later Steller—were part of the Academic Group, one of three groups comprising the Second Kamchatka Expedition. Hartley gives the impression that they were a separate group, accompanied by some six hundred men (150), which was actually the number of persons assigned to the entire expedition (J. L. Black in Wood, 61). She quotes only Steller's negative comments about the native Kamchadals on Kamchatka, leaving out the following less simplistic characterization: "The Itelmen are equipped with an excellent intellect, a lively imagination, and a prodigious memory, but lack all judgement. Their intellect is apparent from their amazing and amusing ideas, reasoning, and inventions, and their lively melodies; their memories from a thousand superstitions; their poor judgement from their theology, morals, and understanding of nature" (*History of Kamchatka*, 222).

Wood, Alan, ed. *The History of Siberia*. New York: Routledge, Chapman and Hall, 1991. Essays on Siberia, devoted to aspects of historical development from the Russian conquest in the sixteenth century up to and including the revolutions of 1917 and the civil war.

PLANT INDEX

alders, small: 127; location of unsuitable for growing grain, 88
alpine bells, 127, 131, 136n7
anemone, narrow-leaved, 132, 137n15
Arabis stelleri (a species of rockcress), 177
Artemisia stelleriana Besser (beach wormwood or hoary mugwort), 177
ash, mountain, 162, 164n2
asphodel, false, a species of: drawing by Berckhan, 132
aster, beach (beach fleabane), 162, 164n2
avens, eight-petal: mountain overgrown with, 133, 137n16

bellflower, clustered: prepared meal from, 103; spotted, 127
birch, dwarf bog, 126, 127; nothing but, 178
birch, Japanese white, 36, 76, 111, 120, 127; bark basket to die in, 77; where it grows, 86, 88
bishop's cap, naked, 133, 137n17
bistort, alpine, 130
bittercress, 133, 135, 138n20
bladderwort: lake overgrown with, 124, 125n10
blueberries, alpine, 132; Cossacks use for dye, 183; enjoyed eating, 141; paid for, 183
burnet, great: prepared meal with, 103
buttercup, xx; Gmelin's, vii; new species and seeds collected from, 141, 151n8; started to bloom, 110, 118n6
butterwort: on high mountain, 133, 137n17
byssos (algae): where not found, 132

catchfly, Nottingham: Berckhan painted, 116
celery, wild: causing strong appetite for sex, 162, 164n
chickweed, common: started to bloom, 110, 118n6; water, 151n6
chives, 124; broadleaf, 129

cinquefoil, marsh, 104; rock, collected ripe seeds from, 130; with long runners, 124
clematis, 121
cloudberries, 150; Steller picked, 156
clubmoss, 156, 159n4
coltsfoot, sweet, 129; with longish leaves, 131, 137n12
columbine: a species of, 119; small-flowered, 121
compact dock: for dish of greens, 103, 109
coralroot, northern, 119
Corydalis (*Fumaria*), 130, 135
cow parsnips (*puchki*), 124, 125n11, 192; at mouth of the Urak, 162, 164n2
currants, red: abundance of, 128; first since the Aldan, 140

dogwood, dwarf Swedish, 162, 164n2; Siberian, 124, 125n8
dragonhead, 124, 125n12; Steller's, 189

fern (*glistnik*, R), 72
fireweed: cooked red shoots of, 104, 106n7

gentian, 135, 138n19; collected seeds from, 141, 151n6; near Okhotsk, 160, 164n2; star, 130; Steller fond of, xx
grass: arrow, 133, 137n16; *Carex*, short, thin and hard, 150; depends on floods, 108; dog ate, 123; gathering, 91, 92n8; good, 75, 156, 162; *Limnas stelleri* Trin., 190; scurvy, 162, 164n2; used to be better, 124; used to stack fish filets, 167

heathers, mountain: collected seeds from, 162, 164n3; two rare, 133
hemlock, water (*omeg*): harms cows, 113; horses immune to, 124
horseradish (dyers' woad): fields overgrown with, 121, 125n3; Siberian, 124

207

horsetail, common: made salad from, 103; leafless, used to scarify eyes, 111

Indian paintbrush, northern, 126, 136n1
iris: Japanese, 127, 136n8; wild, 126

jasmine: decoction for treating gonorrhea, 114; greater rock, 104; northern, 129, 137n16; with pointed rough-haired leaves, 133, 137n16

Labrador tea, Northern, 104, 133
larch, Dahurian, 36, 120, 124, 130, 142, 143; blackest pelts found in forests of, 111; bridge made from, 148; densely grows, 86; grass growing in forests of, 190; good wood, 76; least suitable for growing grain, 88; on top of permafrost, ix, 141; petrified, 126
leek, Steller's, ix, 189
lettuce: from seed lost enroute, 143, 162; lamb's, silverweed tastes like, 115
lichen: great abundance for reindeer, 150
lily, sarana, 162, 164n2; Siberian, 116, 118n12, 126, 136n1; water (*uentshuelue*), rhizomes of, 123, 125n7
lingonberries, 150
lousewort, a species of, 124, 126; fond of, xx; lesser, 124, 125n9; red, 132, 133
lovage, 124, 125n13
Lychnis: with azure flowers, 127, 129, 136n6

marsh orchid, flecked: first orchid with a long spur, 128
marigold, Arctic marsh, 131, 137n12
meadow rue: with a purple-turning flower, 124
milkvetch, 104, 127, 131; greater bog, 130; prepared meal from, 103
moss: abundance on mountains, 132, 142, 144, 145, 150; moss-like growth on old pikes, 111; sphagnum, 133, 137n17, 145; used to light lamps, 109; white cushion, 145
myosotide: collected seeds from, 141, 151n6

Onobrychis (legume), 122, 125n5
oyster leaf, 162, 164n2

pine nuts, 70
pine, Scots, 111, 120, 128; bark as food (*sosna*), 120, 128, 193; good wood, 76; on mountains, 36, 86, 124
pine, Siberian, 36; blackest pelts among, 111
pine: Siberian dwarf (*slanets*): cover disintegrating limestone mountains, 153; cover rough sandstone cliffs, 143; good wood, 76; lesser quality pelts among, 111; on top of mountains, 132
poplar, Mongolian, 140; tree of the river plains, 139
poppies, Iceland, 119; with orange-red flowers, 133, 137n16
Pyrola, lesser (probably wintergreen sidebells), 124

red-capped scaber stalk: first mushroom found, 143
rhododendron: rose-red blossoms, 162, 164n2; sulfur-yellow flowers, 133, 137n17
rhubarb: where it grows, 129
rockbrake, Steller's (a fern), 1, 135, 138n21, 189
rockcress: started to bloom, 110, 118n6; Steller's, 177, 189
rush, a species of, 131, 137n12

sage, Arctic: Steller smoking fuzz of, 123
Saxifraga stelleriana, 127, 177, 190
saxifrage: alternate-leaved golden, 190
saxifrage, bog, with yellow spotted flowers, 130
saxifrage, purple mountain, 156, 159n4
saxifrage, tripartite with rough-haired leaves, 132, 137n14
saxifrages, unidentified, 135, 136n2; collected seeds from, 155, 156; had sketched, 144
saxifrage, yellow dot, 127
Scorzonera: Yakuts eat roots of, 116, 118n10
seaweed: various types, 164
Senecio, 156, 159n5, 164n2
silverweed: Yakuts eat growths on roots, 115
skullcaps, 124
speedwell, Steller's, 190

spirea, false, 127, 136n4
spring beauty, 137n18
spruce, Siberian, 36; lesser quality pelts among, 111; good wood, 76; mountain covered with, 86, 112, 130
St. John's wort, 127
sweetvetch, Alpine: (photo), 2; same as Russian *sardana*, 127
sweetvetch, Arctic: dried roots for bread, 103, 106n6
Symphytum (comfrey): collected seeds of, 155

thistles, plume: fields overgrown with, 121, 125n3
Thysselinum, 124

violets, dames: with white flowers, 122, 133; small yellow, 135

willows, 88, 127; bark, eaten with roe, 168; grow on Horse Island, 120
wintergreen: liverleaf, 121; sidebells, 124; single delight, 127n13

INDEX

Academy of Sciences, 4, 6, 9, 20, 100
adaptability of people, 60
agate, black, 129
Akachan River, 144, 145
Aldan River, 130, 131; arrived at, 127; fish in, 72; forded, 128; meaning of name, 124; plants found on, 127, 134, 135, 136, 140; Yudoma and Maya flow into, 149
Aleksei. *See* Danilov, Sofronov
Amga River, 124, 131; description of, 126; soil along, 127
Amur River: dog salmon in, 166; find out about Gilyaks along, 19; Yakuts hunt sable on, 113
Anadyr River, 73; yasak paid by people living along, 47
Anadyrsk, Anadyrskoi Ostrog, 72–73; belugas hunted, 170; thinly populated, 109
Ancha River, 140; permafrost recorded near, ix
Anga Rivers, 85
Angara River, 47, 60, 81; description of, 27, 29, 30–31, 32, 33; fish and fishing in, 33, 34, 38n7; hunting along, 71; landscape along, 33, 34, 36, 37; settlements along, 72; through Irkutsk, 37, 39–40, 42, 52, 56; iron smelting and value of, 50, 64, 72, 90; levies on people along, 91, 92n2. *See also* Upper Angara

Baikal omul, 64; fishing for and value of, 63; native to and endangered, 34; preserving, 202
Baikal seals, 64, 67–71; blubber, 68; comparison to harbor seal, 67; different kinds of, 68, 70; hunts for, 68, 71; milk used by Tungus, 68; skins in trade, 54, 68–69, 71
Baikal sig, 33; promyshlenniks fishing for, 63, 202
Balaganskoi Ostrog: fish found below, 29, 34

Barguzin (Barguzinskoi Ostrog), 47, 70, 183; best pelts, 111; Cossacks moved to, 60; Steller's trip to, 180
Barguzin River: fishing, 61, 64; open to hunting, 68, 69
barrels: for fish, 62, 63, 167; holding brandy, 113
bears, 59; ate on dead whale, 162; compared with sea lions, 77; killed by Captain Spangberg, 156
beavers, 61; attacked by dogs, 77; pelts, 54
Beasts of the Sea (De Bestiis Marinis), xvii, xxiin3, 180, 181, 200
Belaya River, 139, 142, 150, 177; cotton mill and dyeworks on, 65; iron smelting on, 50; now called Khanda, 65; traveling along, 128–133, 136n3, 137n18
belugas, caught: at Udskoi and Anadyrskoi Ostrogs, 170; in the Ural, 72; with nets, 76
Berckhan, Johann Christian, painter: celebrating, 122, 144; drawings of plants, 116, 132, 133, 135, 138n19, 202; horse dies, 124; on a burial mound, 136; out on the ice, 100, 101; quarters in Yakutsk, 107; rank and support, xix, 10, 13, 14; shot a young loon, 130; traveling, 81, 117, 119, 123, 145, 148, 163, 180, 182; in the dark, 146. *See also* names of individual plants
Bering, Vitus, Captain Commander, vii, xii, xxiv, 1, 17, 181, 195; correspondence with, 17, 22; Pisarev, his evil spirit, 196; sailing out of Okhotsk, 172; second expedition, 3, 4; Steller's first meeting with, xii, 158
Bering Island, x, xvi, 181, 200, 201; pelts from, 5; recovered skeleton, xi
Bering Strait, x, 199
Bibikov, Aleksei Yur'evich, Vice-Governor of Irkutsk, 46, 110, 174, 195; Steller's party accompanied by, 81
birdshot needed, xxi, 186
bismuth, 164

211

black room, 149, 151n15
blubber. *See* seals *and* whales
bobylskie (peasants), 90, 191
Bogul'deicha River, 65, 69, 83; mouth of, 71
bolaric earth. *See* sour cream earth
Bol'sheretsk/Bol'sheretskoi Ostrog, 19, 75, 77
brandy, xix, 47–48, 116, 117, 120, 119, 149, 154, 176; cherry brandy, 116; distilleries, 47, 48, 65, 81, 94; distribution, 47; double, 41, 47, 112, 143, 202; loss of buckets of, 143; new bottles ordered, 108; police oversight, 43; price, 41, 112; prize at target-shooting match, 152; smugglers nabbed, 111; station for distribution and taxation, 40–41, 192; used for preserving specimens, 202, 204; ways of cheating, 48, 112–13
bread, 62, 65, 86, 101, 128, 155, 166, 170n2, 186; Aesop's loaves, 57; grain for, 91; *iukola* as substitute for, 167; joy of having, 149; no taste for, 126; sweetvetch roots suitable for baking, 103
bullhead (*pizda*), 37
burbot (*nalim*), 34; in the Aldan, 129; in the Amga, 124; in the Ilga, 90; in the Ushakovka, 36; in the Yudoma, 149
Buryats, 39, 54, 60, 61, 83; desired information about, 15; meaning of name, 39; sell game, 37; unaffected by epidemic, 84; use of seal blubber, 68; venerating *Shamanski kamen*, 32

capelin or candle fish (*ueki*), 169, 171n11
caravan: financed by, 47; physician to, 12, 81, 195; trade with China, 40, 45n3, 49–50
capercailles, 37
carp, crucian, 72, 120, 135; 142; blood-red, 111; dormant, 72; meal of, 121, 140; sly, 72; Yakut driver's name, 147
cattle: at Okhotsk, 156; butchered, 122, 125n4, 128; "food on the hoof," 6, 105, 107, 124, 128, 141, 149, 155; Gilyaks have, 114; lack of, 120; Yakuts' loss of, 135
char, Arctic (*kundsha*), 169
Chernaya River, 73
Chechuiskoi Ostrog, 99
Chirikov, Aleksei, Captain, 195, 198; his ship, 172, 173, 178; met in Okhotsk, 158

Chivirkui River, 61, 63, 64, 70
Chukchi, 107, 113; exaggerate their numbers, 109, 118n2, 118n5
clay, 20, 156; cliffs/mountains, 89, 95, 131, 162; for ovens, 149; for pottery, 23; mineral, 88; soils, xii, 16; sour-cream earth, 162–163
climate: cannot grow grain, 48; effect of differing ones, 59; protective, 44; much snow, 110; terrible, 5
coal: layers of, 126
coot, Eurasian, 120, 121
Cossacks, xv, 31–32; 69, 73, 87; chief, 107, 111, 116, 174; definitions of, xxiin4, 8n1, 191, 192, 193; earliest explorers, vii, 2; founders of Irkutsk, now few, 60; police chief, 42; origin of, 45n6; Steller appreciates, xv, 31–32
crabs: shall describe, 18; shall preserve, 21; found two special, 163
Crown, the: accounting to, 21; books for Gorlanov, 23; distilleries, 47; items received from, 10, 11, 14, 17, 22–23; monopoly on trade, 40; peasants, 61; secrecy governing and ukases, 22; Steller costs it less, 175
crows: feeding on fish, 166
cuckoo, 118n11; starts to call, 122
curiosities: box for storing, 183; ordered to be collected, 16; preserving, 23, 191; Russians' liking for, 54; sheet of ice, 141
customs duty, 40, 49, 50, 83; station, 40, 62, 83

dace, Eurasian (*yelets, yeltsi*): caught in Lake Baikal, 33; in the Amga, 124, in the Angara, 33, in the Ilga, 90, in the Ushakovka, 36; Yakuts deprived of, 120, 124
daily journal to be kept, 21
Danilov, Aleksei, sluzhiv, 117, 123, 195; back to Yakutsk, 116; brought news and delivered horses, 111; Steller wrote instructions for, 163; with Steller to Okhotsk, 106; 117, 123, 195
Daurken, Steller's horse, 145, 152
Daurkin, Ivan, Secretary to Yakutsk voevod, 107, 115, 117
deer and red deer: hunted by promyshlenniks, 36

de la Croyère, Louis Delisle, Professor of Astronomy, 5, 16; 195; his wife, 106, 149; Steller visited, 158, 161, 163; strange behavior, 106

derevnya (small village), 89, 90, 91, 93, 94, 95, 96, 97, 100, 101, 191; definition of, 72; naming of, 87, 95-96

Devier, Anton Emmanuilovich, Commander of Okhotsk: arrival in Yakutsk, 110; meeting on the trail, 139; visits with, 160, 163, 164; cleaned up Okhotsk, 166

dogs: Berckhan's, 145; "daughter of a dog," 146; dead on streets, 43; dragged corpses, 77, 78n3; gods of, 147; history of, 59; sled, 10, 66n1, 114, 154, 168, 201; Steller's, 123, 158; swimming, 129; trade with China, 57; Yakuts barking like, 133

dolphins (marine pigs), 170

doshcheniks (boats), 97, 111, 191; Angara's banks full of, 37, 40; drawing, 31; for journey from Irkutsk to Yakutsk, 12-13; full of saiga horns, 53; in trouble, 102; ordered one made, 97; promyshlenniks' use of, 61, 62, 64, 69, 70

ducks: lakes full of, 130, 135; northern eider, 1; sleds full of, 37; tufted, female shot, 130

ducklings, 113

duty. See customs

eagles, 39, 44n1-45; Steller's sea, x, xiiin3, 1

earthquakes, 20; big one, 71, 73n1

epidemics: along the Lena, viii, 84-85, 88, 90, 91; to be recorded on Kamchatka, 20

ermine: large numbers of, 87

Eurasian ruffe: absent in Siberian rivers, 29, 34, 129; in the Ilga, 90; rigidity of dorsal fin, 29

exiles, 2, 36, 60, 107; contributing to prostitution, 43

flatfish (*kambala*), unidentified), 169

flints: earth wax used in place of, 129; paid for fifty, 183; Samoilov to provide, 115

flooding, 37n2; of icy streams, 150; necessity of, 120; on the Amga, 124; on the Angara, 30; on the Belaya and Yuna, 130; on the Lena, 108, 97; to escape, 87

fog: in the mountains, 133, 139; in winter, 30, 108

food rations (soldier's, sluzhiv's), 10; Steller responsible for, 6

fox, arctic, 61; to be obtained alive, 16

French disease (Frenchmen). 66, 151n14; has become naturalized, 43; French breasts, 44, 45n8; Yakuts infected with, 114,

Gardebol, Simon, assayer, 20, 113, 195; lazy and unreliable, 155, 174; loaned Steller horses, 115; instructions to Steller about, 18-19; Steller met and dined with, 107, 108

geese: whole sleds full of, 37; snow, 103

Geleitukase, 13, 18, 191

geography: research of, 4, 10, 18; of Yakutsk district, 17

Giliashev, Dmitrei, huntsman, 10, 14, 195; issued a rifle, 23

Gilyaks: description of, 75; of interest to ethnographers, 177; research, 19; trade with Yakuts, 113-114

Gmelin, Johann Georg, Professor of Botany, 5, 64, 158, 163, 180, 191; controversy with Steller, 105, 174-75; documents, 97, 202, 204; impossible request to Steller, 91; instructions to Steller, xv, 9; plants, vii, 33, 86, 116, 127, 128, 158, 199; poor health, 6

goiters, 94, 98n1

Golousnaya River, 34, 69; fissures in ice at mouth of, 71

Gorlanov, Aleksei Petrovich, student, 9,14, 195, 200, 202; books issued to, 23; concerning horses, 106, 116, 135; his driver's name, 147; duties, 7, 10, 15; traveling, 81, 117, 124, 144, 149, 180, 182

gostinii dvor, 37, 38n8; 40, 41, 52

grain, 48, 85, 140; barley and rye, when to plant, 88; for brandy, 47, 49; growing regions, 37, 81, 83, 86, 87, 88, 91, 126; market, 41; not on Kamchatka, 140; prices, 37, 88-89

grasshoppers, 120

gray paper, 14, 23, 185; Chinese substitute, 143, 181

grayling: looks different from Arctic, 154; in the Aldan, 128-129; in the Amga, 124; in the Ilga, 90; in the Urak, 154, in the Yudoma, 149; thrown up through ice fissures, 71

grayling, Arctic (*charius*), 74n2, 155, 169; carrying a string of, 34, 37; in the Aldan, 128–129; in the Amga, 124; in the Ilga, 90; in the Ushakovka, 36; in the Yudoma, 149; resembles Dolly Varden, 169
Great Northern Exedition. *See* Kamchatka Expedition (Second)
grouse, 127; black, 37; hazel, 37; Siberian, 76
gudgeon: in the Ilga, 90
gulls: eating dead fish, 166; juvenile, 173; on the Yuna, 139; painted Shaman's Rock white, 32; shrieking, 67; two kinds of, ix, 173
gunpowder, 11, 23; gift to old man, 101; spoiled by dunking, 143; storage in Irkutsk, 40; too coarse to use, 186

Halle, 3; botanical excursions around, xx; orphanage in, 63, 66n4; Steller a student in, 4
hares: fell to death off Pine Cliff, 99; in Yakutsk region, 120; on the Uda River, 75; Yakuts have to live on, 135–136
hawk, white: a northern goshawk, 127
hay, 65, 87, 91, 108; good hayfields, 36, 72, 89; hay market, 41
head tax, 47, 88, 90; definition of, 191; who pays, 39, 48, 81, 87
Hencke, Carl (Henks), caravan physician, 81, 86, 110
High Governing Senate, 7, 20, 46; Steller's reports to, 14, 100, 186; ukases from, 9, 11, 17, 21, 22
hogs raised in Birulka, 86
horses: arrangements for travel with, 10, 18, 105–106, 107, 110, 111, 116; bones left by Yakuts, 133; butchered, 144; getting across rivers, 124, 128, 129, 144, 149, 156; gift of, 110, 122; in caravans, 45n3; lack of fodder, 145, 150; letting them rest, 130, 131, 139; loading of, 115, 117, 121, 122, 136n8, 140, 174; loss of, 121, 122, 128, 129, 130, 135, 139, 144, 146, 152; mishaps with, 131, 135, 148; stations for exchanging, 66n1, 94; trade in, 56–57; Yakuts eat, 114, 134
Horse Island, 119
hot spring, 70–71

huts (wayside/winter huts): along the Angara, 32, 34; at mouth of Chernaya, 73; blubber used to light, 68; caretakers of, 65; earthen, 119, 127; first one on road to the Lena, 83, 153; Irkutsk started as, 60; made of foliage, 150; promyshlenniks use, 62, 64, 71. *See also* way stations, also *zimov'e*

ice: blocks on river bank, 101; boats adrift in, 31, 70; breakup, 97; effect of earthquake on, 71; freeze-up, 33; jams, 102, 103; jumping across floes, 101, 102; patch, 141–142, 144, 151n7; points on the Belaya River, 131; rivers as roads, 29; seals on, 70; traveling on the ice-choked Lena, 99–104; Yakut superstition concerning it, 73
Ilga River, 90
Ilim River, 33
Ilimsk (Ilimskoi Ostrog), 33, 46; District, 89, 99
indigenous peoples. *See* natives
inozemtsy (foreigners), 13, 23n2, 191
interpreters: Gorlanov as, 7; Klimovskoi as, 10; of native languages, 13, 19
Inya River, 169, 172
Irkut River, 27, 34, 60; origin of name, 39
Irkutsk: amenities of, 36–37; churches, 39, 41–42; fog over, 30; fortifications, 39; city gates, 40, 42; inhabitants, 60–61, 65, 69, 72, 91, 112; its start, 60; location, 33; nickname for townspeople, 59; prevention of fires in, 44; Provincial Administration's obligations outlined, 5, 12–15; weather, 29–30
iron: along the Amga, 126; as government income, 50; at Kamenka, 64, 71, 90; at mouth of Bogul'deicha, 71; ferruginous soil along the Urak, 155; found on Kamchatka, 113; on the Talovka, 71; the Ushakovka's, 34, 71. *See also* smelters/smelting
iukola (dried fish), 167, 170n5

jasper, green, 129, 132, 133, 155
jay: Eurasian or oak, 139, 150n2

Kachega: about, 84–85; location, 83; region around 86, 88–90; today called Kachug, 88

Index | 215

Kalmyks: trade and war with the Chinese, 56–57

Kamchadals: paid yasak, 47; use of salmon and blubber, 167, 168, 170

Kamchatka, 6, 9, 21, 73, 116 arrival on, 173; ores found on, 113; travel arrangements to, 15–16, 18, 19, 105–106, 111; what to investigate, 19–20. *See also* Krasheninnikov

Kamchatka Expedition (Second), xv, 3, 40, 48; added to bureaucracy, 40; negative impact of, 42, 88, 112; money transport for, 103; "proper evaluation" of, 134; purpose of, 4–5; secrecy imposed on, xi

kastak. *See* brandy distillery

Khanda River. *See* Belaya River

Khitrov, Sofron Fedorovich, helmsman: groundings, 157, 172; meaning of name, xii; Steller disliked, 174

Kirenga (Kirensk, Kirenskoi Ostrog): arrival in, 97; 100; Lena River at, 96; Monastery of the Trinity, 97

Kirenga River: ice dams on, 97

kislaia ryba. *See* sour fish

Klimovskoi, Fedot, 14; interpreter of Yakut, 10, 13; keeper of accounts, 10, 15, 183–184

Korff, Baron von, 9; Steller's letters to, 14, 38n7, 175, 202

Koryaks, 73; how they treat dead shamans, 108–109; smallpox among, 109; Steller's instructions concerning, 18, 19

Krasheninnikov, Stepan Petrovich, student, 12, 14, 18; instructions for, 6; research, 19, 20, 160, 163

Krasnoyarsk, 46, 60, 129

Krest, 32, 36, 37n3, 39; 42

Kukhtui River, 168, 169

kumis (mare's milk), 121, 122, 147

Kunstkammer, 16, 17, 23n3, 32; preserved specimens to, 21

Kurile Islands, 5, 163; natives on, 72, 170

Kuta River, 81, 83, 85, 94; in summer too small for a raft, 95

Kyakhta, 81, 181; plants collected around, 116; Treaty of, 196

Kyakhta River, 46, trade in camels on, 56

Kychkin, Dmitrei, Yakutsk dvoryanin, 111, 113, 115, 163

Lake Baikal: fish in, 33, 34, 63; fishing on, 61–64; source of the Angara River, 29; Upper Angara feeds it, 30; freeze-up and break-up, 31; iron smelted around, 50; ostrogs around, 60; Steller explored the eastern shore, 67–73

Lake Baikal omul, 64; brandy for specimens, 202; fishing for and value of, 63; native to, 34; now endangered, 34

Lake Kurile, 181

lake minnows, 123, 135, 142; active in winter, 72; in the Ushakovka, 36; Yakuts deprived of, 120

Lamuts (Evens), 19, 47

Lange, Lorenz, vice-governor of Irkutsk, 181, 187

Lau, Johann Theodor, assistant surgeon, 160; tried to save Steller's life, 182

Lena River: break-up, 97; changed course, 119; investigations along, 15; lake-like stretch, 96; Steller to go to the lower Lena, 16

lenok (*lenki*), sharp-snouted: in the Angara, 33; in the Ilga, 90; in the Uda, 76, in the Ushakovka, 36

Listvenishnoe Zimov'e, 32

mammoths: bones on the lower Lena, 16; Yakuts' beliefs about, 73

marble: ice-polished, 104; black, 132, 133; liver-colored, 133

marcasite, 164

Marikan River, 160, 162, 167, 169

marine sponges, 164, 170; Krasheninnikov's description of, 19

merchants: and promishklenniks, 61, 64, 68; huts named after, 32; in Irkutsk, 41, 60; in the China trade, 53, 56; in the rhubarb trade, 49, 50; not harmed by natives, 109, 113; operate distilleries, 47, 48; pay head tax, 92n1; pay prostitutes well, 43; rapids costly for, 33; role in colonization, 61

merganser, common or red-breasted: female shot, 12

Messerschmidt, Daniel Gottlieb, 4, 180

meteorological observations, 9; instruments in Irkutsk, 12

mica (*sliuda*): black, 93; "hunting" for, 64; large windows of, 44, 45n9; trade with, 53, 61; price of, 183

mills: blubber used for greasing, 68; cotton mill on the Belaya, 65; Dementiev's, 83; Glazunov's, 72; Kranin's, 81; *mutovka*, 95–96; near Kachega, 84; on the Kaya River, 72; Ushakov's (Pivovarov's widow's), 34, 42, 60

millstones, 90, 94

minerals: Steller instructed to research, 4, 16, 21, 186, 187n2

mining: pits left, 71; regulations, 186; Steller's interest in, 179; tools left in Yakutsk, 17

moose, 36; antlers, 75

mosquitoes: effect of long days on, 111; travelers plagued by, 121, 124, 140

Müller, Gerhard Friedrich, Professor of History, 5; described Irkutsk well, 27; instructions to Steller, 9; letters to, 97, 174, 175; poor health, 6; published about *pisani kameni*, 86; suggestions for taxing brandy, 48

mussels, 164

Mynsicht's Elixir, 143, 151n10

natives (indigenous peoples), xi, xii, 1, 7, 10, 191; Aklanskoi and Kamenskoi ostrogs, 73; food fond of, 168, 170; loan sharks take advantage of, 91–92; medical practices, 111, 114, 162; not to be executed or tortured, 8n4; relationship with invaders, 2, 3; replacing "heathens" with "natives," 32; role in China trade, 56–57. *See also names of individual tribes*

nelma. *See* sheefish

Nerchinsk, 46, 52; inhabitants of, 47, 49, 50; 49, 50; treaty of, 78n2

nerpa, nerpi. *See* Baikal seals, also seals

Nikolski (Nikolskaya Zastava), 29, 31, 32

northern lights, 151n12; seen on the Kolyma, 76; brightness of in Turukhansk, 110

Okhota River, 19, 157, 160; bismuth and marcasite on, 164; fish in, 165, 166, 168, 169

Okhotsk: arrival in, 158; commander of, 46, 60–61, 110, 148, 170n3, 196; conditions for departure to, 18; difficult post, 61; fishery at 165–170; galleon, 163, 164, 172–173; inhabitants of, 60–61; instructions concerning, 9, 11–21; preparations for transport there, 108, 115, 122; provisions expected to be there, 10; transport to, 154; unproductive land, 48, 75

Okhotsk, Sea of: porpoises in, 160; preserving fish from, 185; rivers flowing into, 169; sailing into, 172; Steller's first view of, 157; width of, 75, 77n1

Okhotskoi Ostrog (map), 157

Olekma River, 113; breakup, 104

Olekminskoi Ostrog, 103–104

Ol'khon Island, 63, 64, 69

Orlenskaya Sloboda, 93–94

ostrogs (forts): each had a chapel, 2; definition of, 8n2; along route to Irkutsk, 10; in Irkutsk, 40; across and around Lake Baikal, 50, 60. *See also under names of ostrogs*

Ovsianikov, Stepan, instrument maker apprentice, 144; almost drowned, 149; brought Steller's horse, 128

Oyok/Oyoskaya Sloboda, 81, 83

palisades, 8n2, 39

partridge, Daurian, 37

pastures: excellent, 120, 128, 155; inundated, 30; marked by posts, 121; with "message" boards, 131

Pavlutskoi, Dmitrei Ivanovich, Major, 107, 110, 163; information about the Chukchi, 108–109

pay (salary), 6, 10, 13; annual for each crew member, 14; for Gardebol, 17; for helmsmen, 104; for servant, 97; frustration over, 56; manner of payment for Crown employees, 60–61; Steller's, 14; villages as pay, 87

pearls, impure, 164

peasants (farmers), 61, 85, 177, 191, 192; houses, 89, 94–97, 154; Tomsk pride, 59; small villages, 90

Peledui River: icy banks, 100

Peleduiskaya Sloboda, 100

Penzhina River, 72

perch, European (*okuni*), 34; in the Aldan, 129; in the Amga, 124; in the Ilga , 90
permafrost, ix, 141
Peter the Great, 4, 8n3, 42, 66n3, 92n1, 187n1; established Kunstkammer, 23n3; standardized arshin, 193
phosphorescence: of salmon, 168; of sea raspberries, 172-173,
pike, northern (*shchuki*): big in lakes, 72; in the Aldan, 128; in the Amga, 124; in the Angara, 34; in the Ilga, 90; very old, 111; Yakuts deprived of, 120
pipe, 104, 135, 176; mouthpieces commissioned, 115; smoking in place of food and/or bed, 144, 146, 149
pisani kameni (painted rocks, petroglyphs), 86, 89,
pitch: in the mountains, 126; horses' hoofs sealed with, 111
Plenisner, Friedrich, Corporal, 160
podval (brandy storage cellar), 40, 47
podvoda, podvodi, 6, 81, 105; horses for, 18; need for extra, 7, 12; Steller and crew to receive, 10, 13-14
podvodchiki, 106n3, 123; children employed as, 94
Pokrovsky Monastery, 104, 119; maps, 82, 105
police, 42-43, 46; Steller's judgment of, 44; voevod has police powers, 8n5
political history, research of, 9, 10, 16, 18, 20; on Kamchatka, 19; the Buryats', 15
porog/porogi (rapids): on the Tunguska, 33
porpoise (pig of the sea): dissected, 160
porsa (fish meal): how eaten, 168; how made, 167, 170n5
posad ("suburb"), 41, 192
posadskie: church built by, 41; pay for dwellings, 87; pay head tax, 92n1; smelt iron, 50
Posolsky Monastery, 68, 70; area owned, 69, 83; location, 31, 64
Posolsky Monastery Village, 81, 83
prikazchik, 73; definition of, 13; Gabichev sent quarter ox, 103; places that have, 72, 89, 90, 94
progon (road toll), 10, 49, 117; Steller to receive for travel, 13, 14, 21

promyshlenniks, xv, 2, 13, 36, 41, 50, 60; fishing cooperative, 62-64, 69; fishing earnings, 63; not allowed to marry, 39, 43; occupations, 64-66, 68-72, 110; places of origin, 61; seasonal workers, 61, 95-96
prostitution (whoring): causes of, 43, 66; effects of, 43-44, 66, 77, 91; Steller's proposed solutions to, 44
protoki. See river channels
provisions (food supplies): costs of, 155, 184; endangered by ice, 102; for Krashenninikov, 12; logistics, xii, 11, 13-16, 18, 84, 88,106, 108, 154; paperwork required for, 6, 163; problems with, 48, 88, 154
pud, 63, 193; of rye flour, 37

rafts, 13; adrift in ice-choked river, 102; arrival in Yakutsk, 108; given to the voevod, 114; to be built, 90; used to transport salt, 95
rapids. See *porog/porogi*, also *shivera/shiveri*
Ray's *aphyam aculeatam*: Steller caught, 169
raznochintsi (commoners), 68, 90, 95
reindeer, 75, 114, 135, 150; as a human name, 147; carrying shamans' bones, 109; clacking hooves, 72; jerky, 136; milk used by Tungus, 162
rhubarb: trade with, 40, 45n2; where it grows, 129; word prohibited, 49. See also trade
river channels (*protoki*), 101, 104, 135, 192; on the Angara, 31; on the Belaya, 131; on the Okhota, 157; on the Urak, 154, 155, 156; the Vitim's, 99
roach, common (*plotva*): in the Angara, 33, 34
Rozvodnaya: Greater Rozvodnaya, 42, 72; Malaya Rozvodnaya, 39
Russian Orthodox Church, 2; archbishop's residence, 37, 41; churches in Ust'Ilginskoi Ostrog, 90; in Ust'Kutsk, 94. See also churches in Irkutsk

sables: as yasak, 8n4, 114; hunted , 36; dyed pelts, 54, 77; as gift, 104; hunt for, 61, 64, 70, 75, 100, 113-114; quality of pelts where, 110-111

saddlebags, 17, 18, 108
saddle blankets, 139
saiga, 55, 57n2
salmon, dog or chum *(keta)*: entering rivers, 169; growing teeth, 166; at mouth of the Uda, 76
salmon, red *(nerka, lomok)*: first to enter rivers, 168; better than dog salmon, 169. See also *iukola, porsa,* salt, sour fish
salt, 63, 64, 98n1, 121, 184; from underground, 163; salted fish, 34, 62, 65, 166–168; salted meat, 62, 149; saltworks, 95; trade in, 51; white, exuded, 120
Samoilov, Grigorei, miner, 10, 14, 106, 115; equipment issued to, 23
sandstone, 95, 143; gray, 32, 126, 127; cliffs of red, 85, 89
Saturn-Jupiter Saturday, 152, 158n1
schist, 134
Schnurbuch (ledger), 10, 15, 21–22,
scoter, white-winged *(turpany)*, 113
sculpin, antlered *(byki)*, 169, 171n12
sea lions, 1, 181; fall from cliffs, 77; Steller's, xi
Sea of Okhotsk. See Okhotsk, Sea of
sea otters, xi
sea raspberries, 163; glowing, 164, 172
sea stars, 163; glowing, 76
sea urchins, 163
seals: harbor, 67; around Okhotsk, 165; swimming up the Okhota, 170. See also Baikal seals
seeds: cataloged, 163; collected, 130, 134, 139, 140, 141, 155, 156, 162, 186; descriptions of, 200; lost in shipwreck, 14; to be collected, 21. See also *individual plants*
Selenga River: fishing in, 31, 64, 69; open for hunting, 68
Selenginsk, 46, 62, 108
Senate. See High Governing Senate
shamans, 15, 86, 108, 146, 151n14; *Shamanski kamen,* 32; *Shamanskoi Porog,* 33; Steller guided by drumming, 122; predictions, 116
Shcheki, 99, 106n1
sheefish *(nelma)*: in the Penzhina, 73; in the Ural (Yaik), 72
shipyards *(pristani)*, 92; at Ust'Kutsk, 95

shivera/shiveri (big rapids): in the Angara, 31; in the Tira, 96; in the Tunguska, 33
Siberian Office (Sibirskii Prikaz, Siberian Government Authority), 3, 8n3, 8n4, 5, 18, 40, 42; appoints voevods, 46
silver: Gilyaks use, 75; mines, 51; silversmiths, 65; trade with, 53
Skornyakov-Pisarev, Gregorei Gregor'evich, Commander of Okhotsk, 156, 166; known for his vicious temper, 170n3; replaced by Devier, 148; wanted impossible link to the Urak, 152
sled dogs. See dogs
sleds, 6, 10, 77, 81, 114; with game for sale, 37; winter provisions brought by, 154; women and children drive, 94
sliuda. See mica
slobodas: around Irkutsk, 37, 48, 91; definition of, 38n6; development of, 61. See also *individually named*
sluzhivs, xix, xxiin4, 2; Cossacks now called, 60; how employed, 61; to be requisitioned, 10, 11
smelt *(koriukha)*, 169
smelters/smelting, 50; 91, 112; on Kamchatka, 113; promyshlenniks involved in, 64, 65, 71, 72, 93. See also iron
Sofronov, Aleksei, Steller's servant, 114, 117, 121, 123, 142, 144
soil: best along the Angara, 37; clay, 131; ferruginous, 155; loam, 88; mammoth bones in, 16; on top of permafrost, 141; peat, 127; siliceous, 155; universal, 155, 159n3. See also clay
sour cream earth *(zemlianaia smetana)*, 162–163
sour fish *(kislaia ryba)*, 168. See also fish for dog food
Spangberg, Martin, Captain, 5, 17, 19, 101, 106n8, 152; had told about famines, 162; Steller traveling with, 114, 155–158; 160; Steller visited, 105, 107, 108
specimens, 6, 21, 164, 181n1, 195
squirrels, 87; ground, 103; quality of pelts, 110–111
station. See taxation *and* way stations

Steller: as physician, 85, 95, 114; health, 134, 143, 162; medical training, 179–180; peasant smock, 126, 153, 158; spectacles, 145

steppe, 81, 86; Cossacks originated from, 45n6; iron under, 71; Kosaya or Sloping, 83; no agriculture on, 88; flowers on, 107, 118n10, 136n1

sterlet: in the Aldan, 128; in the Amga, 124; in the Angara, 33, 38n5; in the Lena, 96

sticklebacks: near Rozvodnaya, 72; sea, Steller caught, 169

sturgeon, common: in Lake Baikal, 68; in the Aldan, 22; in the Amga, 124; in the Angara, 33, 38n5; in the Lena, 96; in the Selenga, 64; in the Ural (Yaik), 72

sturgeon, starry: in the Angara, 33; value of, 63

sturgeon glue, 50, 54

swallow, bank, 39, 92n6

syphilis. *See* French disease

taimen, Siberian: in the Angara, 33; in the Ilga, 90; in the Uda, 76; in the Yudoma, 149

Tatars, 53; Tatar-style stove, 100, 104

taxation: collection station, 83; for brandy, 40–41, 48, 49; in fishing, 63, 64; in mining, 50; property, 61; Steller for fairer, 91, 177. *See also* head tax *and* yasak

tea, 91, 115, 145, 149, 183; brick in the river, 131; cups and pots, 56, 163; fireweed used as, 106n7; Gilyaks have, 75; green, 57; Northern Labrador, 104, 133; Steller enjoyed, 119, 132, 140, 154

tench (*lini*, doctor fish): caught near Rozvodnaya, 72

thunder, 97, 123, 129; thunderstorm, 141

tobacco, 75, 113–114, 122; Chinese, 40, 43; 50; gift of, 110; exchanged for guide, 123; smuggled as red tea, 50. *See also* pipe

Tobolsk, 5, 52, 60; relationship to Irkutsk, 27, 46; Steller in, 182

Tomsk, 32, 60, 180; nickname for townspeople, 59; Tatars, 53; Steller in, 180; trade in, 55, 56

trade: Chinese trade goods, 40; impact on people, 59; in pack animals, 56–57; in pelts, 55; in rhubarb, 40, 45n2, 49; in tobacco, 114

trails: bad, 81, 126, 128, 132, 133, 135, 143, 152, 154; finding it, 117, 122, 145; fires set to dry them out, 131; good, 120, 121, 130, 140, 148; on a mountain, 124; rocky, 154; rudimentary system of, 7; to the Amga, 123; treeless, 127; twisting, 131

translators. *See* interpreters

trapping. *See names of individual animals*

trout: Dolly Varden (*malma*), 169; in the Yudoma, 149; species of, 29, 74n2

Tungus, 54, 62; desired information about, 15; guide to sour cream earth, 162; hunting marine animals, 170; treatment of wounds, 75; use of seal milk and blubber, 68, 170; venerating *Shamanski kamen*, 32

Tunkinski Range, 32–33

Udskoi Ostrog, 19; belugas hunted in, 170

ukases: administrative, 9, 11, 12, 13, 14, 17, 65, 72; affecting trade, 66n3; concerning the students, 21; of prohibition, 22, 39, 49, 64; ordering Steller back, 182; Steller recommends, 87, 92

Upper Angara, 70, 71; larger seals around, 68–69; dangerous, 61–62

Urak River, 152, 156; fish in, 166, 168, 169; headwaters of, 153, 154; mouth of, 162, 163

Uratsky Wharf, 154, 155

Ushakov, Moisei, surveyor, 116, 117, 124, 144; his horse died, 129

Ushakovka (Ida) River, 27, 39, 42, 60; description of, 34; fish in, 36; smelters on, 65, 71

Ust'Ilginskaya (Ust'Ilga, Ust'Ilginskoi Ostrog), 84, 90, 96; leaving, 93; Pier, 92

Ust'Kutsk (Ust'Kutskoi Ostrog, Ust'Kuth), 90, 94, 95, 96

utesi (cliffs), 85, 89

Verkholensk: description of and cottage industry at, 86; salt taken to, 95

villages. *See* derevnya, slobodas

visits with centenarians, 93, 101

Vitimsk (Vitimskaya Sloboda), 99, 100, 126; forests around, 111

Vitim River: mica found on, 64, 93
Vladislavish-Raguzinsky, Count Sava Lukich, 56, 58n5
voevods, 3, 8n6; in Irkutsk, 47; to assist Steller in Yakutsk, 14–18
volcanoes, 20, 131; Windy Mountain, 130

wagtails, yellow, 139
Walton, William, Lieutenant, 154; together with Steller, 105, 158, 163
Waxell, Sven, Lieutenant, 105, 158, 163; floated fast to Okhotsk, 154
way stations, 66n1, 124, 153; Posikov's, 122; second and third on trail to Okhotsk, 120–121; station hand, 117; stationmaster, 122. *See also huts, zimov'e*
whales: Gilyaks hunt, 76; Koryaks to hunt, 18; spermaceti, 18; stranded, 160, 162, 163, 170
whitefish, broad (*chiri*): in the Penzhina, 73
whitefish, common (*sig*): in the Amga, 124; in the Angara, 33; in the Ilga, 90; in the Yudoma, 149
whitefish, round (*valki*): in the Ilga, 90
wolves, 59; heard howling, 141

Yakov, Steller's servant, 116; pay for the year, 97; let go, 117
Yakuts: burial practices, 76–77, 78n3, 135; Chief Mazarin, 104–105; conductors of caravans, 45n3; desired information about, 15, 17; *chokania* (summer festival), 123; language, 10, 124, 148, 168; living off the land, 115, 116, 120; medical practices, 111–112, 114; naming their children, 146–147; netting carp, 72; poverty, 128, 140; refugees in Gilyak country, 75; smithy, 121; solicited information, 100, 121–122, 146; stations, 156; superstitions, 73, 76, 93, 94, 135, 138n22, 142, 146–147; trading with the Gilyaks, 113–114
Yakutsk: arrival in, 105; climate and weather, 108, 118n3; dusk during night, 107; how to proceed upon arrival, 15; inhabitants' character, 120; pleasant location of, 119; rapid plant growth in, 109
Yarmanka: arrived in, 115; horse ran back to, 122
yasak: Chinese do not demand, 75; finances trading with China, 47; quotas established, 3, 8n4; shady deals with, 91–92, 113–114
Yeniseysk: Cossacks, 60, 178; cowhide factory in, 55; former province, 46; nickname of townspeople, 59; sensible choice, 32
Yudoma Cross: ice patch between Yuna and, 142; birch growth, 177; brandy for, 112; stay at, 149; transporting provisions to, 154, 155, 168
Yudoma River, 148, 149, 150
Yuna River: arived at, 135: fast current, 130; floods quickly, 129; Mongolian poplar found along, 139; ice sheet at half-way point, 142
yurts: Koryaks', 109; in Irkutsk province, 46; on the Amga, 124; Russian fishers', 156; station yurt, 121; wooden, 83. *See also names of indigenous peoples*

Zaborovskoi, Aleksei Eremeevich, Yakutsk voevod; Steller called on, 105; dinners with, 107, 108, 110, 115
zaimka/zaimki (farm, small village): definition of, 34, 193; individually named, 72, 81, 83, 86, 87, 94, 95, 116, 183; near Irkutsk, 34, 36; on the Peledui, 100
zemlianaia smetana. See sour cream earth
Zhigani: Steller describes birds from, 108, 111; *porsa* from, 167
Zhilkina Village: archbishop's beautiful building in, 37, 52
zimov'e/zimovia (winter huts): definition of, 37n1; illustration of, 84, 95, 193; first on trail, 83; system of, 7. *See also huts, way stations*

MARGRITT A. ENGEL is Professor Emerita of Languages at the University of Alaska Anchorage. She is translator of *Journal of a Voyage with Bering, 1741–1742* and *Steller's History of Kamchatka*.

KAREN E. WILLMORE is Professor Emerita of Languages at the University of Alaska Anchorage. She is translator of *Steller's History of Kamchatka*.

JONATHAN C. SLAGHT is the Russia and Northeast Asia Coordinator for the Wildlife Conservation Society. He is coeditor and translator of *Across the Ussuri Kray: Travels in the Sikhote-Alin Mountains*.

www.ingramcontent.com/pod-product-compliance
Lightning Source LLC
Chambersburg PA
CBHW031808220426
43662CB00007B/576